Roxanne Markoff
April 1986

Mind in Therapy

MIND IN THERAPY

Constructing Systemic Family Therapies

BRADFORD P. KEENEY

JEFFREY M. ROSS

Basic Books, Inc., Publishers *New York*

Library of Congress Cataloging in Publication Data

Keeney, Bradford P.
Mind in therapy.

Bibliography: p. 261
Includes index.
1. Family psychotherapy. I. Ross, Jeffrey M., II. Title.
RC488.5.K44 1984 616.89'156 84-70679
ISBN 0-465-04612-6

Printed in the United States of America
Designed by Vincent Torre
10 9 8 7 6 5 4 3 2 1

To our families—

Melissa and Scott; Kristie and George

Contents

PART II

STRATEGIES FOR ORGANIZING THERAPY

Acknowledgments

THIS BOOK would not have been possible without the generous contributions of clinical material from Olga Silverstein, John Weakland, Jay Haley, H. Charles Fishman, Gianfranco Cecchin, and Luigi Boscolo. We especially thank them for their support. John Weakland's case study, which originally appeared in *The Tactics of Change* (1982), is reprinted by permission of Jossey-Bass Publishers, and Olga Silverstein's case study in chapter 1 originally appeared in *Family Systems Medicine* (Keeney, Ross, and Silverstein 1983) and is reprinted with permission. In addition, parts of chapter 2 have appeared in our article "Cybernetics of Brief Family Therapy" (Keeney and Ross 1983) and are reprinted by permission of the *Journal of Marital and Family Therapy.*

Various organizations and institutions have contributed, in their own special way, to this book. We acknowledge the Project for Human Cybernetics, the Ackerman Institute for Family Therapy, the Philadelphia Child Guidance Clinic, the Department of Human Development and Family Studies at Texas Tech University, the Galveston Family Institute, the Department of Psychiatry at Cornell Medical College, the Department of Child Development and Family Studies at Purdue University, and the Family Therapy Training Program at the Menninger Foundation.

We particularly thank our editor, Jo Ann Miller, for her masterful guidance and encouragement. And finally, we are most grateful to Melissa Keeney, who served as first critic and advisor.

Mind in Therapy

About This Book

"That's another thing we've learned from *your* Nation," said Mein Herr, "map-making. But we've carried it much further than you . . ."

"We actually made a map of the country, on the scale of a *mile to the mile!*"

"Have you used it much?" I enquired.

"It has never been spread out yet," said Mein Herr: "the farmers objected: they said it would cover the whole country, and shut out the sunlight! So we now use the country itself, as its own map, and I assure you it does nearly as well."

—LEWIS CARROLL
Sylvie and Bruno Concluded, 1893

ONE of the most exciting and fruitful forms of therapy to appear in recent years is systemic family therapy—the perspective that emphasizes treating the patterns that connect the problem behavior of one person with the behavior of other people.* As an ever-widening body of literature suggests, this shift in focus from individual behavior to social patterns of organization has been enthusiastically greeted by a variety of practitioners.

Unfortunately, this enthusiasm is too often accompanied by bewilderment with the wide array of practical techniques and theoretical explanations available. Ideally, a practitioner should have a map that allows direct access to the various orientations to systemic family therapy. With this outcome in mind, we set

*Relevant social patterns that organize problem behavior do not always include family members; thus it may seem more accurate to speak of "systemic therapy." However, since family members usually participate in the social patterns organizing problem behavior, we prefer the term "systemic family therapy."

forth a unifying conceptual view that enables both novices and experienced clinicians to draw upon the multiple resources of diverse systemic therapies as a means of enhancing the organization of clinical strategies.

This book explores how therapists construct systemic family therapies. As we look closely at several clinical case studies—including the treatment of migraine headaches, a depressed family, an anxious musician, and an anorectic mother—we discover that, despite their differences, each of these therapies was constructed upon the same basic premise. In each case the therapist has conceptualized and treated symptoms and problems as part of a more encompassing systemic pattern of organization. Each of the therapies, however, has a unique way of constructing its own particular view of what constitutes a systemic pattern of organization.

Sometimes these patterns involve the immediate family system, as in Olga Silverstein's treatment of a girl's migraine headaches by having her whole family set aside a time for worrying. Or the pattern may extend to multiple generations, as in H. Charles Fishman's treatment of a three-generation family in which the identified patient has had anorexia nervosa for twenty-five years. The clinical case of John Weakland, on the other hand, demonstrates that the pattern for organizing problem behavior need not include the family system.

The purpose of this book is to set forth how several major therapeutic orientations construct their unique systemic views for use in organizing treatment. Clearly identifying and articulating these views and strategies requires a theoretical perspective that is not exclusively tied to any particular type of therapy. We therefore present a general view of diverse approaches showing their differences and similarities.

In the first section, Theoretical Foundations, we describe the theoretical basis for identifying therapeutic patterns. In chapter 1, we present a fundamental distinction between two ways of looking at patterns that underlie therapeutic communication. We distinguish between *semantic* frames of reference—looking at communication in terms of meaning—and *political* frames of reference—examining communication in terms of organizational consequences.

For instance, when a therapist asks a client to *explain why* he has a problem, he is asking for a semantic frame. The client may subsequently attempt to construct a particular meaning for his situation. He may point to traumatic experiences in his past, to character disorders, social constraints, or he may even construct an elaborate explanation as to why he has no explanation. Should the therapist shift to asking the client to *describe what* is actually happening, he is proposing a political frame of reference. The client may then specify who is doing what to whom. From these descriptions an overall view of the politics of his problem behavior will begin to emerge. All therapists ask questions that interweave semantic and political frames of reference.

Chapter 2 specifies a cybernetic view of multiple communication in therapeutic intervention. By "cybernetics" we mean the organization of communication systems in terms of how they address both change and stability. A cybernetic view allows us to see how successful therapeutic interventions juggle a family system's requests for change and stability in a complementary fashion. Whereas semantic and political frames of reference provide a general approach to examining communication in therapy, the cybernetic organization of multiple communication provides a more finely focused view. We will use this view to more clearly discern the systemic structure of therapeutic interventions.

Thus, chapters 1 and 2 provide theoretical lenses—one for general viewing, one for a sharper vision—to bring into focus the basic patterns of therapeutic interventions. Using these lenses, the next section of the book provides several pictures of the general strategies used to organize systemic family therapies.

In all therapies some underlying distinction directs and organizes how a therapy is to be constructed, maintained, perceived, acted upon, interacted with, understood, and changed. The strategies we analyze present three major distinctions that have been used to organize systemic therapy: (1) a problem-solution interactional focus; (2) a triadic social relations focus; and (3) a contextual meaning focus.

Historically, one could argue that each of these perspectives has been associated with a particular approach to systemic therapy. For instance, the work of Paul Watzlawick, John Weakland, Richard Fisch, Lynn Segal, and their colleagues has principally addressed the complementary relation of problem and problem-solving behavior. Jay Haley, Braulio Montalvo, Salvador Minuchin, H. Charles Fishman, and their colleagues, on the other hand, focus more on the structural organization of triadic relations in the social context of the family. The more recent work of Mara Selvini-Palazzoli, Gianfranco Cecchin, Giuliana Prata, and Luigi Boscolo attend to the contextual meanings that frame the politics of troubled families.

Each of these orientations specifies a unique way of drawing distinctions that construct and organize therapy. Although the organizing distinction may be different for each, all approaches do, in fact, respond to behavioral problems, triadic social relations, and contextual meanings. One cannot not behave, not relate, and not mean. For instance, although some orientations claim to be radically committed to viewing observable behavior, they may still put that behavior in context by placing it within some cognitive frame.

Chapters 3, 4, and 5 examine the major schools of systemic therapy and delineate their basic distinctions in organizing therapy. To differentiate these prescriptions for therapy requires noting how they embody what we characterize as "laws of therapeutic form" and patterns of "multiple communication." Each strategy is described and analyzed in terms of how it prescribes and constructs: (1) relevant distinctions and complementarities; (2) semantic and political frames of reference; and (3) cybernetic patterns of multiple communication. In addition, full-length case material and extended commentary are presented for each systemic orientation.

The particular orientations to systemic therapy we analyze are chosen because of their direct connection to the ideas of communication and cybernetic theory. We specifically use the term "systemic family therapies" to identify the different therapeutic approaches that arise from this paradigmatic base. Although other family therapy approaches are somewhat connected to this same tradition of ideas, the therapies we examine are probably the most clearly committed to a cybernetic view of human communication and context.

When we say that therapy is organized in terms of pattern, it is important to know that we are referring to what Gregory Bateson (1972, 1979) called "mind." The *cybernetic organization* of living process, whether amoeba, redwood forests, human beings, social groups, or whole planets, specifies this definition of mind. "Mind in therapy," thus points to the cybernetic organization of events that therapists and clients embody (see Keeney 1983). This pattern of organization connects therapist and client in a way that successfully addresses both corrective change and stability. The view of mind as synonymous with cybernetic system is a major insight that has profound implications for the understanding and practice of systemic family therapies.

This book is primarily directed to those interested in learning what is most basic to the practice and understanding of the major orientations to systemic family therapy. In addition to offering a detailed analysis of each of these therapeutic orientations, we provide an overarching view that allows a clear perspective for comparing therapeutic strategies. These maps and strategies should help a clinician organize his work to draw more fully on his own unique resources.

Before proceeding, we offer a story to remind us that the relation between clinical practice and map making (sometimes called art and science) can be rewarding:

Once upon a time there was an enchanted forest where a beautiful lady found she could talk with deer. She would spend hours and hours talking with her deer, sometimes laughing and playing with them.

In the same countryside also lived two young scientific explorers whose habit it was to wander about discovering new places and things. They were by nature very curious and enjoyed making technical drawings of what they found.

And so it happened that the explorers encountered the lady and her deer. Time and time again she would spit out insults to them, saying they did not really understand what she was doing and they had no right to invade her unspoiled territory. They, in turn, would maintain it was their duty to study her world and she should be grateful.

For years and years this exchange went on. Nearly a century passed.

One day the explorers accidentally left a drawing at the side of a great oak tree where the lady discovered it to her surprise. It looked like a map to her. Unable to subdue her curiosity she examined it and realized, to her amazement, that if looked at with a sort of squint, the map took on a kind of beauty.

At the next confrontation she teased the explorers, telling them of her discovery. She proclaimed that they were not that different from her. This confused the explorers. They were pleased with the possibility that she may have understood what they were trying to accomplish, but they could not imagine what she had in common with them. After all, they seldom wasted time trying to talk with deer.

One afternoon the somewhat confused explorers decided to play a trick on the lady. While she was sleeping, they quietly and carefully made a drawing of her body. They then arranged to lose this sketch where she would find it.

The next week they came to her asking if she had, by any chance, found an important document they had lost. They went on and on about its importance. The lady listened seriously and then asked them to describe what the document had contained. They paused and replied, "It is a sketch that formally shows how you are as scientifically interesting as anything we have ever studied." The lady responded warmly, "I have always known that." And she began to smile.

Since that time, villagers say, the three can be found roaming other forests, talking, playing, and laughing. Occasionally, they leave a sketch for someone else to find.

PART I

THEORETICAL FOUNDATIONS

CHAPTER 1

Laws of Therapeutic Form

Draw a Distinction!

—George Spencer Brown,
Laws of Form, 1973

THE BIOLOGIST John Lilly once devised an intriguing experiment to demonstrate how people participate in constructing their experience. He recorded the word "cogitate" on a tape so that it is repeated over and over again: cogitate, cogitate, cogitate, cogitate. . . . When people listen to this tape a strange thing happens: after several moments, they begin hearing other words. At a conference of the American Society of Linguistics, Lilly played the tape and the group heard some 2,361 words, imaginary and real: *agitate; arbitrate; artistry; back and forth; candidate; can't you stay; catch a tape; conscious state; count to ten; Cape Cod, you say; cut a steak; got a date; got to take; gurgitate; marmalade. . . .*

In general, *what* one perceives is a consequence of *how* one participates in perceiving, which, in turn, is a consequence of one's social context. With respect to Lilly's "cogitate" experiment, a person's report of what he hears reveals more about him and his context than what is on the tape. For some neurophysiologists the most commonly perceived word is "computate," whereas for therapists working in mental hospitals Lilly found it to be "tragedy." Lilly humorously adds that when he presents the tape to a group with which he hasn't achieved a good rapport, he himself hears, "stop the tape."

Constructivism

The perspective that emphasizes an observer's participation in constructing what is observed is called "constructivism" (see Richards and von Glaserfeld 1979). In a constructivist perspective all descriptions of families and family therapy are seen primarily as information about the observer or community of observers. In other words, listening to what a family therapist claims he perceives in therapy tells us more, or at least as much about the therapist (the observer) as about the family (the observed). This shift in perspective, what the cybernetician Heinz von Foerster (1981*b*) calls the move from emphasizing *observed* systems to emphasizing *observing* systems, is our starting point.

The idea that what we perceive and know is a product of our participation with the observed is not new. That our contemporary scientific culture has found a different way of exposing this view is new. For these philosophers of science, "human knowledge in general, and science in particular, is not engaged in uncovering certainty, truth, or reality, or any of the bugbears of dogmatic science" (Richards and von Glaserfeld 1979, p. 39). For Arne Naess (1972, p. 88), "anything is possible," and for Paul Feyerabend (1970, p. 301), "any idea can become plausible." In addition, a tradition of thinking has emerged that enables us to articulate and understand a constructivist view through a formal language based in mathematics and logic. One of the principal architects of this formal constructivist position is George Spencer-Brown (1973, p. v), who concluded that the basic forms underlying our experience—whether linguistic, mathematical, physical, biological, or musical—can be discovered by retracing how we initially draw distinctions.

From a constructivist position, the practice and understanding of systemic family therapy requires that we fully embrace the basic distinctions underlying it. We will therefore begin specifying our model of systemic family therapy by outlining its most basic distinctions.

Before doing so, however, we need to note that we have found it useful to distinguish between two contexts in therapy: what we call "formal understanding" and "practical strategy." In the first the primary purpose is to achieve formal theoretical understanding, whereas in the second the primary purpose revolves around practical advice and strategy for organizing one's action in conducting therapy. Confusion may easily arise in a conversation where the intention of one is to formally understand through theoretical abstractions while the other is focusing on concrete descriptions of practical strategy.

As a conceptual exercise, imagine clinicians wearing traffic lights: one light indicates to his colleagues (as well as himself) that he is presently in the context of formal understanding, another light indicates his shift to emphasizing practical strategy. A third light signals those times when he struggles with the *relation* between formal ideas and practical action. If clinicians could keep track of their thinking context for any given moment, a great deal of misunderstanding and impractical advice could be more easily avoided.

In this chapter and the next, our primary purpose is to address theoretical maps for formal understanding. At the end of each chapter we demonstrate through the analysis of case studies how these maps relate to clinical action. In the remaining chapters, we shift to clinical strategy. However, our specification of clinical strategies necessarily depends upon a particular foundation of formal understanding.

Semantic and Political Frames of Reference

The distinction between semantic and political frames of reference underscores two ways of viewing *human communication.* We use the term "human communication" to include "*behavior* in the widest sense: words and their non-verbal accompaniments, posture, facial expressions, even silence" (Jackson, cited in Watzlawick and Weakland 1977, p. 7). Following Paul Watzlawick (1964, p. 2) we also agree that human communication involves "the way people affect each other by the message character of their behavior, of the ways they confirm or disconfirm, inspire or drive one another crazy." Given this view of human communication, how can one distinguish relevant differences of communication in the context of systemic family therapy?

A clue to answering this question came from a statement by Heinz von Foerster. In describing Gregory Bateson's communicational paradigm, he (1981, p. viii) noted that Bateson "ignores semantic links" and alerts us to what he calls the "strategic, political, functional, interactional consequences" of communication.

What is important in von Foerster's analysis is that he suggests two ways of seeing communication. Although he is clear in calling one of these frames of reference, "semantics," he is less certain what to call the other view. Instead, he uses a string of terms —strategic, political, functional, and interactional—for the other frame of reference. However, in family therapy, "strategic," "functional" and "interactional" are loaded terms—they tend to be seen as indicating particular orientations and approaches to the practice of therapy. "Politics," on the other hand, may be the most distinct term for therapists. The dictionary defines politics as follows: "a science dealing with the regulation and control of man living in society" (Webster's *Third International Dictionary*); "the science dealing with the form, organization, and administration of a state or part of one, and with the regulation of its relations with other states" *(Oxford English Dictionary).*

It is intriguing to note that these descriptions are very similar to the definition of a term Plato called "cybernetics." In *Euthydemus* and *Cleitophon,* he uses "cybernetics" to denote "the art of steering men." In *The Republic* Plato uses it to specify the idea of "governability." Similarly, André Ampère uses "cybernetics" to describe the concept, "politique proprement dite." In other words, cybernetics is concerned with "the very art of governing and of choosing in every case both what can be and what must be done" (Mihram, Mihram, and Nowakowska 1977, p. 411). Clearly, the correspondence between "politics" and "cybernetics" is historically rooted.

We have therefore adopted the notion of a *political frame of reference* to indicate the cybernetic organization of communication in human relationship systems. With this frame, the contributions of Jay Haley's (1976; 1980) strategic orientation and Watzlawick and associates' (1974) interactional view, among others, can be more clearly understood as underscoring the politics of communication: who-does-what-to-whom-when; or more specifically, the cybernetic organization of therapy.

A classic example of a political frame of reference in family therapy involves the calibration of marital interaction by a symptomatic child. An escalating argument between a husband and wife, for instance, may reach a point where their child has an asthmatic attack, which diverts the marital interaction and in this way calibrates the degree of escalation their arguing may reach. Different approaches to family therapy have described this pattern in different ways. Salvador Minuchin (1974) often depicts this situation as a social triad in which the child's asthma "detours" parental conflict. In other words, the parents' argument is sidetracked by the need to attend to their child. However this particular pattern is described, its specification is within a political frame of reference.

A political frame of reference, however, does not necessarily imply social power or hierarchy. These terms are actually semantic frames that give meaning to political frames of reference. With respect to the notion of hierarchy, Haley (1976, p. 106) notes that it is a "product of our thinking and not of the nature of organization": horses entering a barn in a certain order do not necessarily imply a social hierarchy or "pecking order." Specifying the sequential organization of the horses as they enter a barn is a way of pointing to a political frame of reference. To say that the pattern represents a hierarchy of status or power is to introduce a semantic frame that provides a particular meaning for an observer. The choice of semantic frame therefore reveals less about the horses and more about the intent or purpose of the observer.

In family therapy the same line of reasoning holds. A sequential pattern of behavior indicates a political frame of reference; whereas any description of such a sequence in terms of social power shifts one to a semantic frame of reference. Descriptions of social power again tell us more about how a therapist constructs meaning than about how a therapeutic context is organized.

Suppose a mother tells her son to pick up his toys after dinner. Upon entering his room the boy has a temper tantrum, throwing his toys and yelling insults at his mother. His father subsequently enters the boy's room and tells him to not be upset and he can wait until the next day to organize his room. The boy's tantrum stops, and the parents get into an argument over how to discipline their son.

The sequential tracking of who-does-what-to-whom-when in this scenario indicates a political frame of reference. Should a therapist ascribe a particular meaning to this sequence, or to part of it, the frame of reference then shifts to semantics. To say that the mother and father (or mother and son) are engaged in a power struggle, for instance, is to construct a semantic frame of reference around this particular political scenario.

A mistake in categorizing (or logical mistyping) sometimes occurs when a family therapist discusses a semantic frame as if it were the same as the political frame it contextualizes. With the distinction of semantics and politics, whenever a therapist points to a semantic frame (for example, a power struggle, ego struggle, or resistance), we can always ask the therapist to carefully describe the sequence of action he is naming.

It is important to remember that by considering political frames of reference the relevant patterns and forms that organize social contexts of therapy can be discerned. A political frame of reference provides a view of how communication is organized in a social context. Whenever therapists ask questions that attempt to expose the "reactions of people to the reactions of other people," they are working within a political frame of reference. A major contribution in family therapy has been the way it illuminates the social organization of symptomatic communication. When a whole family is interviewed, it is impossible to avoid stepping into political frames of reference. If a mother is asked what brought the family to therapy, her response will be followed by the responses of other family members. In this way, a political frame of reference is enacted in the session.

Heinz von Foerster's statement about the Batesonian shift from the semantics to politics of communication may seem to suggest a disposal of semantics. We believe, however, that all therapies, including systemic family therapies, construct semantic, as well as political, frames of reference. Semantic frames involve viewing communication as the specification of *meaning*. At most first sessions, the therapist asks the family why they have come for help. In effect, he invites them to construct a semantic frame that defines why they need help. The family may respond that their son is being delinquent, that the family can't communicate, or that the husband and wife can't seem to stop disagreeing. All of these descriptions are semantic frames of reference that provide a view of the family's sense of their experience.

Dialectic of Semantics and Politics

Although therapists address a great variety of specific frames, they all use both semantic and political frames of reference. This distinction is the basic tool for mapping therapy as a swinging back and forth between semantic and political frames of reference. Some therapists, however, address one frame more than the other. Although their descriptions may emphasize the meaning of past, present, and future events or the politics of past, present, and future events, they all use both semantic and political frames of reference.

Thus any interpretation of von Foerster's description of the Batesonian communication paradigm as a shift from semantics to politics is incomplete. The shift actually involves moving toward a dialectic between semantics and politics. To illustrate this more fully, we offer a story Bateson often used to illustrate metaphor and relationship.

At a conference he attended, a Dutch psychiatrist, lecturing on schizophrenia, announced that "the schizophrenic mind is disordered." As an example, he described a psychiatrist asking his institutionalized patient what the difference is between a ladder and a staircase. The patient responded, "A stocking"—his evidence for a "disordered mind." Bateson asked the psychiatrist to give another word for a run in a woman's hose. The psychiatrist eventually responded, "Ladder." "You see," Bateson added, "the patient could be commenting on the sexual difference between herself and the doctor."

Let us examine this scenario in terms of semantic and political frames of reference. The question regarding the difference between a ladder and a staircase can be seen as more than a request for meaning. It is a communication taking place in the political context of a therapist and client relationship within a hospital. The "patient" knows that the "therapist" is supposed to have expertise in helping her. In this political context, it is odd that the therapist asks questions to which the patient and doctor must know the correct semantic answer. The doctor, in fact, is not interested in the semantics of his question but is pointing to a political frame of reference: the doctor wants to prove a difference between himself and the patient. This difference, of course, organizes the politics of mental hospitals: the doctors and patients must repeatedly prove that they are different. In effect, a semantic frame is enclosed within a political frame:

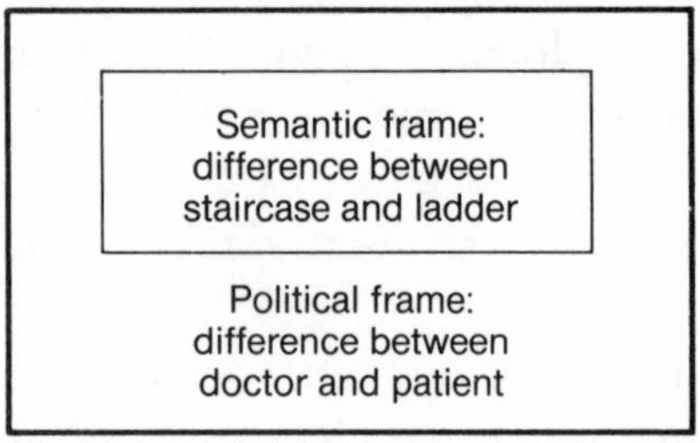

Semantic frame:
difference between
staircase and ladder

Political frame:
difference between
doctor and patient

The so-called crazy message given by the schizophrenic is therefore a transform of the way the therapist packaged his question. By responding, "stocking," the patient uses metaphor to conceal her response about politics in the same way that the doctor had concealed his request about politics.

Relation of Semantics/Politics to Other Distinctions

The notions of semantic and political frames of reference are somewhat analagous to other conceptual distinctions. For instance, Warren McCulloch (1965) differentiated between the "report" and "command" aspects of a message. Gregory Bateson (1968) defined report as a communication describing previous events; command as a communication prescribing later events. The message, "It is raining outside," may be seen as both a description of what has been happening, as well as a prescription for future action—such as getting out one's umbrella.

Paul Watzlawick, Don Jackson, and Janet Beavin (1967, pp. 51–52) re-articulated Bateson's definitions by first noting that "the report aspect of a message conveys information and is, therefore, synonymous in human communication with the *content* of the message." In addition, "the command aspect . . . refers to what sort of a message it is to be taken as, and therefore, ultimately to the *relationship* between the communicants."

The notions of report and command, or content and relationship, are thus defined in terms of the dual aspects of any particular message. Practical problems, however, arise when one attempts to use these distinctions to analyze therapeutic communication. For instance, what portion of communication defines a message (as opposed to a set of messages)? Thinking in terms of content and relationship also implies, as Watzlawick argues, two hierarchical levels of communication "such that the latter (relationship) classifies the former (content) and is therefore a metacommunication" (Watzlawick, Jackson, and Beavin 1967, p. 54).

We prefer an alternative view of communication that sees the relation of what we call semantic and political frames of reference as recursive: each is a frame for the other. In addition, there is a wide variety of communication levels, across both semantic and political frames. One level of content is not necessarily framed by a particular relationship command; instead, multiple semantic frames are framed by (and frame) a wide array of political frames. Most importantly, the distinction of report and command (or content and relationship) presupposes a view of communication in terms of input-output transmission of message material which is being seen more and more as an incomplete and inadequate formulation (see Varela 1979).

The difference between semantic/political and content/relationship (or report/command) can also be understood in terms of different orders of analysis. For instance, consider the statement by a client, *"I have anxiety attacks about twice a week."* From the perspective of report/command or content/relationship, this statement gives a report about the client's experience (a description of content) as well as implicitly suggests or commands that the therapist do something about it (a prescription for their relationship).

If we now re-examine the client's statement as part of a conversation with a therapist, we might find the following:

THERAPIST: Why have you come to therapy?
CLIENT: *I have anxiety attacks about twice a week.*
THERAPIST: What do you mean, exactly, by an "anxiety attack"?

Rather than examine the dual aspects of any particular statement, we can now choose a higher-order view that names the communicational frame of reference within which these statements have occurred. In this case, the statements can be seen as taking place within a semantic frame of reference that requests and specifies meaning.

The frame of reference, however, would be different if the client's statement had been part of the following conversation:

THERAPIST: How often do you have your anxiety attacks?
CLIENT: *I have anxiety attacks about twice a week.*
THERAPIST: Who is the first person, other than yourself, to find out about these attacks?

The statements of client and therapist now can be seen as taking place within a political frame of reference.

For both of these semantic and political frames of reference, an analysis of the client's statement in terms of report/command (or content/relationship) results in the same finding. To understand the *context* of the dual aspects of this singular statement or message, however, requires moving to a view of communicational frames of reference. Here we find that the lower-order distinctions of content/relationship and report/command are always framed by more encompassing semantic and political frames of reference.

We use the terms derived from von Foerster's proposal—*semantic* and *political*—to depict two general ways of viewing human communication. These terms may be seen as a particular case of what Bateson (1979) more generally referred to as "classification of form" and "description of process," respectively. When we name the frame of reference that is the complement to the semantic frame of reference, our choice of name always carries a particular meaning. "Politics," for instance, may signify a wide variety of meanings for different observers. We, therefore, specifically define "politics" as the social organizational consequences of communication in order to construct a particular semantic frame of reference for viewing "politics." In general, since semantic and political frames of reference are always intertwined, any thinking about political frames of reference is always done in some semantic frame and vice versa.

All systemic family therapies involve semantic meanings coupled to the political patterns that organize social interaction. Unfortunately, some theories of systemic family therapy have discounted the semantic frame of reference. Systemic family therapists must reinstate the value of semantics by underscoring its interrelationship with political frames. The various systemic family therapies follow patterns of interwoven political and semantic frames and thereby construct therapeutic realities.

Mapping a Therapeutic Reality: A Case Study of Olga Silverstein

The treatment of a family that initially presented one member's migraine headache as the problem demonstrates how semantic and political frames of reference can be used to map a therapeutic reality. We are careful not to describe this case as "the family treatment of a migraine headache." Although the initial problem was an individual's migraine headache, after the headache was alleviated, other problems and "problem sites" emerged. In effect, the particular problem being treated in this case depends upon when and where an observer decides to punctuate the flow of events. We, therefore, simply acknowledge that the beginning of this family's treatment involved the presentation of a migraine headache.

The case was conducted by Olga Silverstein, a senior clinical faculty member of the Ackerman Institute for Family Therapy, with the assistance of a team of therapists behind a one-way mirror. Although the therapeutic interventions arose out of a group decision-making process, the same strategies could have been implemented by a solo therapist. The therapist could have utilized a "fantasy team," periodically leaving the family to imagine what a consulting team might be saying. Or the therapist could have remained in the room without any consultation, real or imaginary, and have achieved the same results. This case study is not about a team approach to family therapy although the work took place within the context of a clinical team.

The case should not be seen as a particular method for treating migraine headaches. Rather, it is a descriptive study of the communication patterns that organize one particular family's treatment and as a demonstration of how semantic and political frames of reference map and construct a particular family therapy case. The family included a mother, a father, a twelve-year-old son named Jim, and a nine-year-old daughter named Karen. The parents sought therapy in order to treat their daughter's severe migraine headaches. It began as a six-session case, and after a hiatus of two and a half years, involved two additional sessions. Segments of some sessions, which were videotaped, are presented with a running commentary.

SESSION 1

THERAPIST: So how bad are the headaches?

MOTHER: Very bad. They sometimes get her sick to her stomach. Her eyes become half-crossed and she loses control of her eye muscles.

THERAPIST: This is what you've observed?

MOTHER: Yes, she can't see in school. . . .

THERAPIST: It can happen in school?

MOTHER: Yes, quite often.

THERAPIST: What's quite often? Once a week, twice a week?

MOTHER: It had come down to every day for a while. It had

been once a week, then it increased to about three times a week, and then in November it was every day.

This session begins as a symptom or problem-focused therapy. The family has constructed the semantic frame of reference that they have come to therapy for treatment of the daughter's headaches. Using this frame, the therapist focuses on gathering observable behavioral data that will clearly specify what is meant by the term "headache." The therapist, by shifting the questions to address where the headaches happen, as well as their frequency, begins initiating a political frame of reference.

In the next segment, the different statements can be seen as requests for politics or semantics. This analysis will demonstrate how semantics and politics can be used to construct a "micromapping" of therapeutic communication.

THERAPIST: When she comes and tells you she's got a headache or feels like she's going to get a headache, what happens to you? What's your response? *(request for political frame)*

MOTHER: I give her the medication. *(reply is within political frame)*

THERAPIST: Well, what's your first inside response? *(another political request)*

MOTHER: As of now? *(laughter)* It's gotten bad. *(laughter)* I get very upset. *(shift to semantic frame)*

THERAPIST: You get very upset. How upset? *(therapist addresses semantic shift)*

MOTHER: I don't know how to explain how upset, but very . . . You know, up to the point where it's got me down because I don't know what to do. *(semantics)*

THERAPIST: So it's that kind of feeling. . . . You feel helpless. *(semantics)*

MOTHER: Exactly. Yes, what should I do? *(request for politics)*

THERAPIST: "What should I do?" What do you do? *(addresses politics)*

MOTHER: Well, if it's in the early stages and she just gets the stomach thing first, sometimes food helps her, if we can get her to eat. But if it gets into the nauseousness and into the head, then she'll get sick if she eats. We just give her medicine and most of the time she has to lay down; she can't stay on her feet. I stay with her because she's in terrible pain until it's over. *(politics)*

In general the therapist manages to ask questions that begin exposing the social organization of the headache. Knowing the mother's response to the occurrence of the daughter's headache enables the complementarity of problem and problem-solving behavior to be discerned, the perspective initially formulated by Paul Watzlawick, John Weakland, and Richard Fisch (1974). Primarily focusing on the social political consequences rather than semantic meanings of the symptomatic experience is the frame of reference the therapist now uses to organize her questions. (The reader is invited to continue micromapping the transcript in terms of semantics and politics. Our analysis will be limited to underscoring the most critical semantic and political frames that organize this family therapy.)

THERAPIST: Do you tell your husband, or what?

MOTHER: Yes, but most of the time he isn't there because of the hours he works.

THERAPIST: So then, if he is at home and Karen complains that she's going to get a headache, do you take care of her first and then tell him, or do you tell him first, and then take care of her?

MOTHER: I usually take care of her.

THERAPIST: Do you tell him about how upset you get? Do you talk about that?

MOTHER: Yes.

THERAPIST: Yes? Quite a lot?

The therapist has broadened the political context to include the father's participation. The focus remains upon examining the social organization of the problematic behavior.

FATHER: Well, as often as necessary. She's got upset to the point where she would actually cry. And rightly so, because it is a terrible thing to go through and watch this poor child suffer. . . .

MOTHER: She's in terrible pain. . . .
FATHER: And not be able to help her.
THERAPIST: Migraine headaches are awful.
FATHER: But on the whole I think she does everything that she's capable of and everything that's necessary. I think she's a good mother.

The father introduces a new semantic frame and thereby places the discussion about the daughter's headaches and what is done about them in the context of an evaluation of the mother—"I think she's a good mother." The therapist will immediately change her line of questioning to address this shift from politics to semantics.

THERAPIST: *(to mother)* So at first when the doctor told you they were tension headaches you thought, "Oh, I'm doing something wrong."
MOTHER: Yes.
THERAPIST: My poor child.
SON: Well, she does get worried sometimes.
THERAPIST: Do you think she worries about not being a good mother and making her child sick?
SON: No, I mean Karen worries, my sister.
THERAPIST: Oh, *Karen* worries.
SON: Sometimes.

At this point the therapist is attending to more than the relation between problem behavior and problem-solving behavior. Questions are not just limited to defining the problem and who-does-what-when in relation to it.

One way of mapping this therapy is to note that the therapist begins by addressing the semantics of what is communicated by the family and then shifts to a political frame of reference. For instance, when the family requests that the daughter's headache be addressed, the therapist inquires as to what is meant by "headache" in behavioral terms. The therapist then shifts the frame of reference to its political or social interactional context: what do the mother and father do in response to her headaches?

Following this line of questioning, the father steers the conversation back into the realm of semantics by suggesting that their efforts to help "mean" that his wife is a "good mother." The therapist immediately addresses this shift and even proposes the semantic link, "So when the doctor told you they were tension headaches you thought, 'Oh, I'm doing something wrong.' " Following this communication, the son states, "She does get worried sometimes." However, he is referring to his sister rather than his mother. At this point, the therapist will address the semantic frame of "worrying" by examining how it is politically organized in the family.

THERAPIST: What does Karen worry about?

SON: About school . . .

THERAPIST: How do you know that?

SON: She gets worried about a test that's going to happen the next day.

THERAPIST: She tells you that she's worried or she just kinda carries on about it?

SON: Yeah.

THERAPIST: How about you? Do you get worried about school?

The therapist is beginning to shift toward a larger political frame of reference. Each family member will be asked *how* he or she worries and what other members do in relation to it.

SON: No. Not at all.

THERAPIST: You're a good student? Is he, Karen?

DAUGHTER: Yes.

THERAPIST: So he's a good student. You're both in the same school?

FATHER: They were up until this year. Now he's going to junior high.

THERAPIST: So what happens when your sister gets all worried about a test or whatever in school? Do you help her? Do you say anything?

SON: I tell her, like we all tell her, that there's nothing to worry about.

THERAPIST: That doesn't help much. That doesn't help at all. All right. So she worries and Mother worries, and I guess you worry, too.

FATHER: In my own way. In my own fashion.
THERAPIST: What's your fashion of worrying?
FATHER: Oh, I think I don't show my emotions as much as they do. I do my share of worrying.
THERAPIST: Well, how would they know you're worrying about them?
FATHER: How would they know?
THERAPIST: What's your way?
FATHER: I try to be there when I'm needed . . . and I try to help them, help the children with their homework.
DAUGHTER: He helps a lot.
THERAPIST: Would you know that Dad's worrying about you? That's the question. Can you tell?
MOTHER: No.
THERAPIST: Even Mother can't tell when he's upset.
MOTHER: I talk a lot when I'm upset. I have to say what's bothering me. But he, my husband, can carry it quietly and alone and I don't know how he feels.
THERAPIST: Well, anyway, we know what Mother worries about. She worries about not being a good mother. That's one thing.
FATHER: She worries unnecessarily because I think she's a good mother.
THERAPIST: That's about as much help as telling Karen not to worry about being a bad student.
MOTHER: Exactly.
THERAPIST: That's in the same category—reassurance. It doesn't help.

We now know that the family knows when and how the daughter and mother worry. The mother talks a lot, presumably about not being a good mother, and the daughter gets a headache. Note, however, that the connection between headaches and worrying is implicitly accepted in this conversation: it is not directly explained.

We also know that family members attempt to reassure the mother and daughter when they worry—the brother tells the sister and the father tells the mother there is nothing to worry about.

The father and son are silent worriers. No one is able to know (or admit) when they are worrying.

MOTHER: Can you explain to her how she shouldn't worry? That's the hard part. That's what she doesn't know.

THERAPIST: Oh no. She's very good at worrying. Why should she stop that? Listen, some people don't know how to worry; that's not a good thing. Worrying is not a bad thing to be good at. A good worrier is a very important person in the family. Don't you let them try to talk you out of that. . . .

The therapist is now moving therapy from addressing the daughter's headaches to working on the whole family's worrying. Worry is framed as a valuable skill that positively contributes to family life. An assignment will now be constructed around this theme.

Before looking at that part of therapy, let us pause and reexamine the shift that has taken place in this first session. We mentioned earlier that the initial conversation would alternate between semantic and political frames of reference. A diagram summarizes this progression (see figure 1.1).

The beginning questions that organized the therapy concerned the daughter's headaches. This information was framed by a discussion of the social organization embodying her headaches, a shift from a semantic to a political frame. That discussion was then framed as defining the meaning of a good mother. Up to this point all of the session had been explicitly organized around the daughter's headaches. The progression between semantic and political frames can be seen as different ways of seeing her "headaches" in context.

The next change in therapy, however, involved a jump. Therapy moved from a focus on the daughter's headaches to how the family deals with worrying. At this phase, therapy has become more than an individual problem-solving approach and has moved toward a treatment of the whole family: how each member worries and how others know when they are worrying. The session continues to alternate between semantic and political

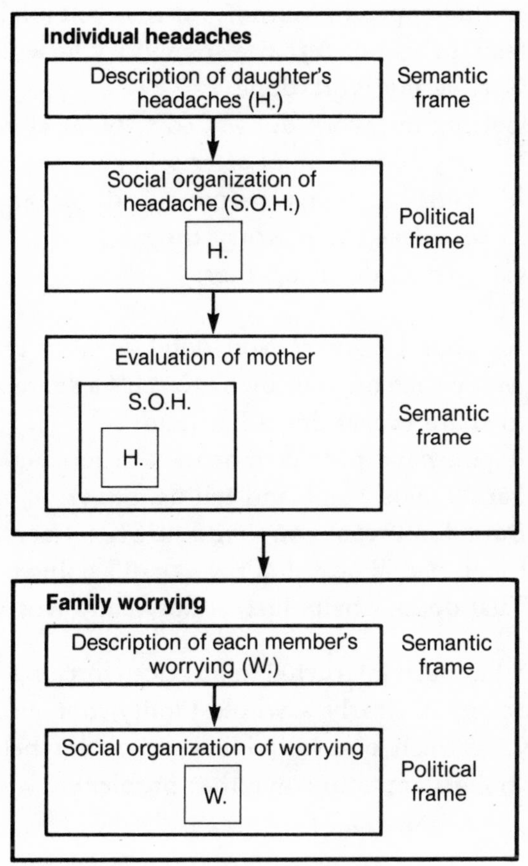

frames of reference, but from now on the central organizing distinction is family worrying.

THERAPIST: I want you to put aside a certain amount of time every day to worry. If you don't worry and try to just put it away, it won't go away. It just sneaks up on you when you don't expect it. It sneaks up in bad places like when you're playing or other inconvenient times. I want you to set aside a time every day and say, "Okay, I'm going to worry right before breakfast." Take five minutes and worry. Think of all the things you have to worry about. For instance, worry that something could happen to Mummy, or that you might fail your tests in school. What else might you worry about?

DAUGHTER: Getting my work done.

THERAPIST: Getting my work done? Okay, what else?

SON: I worry about school after school.

THERAPIST: It's better to worry before so you get it over with. Take a designated worry time.

DAUGHTER: Can we all do it together?

FATHER: Right.

THERAPIST: All four together? You don't want a little private worry time on your own? Karen's a sharer—she likes to share everything all around.

FATHER: If you have problems or they're too big for you to handle, you come and tell us, okay?

THERAPIST: But I don't want you to reassure her. I don't want you to tell her, "Look, don't worry, it's going to be okay." That doesn't help. Just sit down and worry with her.

The family has been instructed to practice worrying. Again, the unit of treatment is clearly a whole family, not just the complementarity between one individual's problem behavior and other members' attempts to solve that problem.

SESSION 2

THERAPIST: How worried did you get?

DAUGHTER: Not that much.

THERAPIST: Not that much?

DAUGHTER: It was hard.

THERAPIST: Was it hard to do? I thought that you were a pretty good worrier. The whole family has been telling me that all you do is worry all the time.

DAUGHTER: It was hard.

THERAPIST: It was hard. Maybe you snuck in a few worries when you weren't supposed to. *(to mother)* What were you doing when they were doing their worrying?

MOTHER: I don't know. I just tried to remind her to worry.

THERAPIST: You would say, "You haven't done your worrying today"?

MOTHER: I wanted to make sure that . . .
THERAPIST: They did it right.
MOTHER: Right.
THERAPIST: She doesn't even think you'll worry right.
DAUGHTER: I almost forgot one day.
THERAPIST: Well, you can always count on Mom to remind you, can't you?
DAUGHTER: Mmm.
THERAPIST: Well, I guess what I'm thinking is that you're really not worrying enough, that you're really not doing a good job at that. And I think that Dad has sort of let down on his part of it. He doesn't sit and worry with you. He does other things.
MOTHER: Should it be an out loud talking thing or a . . .
THERAPIST: Well, it's up to Karen. It doesn't have to be.
DAUGHTER: Sometimes I don't know what to worry about. One day I worried about having to worry. *(laughter)*
THERAPIST: Well, that's a good thing to worry about, but I'm very disappointed because what everybody in the family told me was that you were an expert worrier, and now you tell me that sometimes you can't think of anything to worry about. I'm really very disappointed to hear that. I think this family really needs you to worry for them.

The therapist is using the semantic frame of worrying as a way of getting at family politics. This is made possible by the logic the therapist has constructed involving: (1) prescriptions to worry that imply that the family, particularly the daughter, is having difficulty in achieving "satisfactory" worrying; and (2) the daughter's worrying being semantically framed as an experience the "family really needs." Note that this session again alternates between political and semantic frames.

SESSIONS 3, 4, AND 5

These sessions continued to explore how and whether the family members were worrying. In the fourth session, the daughter announced that she had had no headaches. The therapist quickly responded, "I don't want you to stop those headaches too soon.

That's something I would begin to worry about. . . . I wonder if this week you could plan to have one little headache." The daughter never reported another migraine.

With that development, the father began complaining about the way his wife attempted to stop him from overeating and overdrinking *(political frame of reference).* The therapist subsequently framed her behavior as "being a good mother" to him *(semantic frame of reference).* When the therapist asked what would happen if she stopped taking care of him *(shift to political frame),* he responded, "I'm going to have a heart attack and die." As the complaints of the husband escalate, the consulting team behind the mirror introduces the message that they are worried about the way the therapist is pushing the argument between the couple. The therapist, however, takes the position, "I feel I know you better than they do, and I agree with the kids that nobody is going to cut out on anybody in this family. . . . There's nothing to be afraid of." Upon hearing this, the daughter immediately responds, "If they did it, I would stop them." The therapist then comments, "You would stop them although I don't think it's your job to stop them." The therapist then instructs the mother to increase her "worrying" about the father.

At this point, the therapist and consulting team take two different positions with respect to the political action occurring in the session. The team vaguely expresses concern over how the couple's interaction might be calibrated; the therapist vaguely implies that there is no reason to fear that calibration will involve someone "cutting out." In response to these communications, the daughter announces that her behavior will calibrate them. In effect, the family and therapists have moved to addressing the cybernetic pattern that organizes and stabilizes their interaction *(political frame).*

SESSION 6

MOTHER: Well, you told me to mother him more and when I did, he'd come back and say, "Well, I'll do what I want," and I just didn't know what to do and I think I did something wrong because Karen was instigating. She would say, "Mummy, you're not doing it. . . ."

THERAPIST: Well, she said she was going to help you.

MOTHER: Well, she did *(laughter)* and she'd start something and I'd say, "Okay, I'll say something too," and then he'd snap back and she'd keep going but it made me nervous. . . .

THERAPIST: What made you nervous?

MOTHER: I don't know what I thought would happen. He was getting mad.

The daughter continues to calibrate the escalation of the interaction between the mother and father. Her manner of calibration has shifted, at this point, from migraine headaches to cutting in on her parents' conversations.

Since the original presenting problem had been alleviated, the father decides to terminate the case. The last part of this session addressed the parents' relationship. The father was praised as a devoted and contented father, whereas the mother was depicted as not as happy as he was *(semantic frames).* It was pointed out that this must concern him. He was told to resist his wife's efforts to change him *(political frame),* even though his wife feels that he is turned off *(semantic frame).* The mother agreed with this proposal and went on to say that "he never turns on." Subsequently, the therapist instructed her to turn off a little bit so that he would be able to turn on. As the therapist stated, "He can afford to always be turned off because he knows you're always turned on." The following exchange then took place:

MOTHER: I'm afraid he isn't going to come to. He just feels that I'll be there and I'll take care of him and think of everything.

THERAPIST: But he's right, isn't he?

MOTHER: He is right, but I don't want it to be that way.

THERAPIST: Then we can help you a little bit with that. On the other hand, it's nice to have such a contented husband.

FATHER: She'd rather be a contented wife.

Therapy has thus moved from the daughter's migraine headaches to family worrying to the marriage and calibration of marital interaction by the daughter. The family leaves the session with the therapist constructing multiple semantic frames for the marriage involving good mothering, parental devotion and content, and sexual excitement. These semantic frames are delivered in a fashion that prescribes complementarity for the couple's interaction *(political frame).* For instance, one spouse is instructed to "turn off a little bit" so that the other can "turn on."

SESSION 7 (TWO AND ONE-HALF YEARS LATER)

After two and one-half years, the family returns to therapy. This time the mother complains that she is worrying about her son's performance in school. The therapist reminds the family that two and one-half years ago it was said that the family "needs a good worrier" *(semantic frame)* and that "everybody in this family knows that someone is going to supply you [mother] with something to worry about" *(political frame).*

MOTHER: I'd rather not have the job.

THERAPIST: You'd rather not have the job. Well, who would you like to take it?

MOTHER: I don't know.

THERAPIST: Well, you don't want Karen to. She says no *(laughter).*

MOTHER: No way.

THERAPIST: How about you, Jim? Could you be the family worrier? It'd be a very good thing to do.

SON: How am I supposed to start?

THERAPIST: Oh, it wouldn't be so hard. Karen did such a good job of it; she's a great example. I guess you've forgotten, maybe we have the old tapes. You can come home after school and say, "I don't know if I'll ever get my work done. I don't know what to do about my work. I'm so worried about school."

SON: I worry about that, but I don't worry about them.

THERAPIST: No, just worry about your school work out loud instead of to yourself.

SON: You mean if I had anything that I was worried about

I should just say it out loud? How would that affect her?

THERAPIST: You'd be surprised. You know, I'm sure how that works in this family. As soon as you start worrying, she begins to say, "Oh, Jim, don't worry. Everything's going to be okay. We don't want you to worry." Right? Isn't that the way it works?

SON: How can I start doing it?

THERAPIST: You've got to do a good job. You just can't worry a little. You have to say things like "I can't eat my dinner," "I've got a stomach ache," "I can't get my work done," "I'm so worried about school."

SON: Create worries.

THERAPIST: You really do worry about it, but you just don't tell them. So your mother does the worrying for you since she picks it up. In this family, worry is the theme that gets passed around. You all need a worrier. Your father says he doesn't want the job. Your sister had her share. She's not doing it anymore. Your mother's tired—look at her. . . .

The therapist builds upon the therapy that had been constructed several years ago. Namely, any individual's presenting problem is semantically framed as a problem in how the whole family handles worrying. Within this structure, symptoms can be positively connoted and prescribed. The therapist continues to shift back and forth between semantic and political frames—asking questions that expose both meaning and interpersonal consequences.

THERAPIST: My consultants *(team behind the one-way mirror)* say they're worried. *(laughter)* If you stop worrying about your son, then you're going to start worrying about your husband.

MOTHER: I have to keep finding something?

SON: Sounds logical.

DAUGHTER: Sure.

THERAPIST: Could you say a little more about that?

SON: She's worried about me now. . . . I'm worried about

my dad. Once he broke his ankle and was not working. . . . Now when he goes out in the snow or whatever, I figure something might happen to him. A few times I mentioned it to her, and she said she doesn't worry too much about that.

FATHER: You worry about me? I didn't think he cared.

THERAPIST: You didn't? Really?

FATHER: He never expresses himself to me.

THERAPIST: He just did.

FATHER: He always talks to his mother, he doesn't talk to me. He doesn't open up to me, he doesn't confide in me. I don't know, maybe I shut him out.

THERAPIST: I don't know because it seems he's doing a great job for you though.

FATHER: He's doing a great job for me?

THERAPIST: Yes, he's really doing a great job. . . . He agrees with the group that if Mother stopped worrying about him, she'd be on your back much more. So Jim keeps Mother occupied. Like a guard in football . . . I don't even know the positions on a football team. You tell me. Who's the guy who runs interference for the guy who's carrying the ball?

FATHER: Guard.

THERAPIST: He always gets tackled and you're free to run with the ball.

FATHER: Okay.

THERAPIST: Better him than you.

FATHER: Right!

Let us now review some of the major episodes in this family's treatment. The initial sessions shifted the presenting problem to the semantic frame of "family worrying." Each family member was politically addressed through questions about how he or she worries and the family was told that they need to continue worrying, but in an altered way. Specifically, the daughter was instructed to choose a time to worry for the family and the family was told to worry together. By session 4, the daughter's headaches had completely stopped and the mother began expressing her worries about the father's overeating and overdrinking.

Sessions 3, 4, 5, and 6 addressed the political calibration of the mother and father's interaction by the daughter's behavior. Her calibration behavior had shifted, however, from headaches to verbally interrupting her parents' disagreements. Therapeutic interventions subsequently addressed the positive contribution of such calibration but underscored the possibility that allowing the parents to have a fight might not be bad. Now, two and one-half years later, the role of calibrating the mother and father's interaction has shifted to the son.

Carl Whitaker (1979) has politically defined a healthy family as a social system where all roles constantly shift from member to member. It is clear in the above case that the therapist is implicitly suggesting such a structure for the family—the role of worrying, as well as scapegoat, should be shared. The therapist was able to achieve such a prescription by beginning with a problem-solving focus, alternating between semantic and political frames, and allowing the family plus the therapist to construct a family problem rather than an individual problem.

THERAPIST: Since two and one-half years ago, the family has found a new way to stabilize things in order to make sure that the two of you never really get into it, never really fight things out; I think that's probably very important. And since Karen gave up the job, you're lucky you've got two kids and Jim took over. If you'd stop worrying about your father, then they might have a couple of really good fights.

The therapist has actually given the family a cybernetic description of how they organize their behavior *(political frame):* the children calibrate their parents' interaction in such a way that the parents do not "fight things out." Of course, this description could also have been stated in reverse: the parents calibrate the children's behavior by "not fighting things out." Cybernetically speaking, the combination of both descriptions provides a recursive or double view of this family's pattern of organizing itself.

SON: How would that be good?

THERAPIST: I didn't say it would be good. I'm just saying that

that's what might happen. I don't say it would be bad.

SON: There must be a reason for what you're saying, but I don't know what it is.

THERAPIST: I used to think that it was Mother who the children were worried about and taking care of, but I don't think so any more. I think it's Father. And you think they don't care, but I think they care a great deal and that you're the guy people run interference for. Maybe they think that in some way you can't take care of yourself.

The previous "meaning" of the children's calibration of parental interaction has been that it somehow is connected to doing something for the mother (for example, providing her with something to worry about). In session 1 the behavioral definition of the mother's worrying was that she talked a lot. Thus, through a logic of association, the children's problematic behavior gives the mother something to talk about. Now, however, the therapist is suggesting that their calibrating behavior is also connected to the father—that it somehow protects him.

DAUGHTER: It all makes sense to me.

THERAPIST: So, it makes sense to Karen, too. Listen, Jim, I know it's hard, a big burden to place on you, but if you see that things begin to change a little bit and your mother gets more concerned about your father than about you, then I think you should quickly give her something to worry about. . . .

The therapist continues to prescribe that the family alter *how* they fulfill the political consequences of problem behavior. Throughout the sessions, problem behavior or symptomatic experience per se has never been prescribed or not prescribed. Rather, the political consequences of such behavior have been addressed in a way that accepts and modifies how the family has been organizing itself.

FATHER: I never know what he's thinking or what he's worrying about. Do I give you anything to worry about?

DAUGHTER: I could get a headache.

THERAPIST: Would you do that?

DAUGHTER: I don't want to.

THERAPIST: What could you do?

DAUGHTER: I have a teacher in school that I could always talk about.

THERAPIST: I see, you could start complaining about school. That's very good. Terrific.

MOTHER: She's just like me—she jumped in to save them.

THERAPIST: Who's she saving?

MOTHER: Both of them, I think. She doesn't want Jim to get all the blame and all the problems. Also, she doesn't want her father to get too upset so she's going to run the interference.

THERAPIST: Right. But the group says they feel it should be that way, that the women in this family are stronger than the men, and that it's their job to protect the guys and that's the way it ought to be. I don't agree with that. You might. I may be wrong.

In the first session, the mother and daughter could behaviorally define how they worry, whereas the father and son could not. At this point in therapy, the mother has again provided a distinction between sexes, this time in terms of how they "save" the men. Therapist and consulting team subsequently mirror this split in order to avoid taking either side at the expense of the other. This political positioning helps avoid problematic issues arising from what some therapists would call family "resistance."

FATHER: I don't think that I give anyone reason to worry about me. Do I?

SON: I think you have a crummy life.

FATHER: I have a crummy life?

SON: You work all week and at night you say you're too tired to do anything but sit down and watch TV or sleep. You work around the house but that's no fun. The only fun you get is playing darts every Friday night. I don't think that's a good life.

DAUGHTER: I was thinking that.

THERAPIST: You've had that thought, too.

SON: Boy, it's a real shame for a man to have that kind of life. . . . But what can I do?

THERAPIST: What you can do is make sure that your mother does not get after him about the kind of life he has.

SON: How do I do that?

THERAPIST: The way you've been doing it . . . but put a little more effort in it. . . . Keep her worried about you.

SON: That I can't do.

THERAPIST: That's the least you can do for him. If you really feel so bad for him and worried about him, then what you must do is make sure that you don't add to his burdens by having the two of them really argue or be unhappy with each other.

Again, political calibration of parental interaction by children is addressed, this time in terms of the meaning of preventing "unhappiness." Note that the therapist has waited until the family provided the semantic clues for framing this calibration. Now that it has been presented, therapy can make another logical jump.

THERAPIST: The group wants to know if you think your father is happy with your mother.

SON: Mmm.

THERAPIST: You do. You're sure about that?

SON: I think that he thinks she's a good wife.

THERAPIST: Let me ask you the question the other way. Do you think your mother's happy with your father?

SON: No.

THERAPIST: No. I see. So that's one of the things you're angry with him about.

SON: Um.

THERAPIST: No?

SON: I'm not now because he says he's happy. It's hard for me to believe . . .

FATHER: What is there to believe? What do you think would better my life? If you can come up with that, I would appreciate it.

SON: I think you should do more things than watching TV.

FATHER: Like what?

SON: I don't know what interests you. I guess that watching TV is your main thing so . . .

FATHER: I just asked you, "What do you think would interest me?" More than TV?

SON: I don't know. I suggested lots of things, but you just tell me, "Not now, I'm too tired from work." So you sit down and watch TV for the rest of the forty-eight hours every weekend.

FATHER: I don't think I do that.

SON: Well, you go to church.

THERAPIST: Is this the argument that hangs in the air between you and your husband?

MOTHER: Yes.

THERAPIST: This is the argument that your son is expressing for you?

MOTHER: Yes.

THERAPIST: You think your mother is going to get bored with him and fed up one of these days?

SON: I don't know.

THERAPIST: You're just trying so hard to really help them. You're trying to help them by making suggestions about how he can make his life more interesting. . . . I'm wondering whether you're really more worried that Mother will get fed up with it.

SON: He says he's happy.

THERAPIST: And then he really would be alone and unhappy and sitting alone and watching TV.

SON: I never thought of it that way.

Thus, the son's problem behavior was initially framed as a way of worrying for the family that served the function of calibrating parental interaction. Its positive political contribution to the family was in terms of an attempt to make the father's life more interesting so as to save the mother (and father) from a boring marriage.

At this time every family member has experienced being the

carrier of the family problem. Therapy began with the daughter's headaches and then addressed the mother's unhappiness, the son's school problems, and the father's boring lifestyle. Each problem definition was presented by the family and then played back to the family by the therapist.

In this sense, the family guided the course of therapy, that is, whom the focus would be on, the semantics to be used in describing/explaining their situation, political connections and links across different members, and so on. This therapy has clearly utilized and followed the family's own resources.

LAST SESSION

This session begins with a discussion of the many changes that have taken place in the family including the mother getting a job. Therapy ends with the following exchange, which focuses on the father's participation in worrying for the family:

THERAPIST: I have a long and complicated message from the group. Jim, last time we told you that if you got worried about your mom getting bored with your dad and going off, you would probably do something to help out by having some more trouble at school. First of all, the group wanted to tell you that you're really right on target and you're doing a fairly good job of it. That's to begin with. However, there's more. There have been a lot of shifts and changes in this family and sometimes that's very difficult. Things get all shaken up for a while and your mother's moving out to get a job has not been an easy thing for the family to assimilate. One of the things that has gotten a little out of kilter is Father. He has never worried about anything, because Mother was in charge of the worry department and did so well at it that he was totally free not to worry. Now he finds himself as the sole worrier in this family. He's not used to it and it's very upsetting to him. But, I think that maybe we have learned something by that: when one person stops worrying, the other one starts. In a family it works that way. So maybe it would help you, Father, to give up the piece of worrying you do about your son and his grades because as long as you worry, your son won't. He doesn't have to. So, now we'd like to help you pass the load about his school work to him.

FATHER: Fantastic! *(father throws report card into boy's lap)*

THERAPIST: Exactly. *(laughter) (to mother)* It's going to be very difficult for you to trust the men in the family, either one of them, because you didn't have such a great experience with the men you grew up with.

MOTHER: I know. My two brothers, my father, and my uncles were all alcoholics. . . .

THERAPIST: All along the line. So no matter how much we tell you that these guys are different and no matter how much evidence you have of how dependable your husband is, that he doesn't drink, works steadily, and doesn't let you down and so on, there is that echo of worrying about the men and something happening to them. So although we're not worried about your husband's ability to be a father to his son . . . as a matter of fact, we feel quite confident that that's not going to be a problem for you *(father)* . . . we're concerned that it's going to be a problem for you *(mother)* to trust and not interfere.

MOTHER: It's me! *(laughter)*

THERAPIST: That's going to be a real problem. So what we would like you to do is go back to an original formula. You're going to have to worry again.

MOTHER: In general?

THERAPIST: No, something like five minutes a day.

MOTHER: Okay.

THERAPIST: And in those five minutes, I want you to think or keep a list of all the terrible things that could happen to them. And do that every day.

MOTHER: I will. Once a day?

THERAPIST: Once a day. Maybe just five minutes. Just take five minutes and sit and don't tell them about it.

MOTHER: I have been doing that for a while anyway.

THERAPIST: But you'll worry *specifically* about how they'll fail—about the way in which they're going to fail. There's no way you can stop worrying because you've such a real history of men to worry about.

MOTHER: I understand.

THERAPIST: No matter how much evidence they give you that they're different, there's always that fear.

MOTHER: Definitely.

THERAPIST: . . . of how they won't be.

MOTHER: Definitely.

THERAPIST: Right?

MOTHER: Yes.

THERAPIST: I think that might help.

MOTHER: I'll do that.

THERAPIST: And the other thing: it's also necessary to realize that we don't share Mother's worry, but that doesn't matter.

The explanatory comments that were interspersed throughout the case presentation point to a cybernetic view of therapeutic communication, articulated in terms of laws of therapeutic form. Delineating the process of therapeutic change involved addressing changing patterns of communication rather than reified descriptions of biochemical, psychological, or social components. Therapy was organized to include all members in constructing political and semantic frames of reference. This therapy provided a context wherein the family could change the way they change in order to maintain their stable organization. This change of change required that the therapist accept, respect, and challenge all communication that the family presented.

CHAPTER 2

Multiple Communication in Systemic Therapy

> An inevitable dualism bisects nature, so that each thing is a half, and suggests another thing to make it whole. . . . Whilst the world is thus dual, so is everyone of its parts. The entire system of things gets represented in every particle. . . . The same dualism underlies the nature and condition of man. Every excess causes a defect; every defect an excess. Every sweet hath its sour; every evil its good.
>
> —RALPH WALDO EMERSON
> *The Complete Writings, 1929*

IN HIS BOOK *Mind and Nature: A Necessary Unity* (1979), Gregory Bateson argued that multiple descriptions, rather than singular descriptions, enable one to construct a systemic view of human relationship and interaction. When two people interact, each member has a particular view of his flow of interaction. If an observer combines both of these views, a sense of the whole system will emerge. Bateson called such a multiple view "double description" and compared it to binocular vision. He concluded "that the combination of diverse pieces of information" defines a way of approaching what he called "patterns which connect" (1979, p. 68) and prescribes a particular scientific methodology: "the *manner of search* of the science called 'epistemology' " involves the comparison of multiple views.

The notion of multiple views can be extended to understanding and organizing communication in therapy, and in this chapter we present a particular model of multiple communication for understanding and organizing systemic therapies.

Any discussion of multiple communication in therapy must include a reference to the pioneering clinical work of Milton H. Erickson. A skilled observer of human interaction, he found that different patterns of such behavior as body movement, breathing rate, voice tonality, and speech indicated that people are always part of an organized system of diverse communications. Rather than looking for singular communications, Erickson preferred a more complex and systemic view of multiple communications. Erickson trained himself not only to construct multiple descriptions of communication but to perform multiple *prescriptions.* He became remarkably skilled at both sequentially and simultaneously weaving multiple communications in the course of therapeutic intervention. He would sometimes alter his voice to mark a trance suggestion within a conversation: "Oh yes, Joe, I grew up on a farm, I think a tomato seed is a wonderful thing, *think, Joe, think* in that little seed there does *sleep so restfully, so comfortably* a beautiful plant yet to be grown that will bear such interesting leaves and branches" (Haley 1973, p. 303).

Our view of multiple communication in systemic therapies builds upon the ideas and techniques set forth by Bateson and Erickson. In this chapter we first describe how multiple communications are structured in terms of distinction and recursive complementarity and then present a cybernetic model of multiple communication based on the complementarity of stability and change. Finally, a case study illustrates how this view of multiple communication describes and prescribes systemic interventions.

Distinction and Recursive Complementarity

A wide variety of theoretical positions suggests that experience is structured in terms of pairs, dualities, or distinctions and that "any pattern, value, ideal, or behavioral tendency is always present at any time, along with its polar opposite. Only the relative emphasis given each pole and the ways of arranging their simultaneous expression tend to change" (Slater 1974, pp. 182–83).

We may view therapy in a similar fashion: a particular communication can be seen as half of a more encompassing pair, duality, or distinction. Clients who propose that they want to get rid of their discomforting bouts with depression, for instance, can also be seen as communicating (usually on a different level) that they want to maintain the positive social consequences the depressive episodes provide. Similarly, a request to change one family member can be seen as connected to a request to change (or stabilize) another family member.

For instance, a wife may experience back pains after receiving an invitation to a social party. Although the husband complains that he isn't able to see their friends because of her "condition," one implication is that her symptom serves to protect him from being in a situation that is "too social," something he is unconsciously worried about. When his worry about being with others calms down, his wife may begin approaching social events. This subsequently results in the husband having back pains and the entire dramatic scenario becomes reversed. Any request by one spouse to change his or her symptomatic experience can thus be seen as a simultaneous request to change the other spouse. From a somewhat different perspective, any proposal to change symptomatic experience implies a request to change the way in which they maintain stability in the relationship.

In general, all distinctions propose multiple communications. One cannot speak of change without implying stability, autonomy without interdependence, parts without wholes, competition without cooperation. When any differentiation is made, two ways of talking about its sides are always present: (1) we may speak of their *distinction;* or (2) we may talk about their *connection.* Using our previous example, we might choose to see each spouse as requesting change of symptomatic experience without any consideration for how that change connects with stability of their relationship. Or we may choose to see the complementary connection of change and stability.

As an example outside of therapy, consider the distinction between predator and prey. The logic of this relationship is often specified in terms of a predator attempting to catch his prey where there can only be victory for the predator (unless absence of the predator's victory is seen as victory for the prey). On the level of individual foxes and rabbits, for instance, the fox is usually seen as working for a momentary victory. At the level of species interaction, however, the population size of the fox will be curbed by the population size of rabbits. Each individual victory for a fox may therefore be seen as contributing to what someday will be a loss for the fox population.

This suggests that any distinction cast in terms of victories and losses is incomplete. For the predator/prey dichotomy, a more encompassing system frames it:

(predator/prey)

ecosystem/species interaction

The patterns of species interaction provide the way in which an entire ecosystem is kept in balance. To take the side of either predator or prey is to risk breaking a larger pattern of interaction. As can be seen in the work of Francisco Varela (1979), any distinction with an underlying logic of competition is also part of a more encompassing distinction with an underlying logic of cooperation. For example, "predator/prey" points to a logic of competition, whereas "ecosystem/species interaction" points to a logic of cooperation. If someone asks, "What is the relation between foxes and rabbits?" with what we now know, we can counter, "At what order of process? They battle with each other as individual members, but cooperate with each other as whole species."

In family therapy, requests to unilaterally change one member's symptomatic experience underscores the distinction between who is troubled, sick, or problematic and who is not. From another perspective, the family can be seen as cooperating in such a way that each member contributes to stability of the relationship structure.

All distinctions of therapy can thus be perceived by an observer as either: (1) a duality of excluding opposites; or (2) a recursive complementarity of self-referential sides. "Recursive complementarity" refers to the higher-order view of a distinction where the interaction between its different sides is underscored. Here, the two sides must maintain a difference to interact, while their interaction connects them as a whole system. Recursive complementarity thus points to how the different sides of a relation participate as a complementary connection and yet remain distinct. As the Zen people say it, "Not one, not two."

Any distinction taken as an either/or duality can be reframed as the right-hand side of a more encompassing recursive complementarity (Varela 1979). With this shift, what may have appeared as battling opposites becomes a pattern of interaction stabilizing the organization of a whole system. Battles to eradicate one individual's migraine headaches, as seen in the previous chapter, became transformed into a task requiring the whole family to cooperate in worrying together. In this clinical context, the duality of excluding opposites revolves around the absence or presence of migraine headaches, whereas the view of recursive complementarity underscores each family member's contribution to stabilizing the whole family system.

The distinction between semantics and politics also offers a recursive complementarity when semantic meaning provides for patterns of political organization that subsequently lead back to semantic meaning. Thus semantics and politics feed off each other. When a symptomatic child is labeled a "spoiled brat," family politics will be markedly different than had the child been labeled "psychotic." In such a frame of reference the child's problem behavior needs appropriate parental discipline rather than medical attention. This shift in politics will, in turn, lead to other frames of meaning. Effective parental discipline, for instance, may require that husband and wife find a way of getting together on marital issues that trouble them. This may lead them to a broader scope of interpersonal politics that includes their relationships with their parents, friends, and employers.

Thus, therapies are constructed through the recursive drawing of distinctions and distinctions upon distinctions. In this way, ideas, patterns, and whole mental systems participate in ever-shifting frames of reference. Therapy is a nesting of semantic and political frames interrelated as recursive complementarities.

A Cybernetic Model of Multiple Communication

We define cybernetics as the study of a particular recursive complementarity concerned with the interrelation of stability and change. This view is captured in a statement by Gregory Bateson (1972, p. 381): "all change can be understood as the effort to maintain some constancy and all constancy as maintained through change." For years, theorists and therapists have argued whether families should be seen primarily in terms of processes of change or patterns of stability. Families are described as either change oriented, stable oriented, or a balanced combination of these distinct processes. In cybernetics, however, one can never separate stability from change—both are complementary sides of a recursive coin.

This framing of stability and change can also be seen in terms of Bateson's (1979) notion of "double description." Given two drawings of a cube, each taken from the perspective of a monocular view, a stereoscope can fuse these representations into a double view of higher logical type—both two-dimensional drawings are combined to generate a three-dimensional view. Extending this notion, we can assume that each side of a conceptual distinction can be fused through a cognitive act (analogous to the operation of a stereoscope) that produces a higher-order view. From the perspective of double description, change and stability are seen as two sides of a cybernetic complementarity: families cannot be described as changing without consideration for their stability and vice versa.

Thus, the French proverb, the more things change, the more they remain the same, can be stood on its head: the more things remain the same, the more they are changing. The tightrope walker must continuously sway to remain in balance; the way to remain balanced while standing in a canoe is to make it rock. Applying this perspective to social systems, Bateson proposes, "You can't have a marriage and not quarrel with your wife" (cited in Bateson and Brown 1975, p. 47).

Definition of Cybernetic System

A cybernetic system, whether it involves a man and canoe or a husband and wife, can be defined as follows:

$$\text{cybernetic system} = (\text{stability}/\text{change})$$

The recursive complementarity between stability and change specifies a cybernetic system. Cybernetic systems are therefore patterns of organization that maintain stability through processes of change.*

Cyberneticians have traditionally referred to this pattern of recursive complementarity as "feedback." Stated in our terms, feedback is a method of *stabilizing* a system by recycling into it the *changes* of its past performance. When this definition of cybernetic feedback system is identified as "mind," as Bateson (1972, 1979) proposed, mind becomes immanent not only in simple living systems but also in brains, conversations, and various social contexts. Thus, the double view of change and stability, when appropriately combined, provides a glimpse of mind in therapy.

Seen from the perspective of multiple communication, cybernetic systems provide communications of both change and stability. In therapy, the troubled system can be depicted as communicating a message that requests stability of the system's survival or identity while communicating another message that requests change in the particular way it maintains itself.

Therapeutic Change and Meaningful Noise

One way of summarizing this double view of therapeutic change is to note that it involves a communication about "change of change." Specifically, therapeutic change can be mapped as follows:

$$(\text{stability}/\text{change})_1 \xrightarrow{\quad} \text{intervention}\ (\text{stability}/\text{change})_2$$

*The complementarity between stability and change has been alluded to by Watzlawick, Weakland, and Fisch (1974, p. 1) as "the paradoxical relationship between persistence and change."

where the system at $time_2$ is more adaptive than it was at $time_1$. In effect, the system requests or searches for a way of changing how it changes in order to stabilize its organization as a more adaptive system.

Following Ross Ashby (1956) and Gregory Bateson (1979), all adaptive change requires a source of the "new" from which alternative behaviors, choices, structures, patterns, may be drawn. Although Ashby and Bateson referred to this source of the new as "random," it is important to realize that not all sources of randomness or noise are effective in therapy. Clients, as well as therapists, must *believe* that there is some communication that not only is new to them but has *meaning.* We therefore prefer to speak of this communication as "meaningful noise"*

The term "meaningful noise" suggests a communication punctuated by an observing system. What is "meaningful" arises from the action of a particular observer. If a client believes there is meaning in a communication, his search for meaning will help construct it. Sources of meaningful noise may include references to family history, cultural myth, psychobabble, religious metaphor, and stories about other clients (fictional or not). The descriptions and explanations clients propose or request are the best clues for what form of noise will be useful.

At this point, a more complete model of therapeutic change can be sketched:

(stability/change) / meaningful noise

Here the left side of the expression indicates a cybernetic system that alters the way it changes through the construction of alternative patterns out of meaningful noise. The above expression is therefore simply a recursion of the primitive cybernetic complementarity between stability and change:

stability / change

(stability/change) / meaningful noise

*In a previous work (Keeney 1983), this communication was referred to as a "meaningful Rorschach." We have changed this term to "meaningful noise" because the word "Rorschach" carries distracting connotations.

Thus, meaningful noise points to a higher-order process of change.* At this level, a cybernetic system requests both a change of change and a new way of stabilizing its stability. To do so requires encountering a third communication that provides a meaningful source of the random from which a different, and hopefully more adaptive, pattern of organization can be constructed.

The Cybernetic Structure of Interventions

Using these ideas, different therapies can be seen with respect to how they address and organize the multiple communications concerning change, stability, and meaningful noise. A cybernetic view of multiple communication in systemic therapy begins with the assumption that troubled systems present multiple communications, sometimes taken as contradictory, to a therapist. These communications include: "change us" and "stabilize us." These two communications, when viewed as a double description, mark the recursive complementarity of a cybernetic system. In effect, dual requests for stability and change are a way of indicating that the system is exploring the possibility of altering the way it changes in order to remain stable.

A cybernetic view of therapeutic intervention suggests that a therapist mirror the multiple communications a troubled family presents. Accordingly, therapists may inform families to change *and* stabilize. Again, these messages are not contradictory, nor do they involve a logic of negation, but are connected through a logic of complementarity. An awareness of cybernetic or recursive complementarity in family process brings to light a number of interesting observations long known to therapists. For instance, prescribing a symptom while scheduling another session to work on the problem is a way of requesting both stability and change.

*More specifically, "meaningful noise" is a double description incorporating the two necessary components of *stochastic process* (see Bateson, 1979): a source of the random *(noise)* and a process of selection (an observer constructing *meaning*).

On the other hand, both messages may be proposed to a family that reports symptom disappearance—warning them of a relapse while simultaneously giving them a vacation from therapy.

It often takes profound clinical artistry to simultaneously communicate apparently incongruent ideas to a troubled system in a way that helps the family move toward more adaptive ways of relating. A therapist might smile and wink at the wife, and, at the same time, instruct the husband to continue being a nuisance to his wife because they might not be ready for too sudden a change in their relationship. The advent of brief family therapy teams, however, has made it possible to more easily divide and manage the communications requesting change and stability. With a therapy team, one member can request that things remain the same while another can request change.*

Teams or solo therapists who merely prescribe a symptom or positively connote it will fail if they do not simultaneously (or sequentially) request change. Similarly, congruent commands for change frequently only introduce to therapy that beast often called "resistance." The art of therapy requires successfully handling requests for both change and stability. This requires speaking the complementary voices of change and stability in the language or system of metaphors that the family brings to therapy. The way a troubled family communicates about its situation may inform the therapist how to request and underscore both sides of what they experience as a battle of differences. In the case study presented in chapter 1, the therapist used the semantic frame of "worrying" as a way of prescribing stability and change. The family was instructed to continue worrying (stability), but in an altered way (change).

In the approach to systemic family therapy presented at the end of this chapter, problems and difficulties are seen in terms of how they provide both positive and negative contributions to the system that contains them. Here the advantages or gains of the problem are framed as part of the family's request for stability,

*For instance, the family therapy team work at Purdue University (see Keeney 1981) explicitly used the distinction between stability and change to organize therapeutic intervention. In addition, the recent team work of Olga Silverstein, Peggy Papp, Stanley Siegel, and Marcia Sheinberg at the Ackerman Institute for Family Therapy has demonstrated how different sides of a system's "dilemma" can be addressed by team members.

while the disadvantages or losses are framed as a request for change.

In another way of thinking about change and stability the distinction is made between cooperation and resistance. Here the behavior of clients can be divided between those actions that are seen as cooperating with the therapist's efforts to promote change and those that appear to resist proposals of change. What has traditionally been called "resistance" is now reframed as a system's proposal of stability. With a cybernetic frame of reference, it is not possible to see cooperative behavior without resistance or vice versa: each is only one side of the more encompassing cybernetic complementarity of stability and change.

The Cybernetic Sorting of Multiple Communication

Since there are as many ways of distinguishing change and stability as a therapist's imagination can generate, it is important to emphasize that the practical sorting of clinical communication in terms of change and stability involves keeping an eye on how it leads to possible interventions. From this perspective, communications are looked for that suggest how one should *prescribe* both stability and change.

In our discussion of recursive complementarity, we demonstrated how the distinction of "predator/prey" could be seen as the right-hand side of the complementarity "ecosystem/species interaction." From that standpoint all communication proposed by clients indicating symptomatic or problem behavior can be viewed as the right-hand side of some larger complementarity. For instance, in the case of problematic sibling fights, what appears on one level as a battle between two children may on another level be a form of interaction that helps stabilize a whole family, perhaps by calibrating the intensity of a symmetrical parental relationship.

Sorting multiple communications in therapy can therefore be approached in terms of two steps. First, the troubled system is identified with respect to the major distinction used to describe the reason they are coming to a therapist. For instance, the communication may center around a specific problem, such as a child's headaches. In such a situation, we have the underlying either/or relation: headache/no headache. Experientially there is no such thing as a symptom that is experienced all of the time. Headaches, anxiety attacks, marital fighting, bouts of uncontrolled eating, and hallucinations occur in an off and on (that is, either/or) fashion. Clients can therefore be seen as requesting that their experience not include a particular "A/not A" distinction. They do not mean to only say, "Get rid of my headaches." Instead, they want to alter an experiential universe that repeatedly oscillates between having headaches and not having them.

Another way of viewing the description of a symptom is to note that there are different political consequences associated with its occurrence and its absence. A request to treat a headache, from this perspective, is both a request to change (that is, alleviate) the discomfort of having a headache, as well as to change the problematic political patterns that sometimes occur when the headache is not present. Or we could say this in a different way: a request to treat a headache may be seen as a request to stabilize both the relief experienced when the headaches aren't occurring and the positive political consequences of the headache's appearance.

Given the identity of the presenting communication, the second step is to frame it as part of a larger complementarity. In the case study presented in the previous chapter, this was done by placing a daughter's migraine headaches within the frame of family worrying. The girl's headaches had been discussed by the family in terms of "worrying." That was a clue to the therapist to talk more freely about the larger sequences of action that included the participation of other family members. Worrying was discussed as providing a positive contribution to the whole family. The therapist then used that complementary frame to construct interventions requesting that patterns of worrying change, while the family as a whole was reinforced to remain stable.

The progression of this transition can be spelled out more carefully. First, the therapist uncovered how the political frame of reference embodying the headache involved the participation of other family members. When that political frame was probed, it precipitated the family to start talking about worrying. In effect, the same political frame of reference (the family organization) was attended to, but the metaphor or name of the political frame shifted from headaches to worrying. The advantage of talking about worrying is that the participation of each family member could be more easily addressed than when the focus was on an individual's headache. This new semantic frame enabled the stability of the family to be underscored while the way the family achieved stability could be changed through altering the family patterns of worrying.

Thus, the first step in sorting multiple communications in therapy involves specifying how a troubled system is locked in an either/or logic of "A/not A" (headache/no headache). The oscillation between having symptomatic experience and not having it, whether expressed in terms of symptomatic pain and symptomatic relief, drunkenness and sobriety, anxiety and calm is itself a caricature of a system caught in the dilemma of trying to both change and remain stable. The next step involves discerning and/or constructing a complementary frame that subsumes the problem distinction (family organization/worrying). With that recursive complementarity, the therapist has a logical structure for designing interventions that aim at helping the system adjust the way it changes in order to stabilize itself.

Clinical Application

A troubled system comes to therapy, in most cases, with a request to alter the way it changes in order to stabilize itself. This "change of change" requires a source of meaningful noise onto which new structure and pattern can be punctuated. The therapist therefore provides three, not two, communications to a troubled family: (1) a request for change; (2) a request for stability; and (3) some meaningful noise from which an alternative pattern or structure for reorganizing change and stability can be constructed. Families themselves bring all of these communication resources to therapy.

The therapist's job is to use his sensory processes to discern how these communications are articulated and to mirror them back to the troubled system. This recursive mirroring process has been described elsewhere as "sociofeedback" (Keeney 1983). In effect, the therapist's mirroring or articulation of the different communications of a troubled family enables the system to (re)-calibrate how it maintains its organization. The following case description illustrates this process.

A family presented an overweight twelve-year-old daughter who exhibited uncontrollable eating bouts. All previous efforts by her parents to calibrate her food binges had failed. The therapy team first asked questions that would provide a clear behavioral description of the problem and all attempted solutions. The therapists then moved to asking questions that would expose the family's coalition patterns. And finally, therapy shifted to asking questions that placed the problem in the context of the family's history.

With those levels of data, the therapists, consulting with each other, sorted the information to design an intervention. The most relevant pieces of information included:

1. The problem sequence only occurred between 8:00 and 11:00 in the evening and lasted about thirty minutes. Problem-solving efforts usually involved the mother lecturing and getting into a fight with her daughter at the dinner table (usually around 6:00 in the evening), and then the mother and father discussing her problem the following morning at breakfast.
2. The father usually sided with his daughter against his wife, and the mother often called her mother for advice and consultation about the family's dilemma.
3. The problem began two years ago when the family moved to a new town. They had previously lived near the maternal grandmother and were now several hundred miles away.

With that information, an intervention was designed. The family was told that they must agree to follow the advice without questioning it. After accepting, they were told that no one was to discuss the problem for a week. Instead, they were instructed to perform a task that required the daughter going to her father whenever she knew an eating binge was about to begin. At that instant the father was to put his wife's favorite sweater on his daughter. Then and only then could the daughter begin eating. As she ate, she was to take great care to not spill any food on her mother's sweater. If she did, she was to help her mother clean it after she finished eating. While the daughter ate, the rest of the family was told to concentrate on their deepest and most remote feelings and thoughts for grandmother. They were not to discuss any aspect of the assignment.

In the following session, the family reported that they had followed the assignment for only one night and that the problem had disappeared. They also claimed that things were much better for them in general and that they were planning a trip to Europe with their grandmother for the next summer. The therapists expressed surprise and suggested they could not understand how anything could have improved. After all, they added, the family had not even followed the assignment for the full week. The therapists expressed their interest in watching how "the family's solution" would be tested and challenged during the weeks to come. Follow up phone interviews indicated that the family had no further need for therapy.

With respect to the cybernetic sort of stability, change, and meaningful noise, we can first note that assigning the daughter to continue her eating binges was a prescription of stability. Whereas the maintenance of the symptom was proposed, change was addressed by prescribing an altered pattern in which the symptom occurred. The pattern was modified in terms of: (1) the sequential organization of events; (2) social patterns of interaction; and (3) the frame of contextual meaning. And finally, the specifics of the task, including selection of mother's "favorite sweater," family references to grandmother, and daughter's assigned interaction with father and mother provided potential sources for meaningful noise.

It is important to notice that a cybernetic view of multiple communication is not limited to reinforcing a particular approach to therapeutic intervention but is more generally a way of making explicit the cybernetic patterns that organize systemic therapies. The same intervention might have been designed by a so-called interactional therapist concerned only with disrupting the recursive organization of problem-solution interaction. A so-called strategic therapist might have constructed this intervention to change the organization of coalition patterns in the family. To others the intervention would be structured by another style of systemic therapy that took into consideration the historical context of the troubled system. Or a therapist might have utilized all of the above views (or none of them) to design the intervention.

Connections to Semantic and Political Frames

How the ideas in this chapter are related to the distinction of semantic and political frames of reference set forth in the previous chapter requires some further comment. For the social system of family therapy, the complementary relation between communications of change and stability is a particular way of describing its political frame of reference. On the other hand, the meanings that are associated with a particular political pattern of organization arise from semantic frames of reference. Our use of the term "meaningful noise" thus indicates one way of speaking of semantic frames of reference. Our cybernetic model of multiple communication is itself another recursion or transform of the basic laws of therapeutic form, the distinction and relation of semantic and political frames of reference:

$$\frac{\underbrace{\text{political}}}{\text{(stability/change)}} \Big/ \frac{\underbrace{\text{semantic}}}{\text{meaningful Rorschach}}$$

In the previous chapter, we examined how *communication* in therapy could be seen through two frames of reference: politics and semantics. In this chapter, the view of politics and semantics in therapy is based on *cybernetics* and provides a way to characterize and organize systemic interventions.

Our cybernetic model of multiple communication can be seen as a more finely focused lens usually limited to mapping interventions in systemic family therapy. In the case that follows, this model is used to map particular systemic interventions. However, this mapping is at a different level of analysis than the mapping previously presented. The same case could also be mapped at the level of analysis that specifies semantic and political frames of reference. Similarly, a zoom lens could be applied to the previous case in order to discern the multiple communications arising in its therapeutic interventions.

The reader is invited to map each of these cases in terms of both semantics and politics, as well as the cybernetic model of multiple communication. In the chapters to come we will use both views to demonstrate how different strategies for organizing systemic family therapy can be presented. It should then become more apparent how our two different double views—"laws of therapeutic form" and "multiple communication in systemic intervention"—are themselves the two sides of an even higher-order double view. We think of that view as "mind in therapy."

Mapping Systemic Interventions: A Case Study of Olga Silverstein

This case study uses the multiple communications of stability, change, and meaningful noise in systemic family therapy. The therapist, Olga Silverstein, begins with a problem focus for organizing data-gathering questions. Each family member is interviewed to discern how the presenting problem provides positive, as well as negative, consequences. One member's problem behavior, for instance, may provide a way of stabilizing another dyadic relationship. Such information helps construct a frame of reference which demonstrates the positive social consequences of a presenting problem.

Because it is assumed that all problems provide both negative and positive consequences for all connected social participants, problems are seen as dilemmas. After each family member's dilemma is defined in relation to the presenting problem, these dilemmas are then connected to give a systemic interpretation, story, or hypothesis of how the presenting problem provides a "pattern that connects" the whole family.

In effect, double descriptions of how the presenting problem influences them are created for family members. These multiple views are then connected in a way that ties all family members together as a system. The pattern that connects the whole family may include references to their family history.

In multiple communication, the negative consequences of the presenting problem can be seen as connected to a request for change while the positive consequences are linked to a request for stability. Meaningful noise arises out of the analyses, stories, themes, historical interpretations, and hypotheses the therapist presents to the family regarding how the problem contributes to their being connected. In this case the therapist managed to organize interventions by addressing these communications of stability, change, and meaningful noise in three sessions with the family.

The first session involved a father, mother, and their thirty-three-year-old daughter, Judy. The younger daughter, Mary, was absent, although she had told the therapist on the phone that the family's problem centered around Judy's "depression." The father described Judy as "a daughter who has everything going for her, but who hasn't been able to get started." Judy's problems were seen by the family as connected to her failed marriage, which in Judy's own words had "quickly dissolved."

In addition, Judy had worked in her father's business, which she assumed would be her inheritance. Unfortunately, a major client withdrew his account and "the business dissolved," as Judy put it. Since the business folded, Judy, her father, and her mother "have had nothing to do." Her father's major complaint was that Judy wouldn't make any effort to look for another job. Judy described her present situation as "hanging out" around her apartment, which was on one side fifty yards from her parents' home and, on the other side, next door to her sister.

The mother's attempted solutions involved providing Judy with a wide assortment of suggestions and ideas about what she might do. The father's efforts usually began as "pep talks" and ended with his telling her that she's a "loser" and a "failure." Judy, following her mother's advice, consulted a psychiatrist who was an internationally recognized expert on depression. He diagnosed her as "depressive" and prescribed medication. Another (nonpsychiatric) therapist informed Judy that she was "clearly not depressive." Other problem-solving contexts included Judy's participation in group therapy with the group repeatedly advising her to be less concerned about her family's business and find a new job.

With this information, the therapist turned to the mother and asked if her husband was also depressed. The mother said that he was very depressed and noted that both of them were worried about whether to move to Florida. The father described himself as hating "the cold," while his wife hated "the hot." The mother added that their daughters need to be "settled" before they could even consider leaving. The therapist subsequently asked the daughter whether her mother was depressed and was told that she had been depressed ever since her younger daughter had left home. With further questioning it was revealed that Judy thought her father to be more depressed than her mother, whereas the mother saw the father and Judy as equally depressed.

At this stage of the first session, the mother offered a reference to her family of origin. She had grown up with two alcoholic brothers and a third, mentally handicapped brother. She found herself thinking about how her own mother spent a lot of time crying and praying, something she had been doing more and more herself.

The therapist immediately shifted to the father's family of origin and found that his mother had "given all of us up" when he was twelve years old. She left her husband and "abandonded her six children." He subsequently grew up in foster homes and boarding schools. The father added that his mother had remarried "an alcoholic bum." The therapist then turned to Judy and asked her if her previous husband had been an alcoholic, which she acknowledged.

With this background, the therapist took a break from the session to confer with a group of student therapists who had been observing the case from behind a one-way mirror. She then prepared to structure multiple communications of stability, change, and meaningful noise. The following exchange took place in the last part of the first session:

SESSION 1

THERAPIST: Everything I say now is only based on the information we've gathered in this short time. A lot of it will probably change as we go along. First, I want you to share with your sister what I'm about to tell all of you because she is involved in everything that goes on here. What I'm going to say concerns what keeps this family going along *(change)* as well as what keeps it stuck *(stability)*—two separate things that are very related. It may come as somewhat of a surprise, but at least it's something to think about.

(to father) We are impressed with what you learned from your own family of origin. *(meaningful noise)* Supplying a supermother for this present family was probably the highest priority in your life. *(meaningful noise)* We don't know how you managed to do that, but you did.

(to mother) You are a supermother. *(meaningful noise)* We think you have a lot to do with it—you did it in cooperation with him. The dilemma is that in order to be a supermother you've got to have kids. *(stability)*

(to Judy) The dilemma for you is that you're going to help your father in this task which has been his life's work. *(meaningful noise)* You've got to remain a child. You can't grow up. *(stability)* That's quite a dilemma for both you and your sister.

(to mother) So you've got a problem. I guess it's not going to change until a time arises when your husband is convinced that you will not abandon the children. *(stability)* Only then can you get on with your life together. *(change)*

The therapist begins with the message that her descriptions of what is going on with the family will probably change, thus implying that the family will also probably change. In addition, the therapist marks her comments as concerned with both change ("what keeps this family going along") and stability ("what keeps it stuck") and notes that these "two separate things" are "very related."

The therapist then addresses the family members individually and notes how each of them is connected to the presenting problem and how that connection provides a positive consequence for the family *(communications of stability).* The daughter's depression keeps her at home, which enables the mother to be a "supermother," which, in turn, satisfies the father's need to provide a mother who won't abandon her children. The meaningful noise in this intervention largely arises from the therapist's use of the father's history.

MOTHER: He's had no qualms about getting up and going to Florida.

THERAPIST: Verbally, that's true. You're the one who's going to have to prove that you're never going to abandon these children. *(stability)* Right?

MOTHER: Well, I've always said I wouldn't.

THERAPIST: That's right. You keep reassuring him that you wouldn't. He can afford to *say* that he's going to leave them *(change)* because he knows you're not going to do it. *(stability)* So we're stuck. We're stuck in your being such good parents *(stability)* and that being the first priority.

(to Judy) And that's how you're stuck: How to be a good daughter *(stability)* and grow up at the same time. *(change)*

JUDY: What do we do?

THERAPIST: I don't know, but that's what we're going to try to help you with. *(change)* Will you tell your sister?

JUDY: Oh, yes. I think you'll be surprised when you see the fourth member of the family, the difference in personality.

THERAPIST: Oh, yes. Every single member of the family makes a difference. It changes. So I'll see you next week. *(change)*

MOTHER: Is it advisable that Judy talk too much to her sister because she might be frightened away?

JUDY: I have a very close relationship with my sister. We talk about everything.

THERAPIST: I would say you shouldn't change much of anything right now. *(stability)*

The therapist's interventions in session 1 largely involve the construction of semantic frames that build up a logic for specifying the positive consequences of their situation, thus enabling the therapist to request stability. This, of course, is done in the context of therapy, which by definition is a request for change. The semantic frames thus far include:

Family Description		*Therapist's Semantic Frame*
Daughter's problem behavior	means	she is a good daughter
Mother's reluctance to move	means	she is a "supermother"
Father's reluctance to move	means	he is taking care of mother and children
The semantic frames are then circularly linked as follows:		
Daughter's being "good"	means	she is taking care of father
Daughter's taking care of father	means	he is able to take care of mother
Father's taking care of mother	means	she is able to take care of daughter

When these semantic frames are linked together, different political consequences arise. Framing the daughter's behavior as helping her father to help her mother be a supermother implies a radically different political frame of reference than would be the case if her behavior were simply regarded as "depression." The unit of therapy shifts from treating a sick individual to treating a relationship system that has a particular way of taking care of itself.

SESSION 2

All four family members are present at the second session. The therapist begins by reviewing what she told the family in the previous session and gives Mary an opportunity to provide her views and insights. Mary states that her father had asked her to move out years ago because she was constantly out too late or staying overnight with her boyfriends. The mother added that while she agreed with the father's decision on the surface, "deep down under I never forgave him for kicking out Mary." The therapist underscored the sequence of the two sisters' crises in time, pointing out that Mary was kicked out five years ago and Judy's marriage dissolved three years ago.

With further questioning the therapist found that the father claims to have stopped worrying about Mary and instead only worries about Judy "finding out where she's going in life." On the other hand, the mother still worries about Mary. In this discussion the therapist casually asks the father if Mary's behavior resembles his own mother's. The father acknowledges this and mentions that he hadn't noticed it before. He reaffirms that he's not worried about Mary and is only concerned about Judy, who he again describes as "not knowing where she's going."

THERAPIST: I think she knows where she's going. It may not be the best place for her, but I think she knows what she's doing. Maybe not consciously, but she's being a good little girl to her mother. *(meaningful noise)* That may be the most important thing for this family. If Mary won't do it, then Judy has to do it.

MOTHER: What do you mean, being good to her mother?

THERAPIST: It allows you to remain a mother. *(stability)* If these young women were, at this age, on quite independent courses, your job would be over. *(change)*

MOTHER: I don't think so. We'd still be in touch.

THERAPIST: Yes, but your job of being a protective mother *(meaningful noise)* would be over. Of course, I'm not saying you should lose your children. I'm also not saying that you want things to continue as they are. I actually think it is what your husband wants. *(meaningful noise)*

The therapist frames the behavior of both daughters as allowing the mother to remain a "protective mother" because the father doesn't want to see his children abandoned. This circular pattern will be spelled out over and over again throughout the session. The therapist will take each family member's statements and transform them into additional data for verifying this pattern.

MOTHER: *(to father)* How does that hit you? Does it come across to you?

FATHER: Yes, to a certain extent. We don't worry only about her, because she's a very intelligent woman.

THERAPIST: Yes, she is that.

FATHER: But Judy hasn't really grown up.

THERAPIST: Yes, that's right. That's exactly what I'm saying. You're right.

MOTHER: How can we help us all? We never sit together as a family like this. If we're ever in a car going somewhere, Mary and Judy become little girls in the back seat and chitchat between themselves.

JUDY: We never have talked as a family!

The purpose of therapy has shifted at this point to addressing the whole family rather than any particular member.

MARY: You can't hit Father's nerve and Mother is a screamer. . . . I'd rather keep things pleasant.

THERAPIST: *(to Mary)* I think you have a very good big sister.

MARY: Judy is great. Everyone's focusing on her and staring at her under a microscope waiting for her to do something really great. Unfortunately, she's not really doing much of anything now and that's why there's a lot of concern.

Mary shifts the therapeutic focus back to Judy. The therapist therefore immediately reconstructs the family frame of reference.

THERAPIST: You see, it's really quite a problem because the family came here to get unstuck with where the family is stuck with Judy. *(change)* Everyone worries about that. The problem for me is if we were to help Judy get unstuck and go about her business, I would worry a great deal about your father. *(consequence of change)*

MARY: You would?

THERAPIST: Yes.

MARY: I don't understand.

THERAPIST: On one level he would be delighted.

MARY: Then what's the worry from?

THERAPIST: I worry that your father wouldn't know how to handle your mother once she's not a mother. *(consequence of change)*

The therapist has now added another piece to the systemic interpretation she is weaving for the family. Namely, one uncertain consequence of change involves its effect on the stability of the marriage.

MARY: I think they just have to make a decision about where they want to retire. . . .

THERAPIST: Well, the situation would change if you two were . . . *(pause)*

MARY: Grown up, right?

THERAPIST: The situation would be totally changed.

MOTHER: Supposedly, right.

MARY: Not really. I'd say the lousy parts of the situation would still be the same. As a matter of fact, it might even get worse. *(pause)* The reason why I don't see my parents too much is because I'm doing so many things. . . .

THERAPIST: You also know that Judy is there to take care of things and you can afford to do things. *(stability)*

MARY: No.

THERAPIST: Don't you think?

MOTHER: Sure.

THERAPIST: That's what I meant when I said Judy was a very good big sister.

MARY: You mean that her having contact with the parents takes care of things.

MOTHER: Oh, sure.

THERAPIST: Sure.

The therapist has underscored another positive consequence of Judy's problem behavior: it helps out her sister.

THERAPIST: The dilemma, as I said before, in trying to help a family solve a problem is that when you solve one problem *(change)*, another one may take its place *(stability)* because there's a reason why things are working the way they're working. *(meaningful noise)* Even though I understand that it's very painful and you want it to change, Judy keeps things stable in the family. She's the stabilizer: the family can't change as long as it has a child to concentrate on. Judy is a very good child that way, and I think it's mostly devotion to your father *(meaningful noise),* because I think your mother could manage it. She may even be a bit tired about being a mother.

The therapist now begins spelling out the cybernetic relation of change and stability in this family. The circular pattern that has been previously identified is now described as Judy stabilizing the family by remaining a child. Again, the therapist describes Judy's intent as an attempt to help her father. *(meaningful noise)*

MARY: It wasn't always the way it is now; roles change. Our family has gone through an evolution.

THERAPIST: When you were both little it was a family with two children. Now the family is still a family with two children. *(stability and meaningful noise)*

MARY: We sort of flip-flopped. There was a time when Judy couldn't talk to Father and I was home and had the role of the good little daughter. Judy then got married and for a small amount of time we were both okay. I eventually erupted and became a teenage problem.

THERAPIST: Yes, you do take turns.

MOTHER: Is there anything we as parents can suggest or do?

THERAPIST: No. I've already told you that I think you're a perfect parent. *(stability and meaningful noise)*

MOTHER: Then how can we help Judy?

THERAPIST: You can't. *(long silence)* That's the hardship: the more you try to help her, the more it makes things the same. The more she's a child and the more you help her, the more she behaves like a child who needs help. And the more she behaves like a child who needs help, the more you help her. It keeps that circle going forever. *(stability)*

The therapist is spelling out the recursive complementarity of how efforts to change the problem actually stabilize the problem—the perspective of Watzlawick, Weakland, and Fisch (1974). In cybernetic terms, this is a definition of a self-correcting feedback loop, sometimes called "negative feedback."

MOTHER: What can we do, if anything?

THERAPIST: *(to daughters)* I don't know. I suppose you could continue to take turns. *(to father)* What do you think?

FATHER: We have a girl here [Judy] who is fantastic. I've worked with her in the office, so I know. I can't see how she can carry on such a dull life. She's not involved in anything. . . . If she'd lose herself, she wouldn't think about herself. The important thing is to get so involved that you don't have time to have these thoughts that might come into her mind.

THERAPIST: What kind of thoughts are you worrying about?

FATHER: She's depressed. She makes no effort whatsoever. She's like a little girl who has so much on the ball, but doesn't realize it.

THERAPIST: What kind of thoughts is he talking about? Is he talking about suicidal thoughts?

FATHER: I don't see that.

THERAPIST: That's not what you're worried about?

FATHER: No. My problem is that she has so much time on her hands and she lives a very dull existence. . . . When I see both of them standing on their own two feet, I'll be completely satisfied and can go away and enjoy myself. We're thinking about going to Florida. I think our biggest mistake was allowing these two girls to live next door to us. It would be so much easier and we'd have so much in common if one lived in California and the other lived in Timbuktu.

THERAPIST: *(to father)* You're not hearing me when I tell you that you're the one I'm really worrying about. I'm worried that you wouldn't know what to do with your wife if she weren't relating to you as the mother of these girls. *(consequence of change)*

With this shift, the therapist proceeds to ask the parents what they're presently doing with their own time.

MOTHER: I'm not happy hanging out.

THERAPIST: Do you think your husband is happy hanging out?

MOTHER: No, he's not happy hanging out.

THERAPIST: Nor are you?

MOTHER: I'm certainly not.

THERAPIST: *(to mother)* But you're not retired. Your job as a mother is still operative. *(stability)*

MOTHER: Very low key.

THERAPIST: Well, as much as your daughters will let you.

MOTHER: I'm not as much into Mary's life as she might tell you. I call her very rarely.

THERAPIST: You spend a lot of time worrying about her?

MOTHER: Yes.

The therapist has now found that the mother, father, and Judy all "hang out" and are basically doing very little with themselves. At this point, the therapist takes a break to consult with the observing trainees.

THERAPIST: I've been thinking about what people say about good guys and how they finish last. *(meaningful noise)*

FATHER: I agree with you. That is something I've always agreed with.

THERAPIST: The trouble with this family is that it's got at least three good guys, maybe four. You *(father)* are the best of them all. You win that game. *(meaningful noise)*

FATHER: Well, I know that I can't change at this late stage in my life. I do know from past experiences, especially in my own family. My stepfather, for instance, was an unreliable bum, but he was the most popular one in the family.

THERAPIST: Everyone loved him and took care of him.

FATHER: That's right.

THERAPIST: Too late for you to become an alcoholic? *(change)*

MOTHER: *(laughing)* He can't drink at all. One drink and he's out.

THERAPIST: Your wife is good at taking care of alcoholics. *(stability)*

MOTHER: No, actually I didn't have to take care of my brothers. Having brothers and having children are widely different things. You don't let brothers get to you; you form a barrier.

THERAPIST: *(to father)* Is it too late for you to change?

FATHER: I think so.

THERAPIST: Are you going down a good guy to the end? *(stability)*

FATHER: You don't change when you're past seventy.

THERAPIST: It's not easy at any time. *(pause)* What I was thinking was how sad that there's something you want to do and you feel constrained that you can't do anything for yourself at this point in your life. People at seventy can feel that their time is their own now. *(change)*

FATHER: That's the way I feel now, but unfortunately I haven't been able to do anything. I just keep putting it off.

THERAPIST: That's because you put all the responsibility on your daughters. You say, "If they would shape up then I could do something with my life." You make them responsible for you. *(meaningful noise)*

The daughter's behavior has already been framed as being in the service of the father. Where it was first defined as helping the father maintain a supermother in the family, it is now defined as taking the responsibility for the father's future.

MOTHER: Not really.

THERAPIST: Sure it is. What do you mean, not really?

MOTHER: If he's really serious about doing something with his life, [he should] do it! Even I've come to that point: stop talking about it and do it. If you want to go to Florida, then go.

THERAPIST: *(to father)* What would you do in Florida?

FATHER: I'd enjoy the weather all year round. I'd hibernate in the winter months.

THERAPIST: That's right, but would you just hang out there?

MARY: He would dance.

THERAPIST: Are you a dancer?

FATHER: Yes. A dancer, a golfer, a tennis player, a skater. I used to do quite a bit.

MOTHER: He doesn't any more.

THERAPIST: He's waiting for the girls to shape up. *(change)*

FATHER: No, I don't think so. I've made up my mind that this year is it. I haven't got too long to be around to enjoy these things. I've got to make up my mind fast.

THERAPIST: So?

FATHER: I've made up my mind that I'm either going to rent or purchase a place in Florida that's suitable. Where I'm at now is a very dull existence.

THERAPIST: I can imagine. I know the city.

MOTHER: But there is so much to do if you just want to do it! If you find it dull in New York City, what in the world are you going to do in Florida?

FATHER: You have nothing but people here. No matter where you go, you're crowded.

MOTHER: But you like people.

FATHER: Not that many people. You have to stand in line to do anything.

THERAPIST: *(to mother)* What do you think? Will he do it or is he just talking?

MOTHER: Frankly, I think he's just not realistic.

THERAPIST: *(to father)* Your wife doesn't think you'll do it.

FATHER: She's mistaken. I will do it.

MARY: He'll do it. He always makes the decision.

THERAPIST: *(to Judy)* What do you think?

JUDY: If my mother decides he'll go to Florida, he'll go to Florida.

THERAPIST: *(to Judy)* So, for you, it's a question of what your mother wants. You're the one who can swing it.

JUDY: You mean if I get a job and everything, they'll go?

THERAPIST: You're very decisive in whether your mother decides to go or not. You're the key. *(meaningful noise)* If you feel that your mother doesn't really want to go along or is scared somehow about being alone with him without the two of you, then what you have to do is dig in your heels and complain a lot and get more depressed and make sure you give her a good reason to stay here. *(stability)* Let me tell you exactly how it's going to work. Now this is just an imaginary picture: he's going to be unhappy here and he has this fantasy that life will be different in Florida. Mother feels she knows better. She's scared that she's going to be all alone with him in Florida and he's going to get really depressed. They then won't know what to do with each other and that makes her nervous about going. *(meaningful noise)*

MOTHER: Very good observation because it's true.

THERAPIST: *(to Judy)* And you're going to be aware of mother's worry and help her out by getting more depressed and hanging on her, making her a good excuse for not going. She'll tell your father that she can't leave Judy because she's too depressed. So then they'll stay here. It won't be because she's worried about him, or because he's worried about her, but because they're both worried about you. *(stability)*

The therapist has again used the information the family presents to verify this circular pattern of organization. Judy's problem behavior, previously linked to helping the mother remain a mother, is now more clearly depicted as calibrating the marital system.

FATHER: I think that in due time this will all be ironed out.

THERAPIST: I don't think that time will do it. *(stability)*

FATHER: Really? What makes you think so?

THERAPIST: Because the way it is, is the way it has to be. *(stability)* If you're hanging around waiting for Judy to make the change to free you, that's a pipe dream. That's never going to happen.

FATHER: Right now I have too much time on my hands. If I was involved in something, I wouldn't even think about a lot of things.

THERAPIST: So why aren't you involved? *(change)*

FATHER: I'm too old to get involved in business. It wouldn't pay.

THERAPIST: You could be involved in having a good time. *(change)*

FATHER: That's it. If I can get involved with other people

with a similar lifestyle, I would forget and be myself.

The father's descriptions of his own situation are practically identical to his previous complaints about his problematic daughter.

THERAPIST: I don't think you're going to do it. *(stability)* What I've been saying is that it is more important for you, in the final analysis, that your wife keep on proving over and over again what a good mother she is. *(meaningful noise)* That's more important than having a good time for yourself or taking care of her needs. She's got to be a good mother: first, foremost, last, always, that's the name of the game. *(meaningful noise)* That's an endless game. So I don't think you're going to do it. *(stability)*

FATHER: I could disagree.

THERAPIST: The only way you could disagree would be by doing something different. *(change)*

FATHER: Well, that's what I'm going to do.

THERAPIST: Oh, well, we'll see. I don't think you will. *(stability)*

JUDY: I think he would if he had Mother's support.

THERAPIST: He always has your mother's support. *(stability)*

JUDY: I disagree.

THERAPIST: It's hard to know where it's coming from. It looks as though she isn't supporting him. *(meaningful noise)*

FATHER: There will always be a place for these two girls, incidentally.

THERAPIST: Of course there will. They will always be your daughters. *(stability)*

FATHER: They'll enjoy themselves better.

THERAPIST: That's beside the point. Whether they will or not is beside the point. Can you afford to let them grow up? *(change)*

FATHER: That's the whole thing; I want them to grow up.

THERAPIST: On one level that's true *(change)* but I don't think you can do it. *(stability)*

FATHER: We'll see.

Throughout this session, the therapist has repeatedly used multiple semantic frames to put the family's current problem into context. Any indication that these new frames suggest change is countered by the therapist with the possible consequences of change. On the other hand, any indication that the situation remain the same results in the therapist pointing out the consequences of maintaining the current forms of stability. The therapist thus engages the family in confronting their dilemmas of change and stability. Any change or stabilization of the problem may result in unpredictable consequences at different levels of the family structure. The family is thus presented with views of how their present problem is the fulcrum of a multileveled dilemma. The therapist's task is to fully address those multiple communications regarding their situation.

Thus, any communication by a family member may be countered with an opposite, but complementary communication by the therapist. This interplay of opposites is a sort of dialectical process where the emphasis is on the complementary connection of multiple communications. The therapist, by presenting multiple comments in relation to the family's proposals, contributes to the construction of a pattern that attempts to connect and correct the troubled system.

SESSION 3

MOTHER: Since we started these sessions, I don't contact Judy as much as I used to. I thought it would be a good idea if we would get off her back.

THERAPIST: *(to Judy)* Have you noticed a difference? *(change addressed)*

JUDY: Ummm. Not that much.

MOTHER: You hardly come to the house. It used to be an everyday affair.

JUDY: *I'm* the one who doesn't come to the house.

THERAPIST: So you're the one who has made that change? You come less.

JUDY: Yes, I come less.

THERAPIST: Ah, so both of you have pulled back a little bit. *(change addressed)*

JUDY: Yes.

THERAPIST: There are colleagues of mine behind the mirror whose advice it is that it was a very good thing for Judy to give you every opportunity to be a good mother. Since both daughters really were such good kids, the only thing they could do was give you little problems like dragging their heels. My colleagues think this is not such a bad thing and they think you should continue doing it *(stability)* in order to make Dad feel he has been a better father than his own father by providing this family with a supermom. *(meaningful noise)* They predict that you'll never move to Florida . . . that it will go on this way with Judy continuing to give you enough concern and reason for bringing the family together at all costs *(stability)* even though the time for growing up and separation has come. *(change)*

MARY: But that's not a solution. You're just saying that they can understand us continuing as we are, but that is certainly not what we want to do, otherwise we wouldn't be here.

THERAPIST: Absolutely. I agree with you. I think that would be too bad. The person who would pay the highest price for that would be Judy. Going that way, she would have to get more and more isolated and depressed. *(consequence of present form of stability)* It's too high a price to pay for being a good girl. I think that. I disagree with my colleagues. *(change)*

The therapist has been reinstating the previous frames of reference, noting again how Judy's problem behavior contributes to the stability of her mother, father, and whole family. Now, however, it is pointed out that the way in which she has done this has involved too great a sacrifice of her own self. She has, in other words, risked her own stability in order to stabilize her family relationship system. The implication is that a change must occur in the family in order to take care of Judy.

THERAPIST: But I'm not sure that you're not too good a daughter to ever change that. *(meaningful noise)* I don't know. I somehow feel that you're not going to make that move to change it. That will come from someplace else. *(change)*

MOTHER: I don't understand.

THERAPIST: *(to Judy)* It's going to have to come from one of your parents. The question is, which one? *(change)* I don't think that Judy is going to be the one who's going to make the change. She's just too tenderhearted toward the family. It may not appear that way. For instance, Father might ask, "If she really loved me she'd do what I want her to do." But she is doing what he wants her to do on a very deep unconscious level *(meaningful noise)* which is keeping the family together. *(stability)* If Judy went out, let's say tomorrow, and got a job and had a busy social life, your mother would have no reason to stay. They would have to go to Florida and be alone and have the family come apart—as it appropriately should. . . . *(change)*

MOTHER: But I have made the move. As little as it seems, nobody realizes why I made this move of painting our apartment. What I'm saying now is, "Hey, this is it." As I've said to my husband, we can go to Florida, but I'm staying here in this apartment until I find out which way our lives are going. In other words, I'm not giving up something stable. . . . I'm not fleeing anywhere to some uncertainty until I find out how we are going.

THERAPIST: Here's some advice: when either one of you decides to do something for yourself, it may give Judy permission to do something for herself. *(change)*

MOTHER: It makes sense.

THERAPIST: As long as she has such self-sacrificing parents who can't do anything unless her life is perfect, she's tied into not being able to do anything unless your life is perfect. You're all tied into the same knot. *(meaningful noise)*

With this interpretation, the therapist fully underscores the complementary contributions of parental and sibling systems with regard to how they maintain their present situation. Namely, the self-sacrificing parents are waiting for the daughter(s) to change, while the self-sacrificing daughter(s) are waiting for the parents to change. This knot, in effect, is the family's dilemma.

THERAPIST: There's a sense in this entire family of waiting for permission to move on. Judy will have that permission to move on when you stop sacrificing, and then maybe she'll stop sacrificing for you. *(meaningful noise)* I don't think she'll move before that. . . . As far as the fear of the family coming apart, the family has to change. It's not going to come apart *(stability),* but it's going to be different. *(change)* I know, I've gone through that myself. It's hard in a close family, but maybe it's your time.

The therapist conducted a follow-up interview six months later and found that Judy had taken a job in a financial company and had established a life of her own. The husband announced his decision to move to Florida in order to "save his life," while his wife expressed her "fear" that such a move might "delegate her to old age." The session ended with the couple's decision for the husband to take a trip to Florida to see if he could find a suitable place for them to live.

This case illustrates the use of multiple communications to construct therapeutic interventions. It is rooted to the idea that clients (as well as therapists) are organized by multiple views of their situation. Stories about one's family of origin, in particular, provide profoundly meaningful myths for individuals in our culture. Here we have seen a practical way of using family history as a frame of reference that encompasses problem behavior. As the case demonstrated, any particular frame of reference could always be countered and corrected by another frame. In that way, multiple frames of reference provided self-correction of the multiple communications constituting therapy.

We can now examine how the fine-focus view of multiple communication in systemic intervention and the more general laws of therapeutic form may be used to analyze different strategies of systemic therapy. The chapters that follow emphasize how these theoretical views provide a clear way of specifying the construction of particular therapeutic realities.

PART II

STRATEGIES FOR ORGANIZING THERAPY

CHAPTER 3

Problem-Solution Interaction

> . . . And then what you need to do is to try to do something that induces a change in the patient—any little change. Because the patient wants a change, however small, and he will accept that as a change . . . and then follow that change and the change will develop in accordance with his own needs. It's much like rolling a snowball down a mountainside. It starts out a small snowball, but as it rolls down it gets larger and larger . . . and starts an avalanche that fits to the shape of the mountain.
>
> —MILTON H. ERICKSON
> *Personal Communication,* 1977

The Mental Research Institute Strategy

The strategy prescribed by Watzlawick, Weakland, and Fisch in their book, *Change: Principles of Problem Formation and Problem Resolution* (1974), and by Fisch, Weakland, and Segal in their book, *The Tactics of Change* (1982) is one of the most efficient problem-solving approaches in the history of psychotherapy.* It begins by prescribing distinctions that enable a therapist to identify: (1) the

*The strategy presented here was largely developed at the Brief Therapy Center, Mental Research Institute, Palo Alto, California. For practical purposes, we will refer to this orientation as "MRI therapy" or simply "MRI." The reader should, however, be aware that the Mental Research Institute practices other strategies of therapy and that the work we refer to is only one part of their program.

problem; (2) the history of its attempted solutions; and (3) the frame of reference the client uses to view and conceptualize his problems and solutions.

Political and Semantic Frames

In terms of political and semantic frames, their strategy for organizing therapy thus involves the following sequence.

1. Construct a semantic frame (S_1) that behaviorally defines the presenting problem to be worked on, as well as specifies the goal of therapy in terms of how the problem is to be modified
2. Construct a political frame (P_1) that defines all attempted solutions —by the client, as well as others
3. Construct a semantic frame (S_2) that defines how the client gives meaning to his problematic situation. In particular, find out how the client semantically frames P_1

These semantic and political frames are nested as follows:

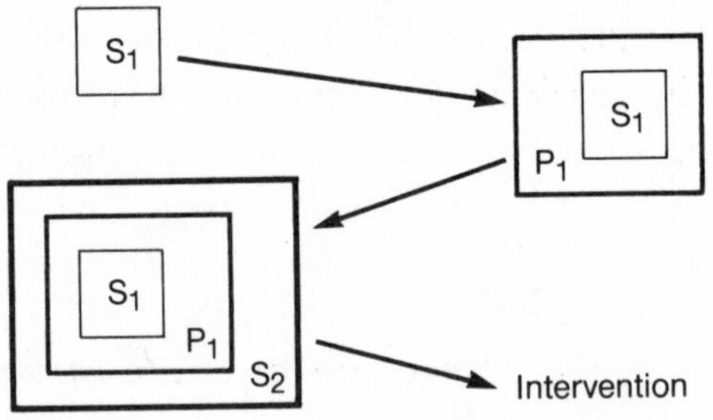

If a family presents a son who is having trouble at school, the first semantic frame would address spelling out exactly what is meant by "trouble at school." A specific behavioral focus would then be constructed for the family. The therapist would also address the political frame that specifies all the people who have been involved in trying to solve the presenting problem. The specific efforts of teachers, friends, parents, and so forth, would be outlined. And finally, the way in which the family discusses the son's school problem will be assessed in order to determine how they give meaning to what is going on. Their very choice of terms in defining their problem (for example, "school trouble") is an indication of how they see their situation.

By constructing these distinctions and frames of reference, MRI therapy is set in motion. In general, the beginning of any therapy sets the guidelines for what distinctions will be used to organize it. Sometimes this means which questions are to be addressed and which ones ignored. In the beginning of MRI therapy, problems and attempted solutions get addressed and specified in behavioral terms. All other questions and information are marked as irrelevant and distracting. The art of conducting therapy at this stage thus has to do with blocking inappropriate distinctions and facilitating the relevant ones. In this way, a particular type of therapeutic approach is developed.

This is true for all approaches to therapy. In the beginning, the most important concerns may be to decide which distinctions are not to be drawn and attended to. In the case of MRI, therapy is to avoid becoming anything other than a problem-solving endeavor. As Fisch, Weakland, and Segal (1982, p. 10) put it, they focus on "the minimum change required to resolve the presenting problem rather than aiming to restructure whole families."

Traditionally speaking, the initial questions of therapy serve to gather "diagnostic information." When enough information has been gathered, the therapist then diagnoses what the problem is and proceeds to design a treatment strategy. Using this view, the initial distinctions and frames of reference we have described in the beginning of an MRI therapy can be seen as an initial diagnostic stage. However, another view of this stage of therapy arises from constructivism. Namely, these initial distinctions, frames and questions *prescribe* rather than describe a therapy. The diagnostician's "data" can always be seen as the constructivist's "capta."

Recursive Complementarities

Whether we see the beginning stage of therapy as descriptive, prescriptive, or both, the next stage is to organize what is done with the derived information. At this point we begin noting how recursive complementarities are constructed. In the work of MRI, the first recursive complementarity is the one between problem behavior and problem-solving behavior. As Watzlawick and his colleagues summarize this relation, "the solution is the problem." More accurately, the relation between a problem and efforts to solve it are recursively intertwined: the problem arises out of efforts to solve it while attempted solutions arise from experiencing the problem.

For instance, *The Tactics of Change* presents a case wherein a woman's concern about her sexual performance, which she had previously found satisfying, developed into a problem following a conversation with her female friends. In her conversation she began to wonder whether she had ever had an orgasm. Since her friends' descriptions of orgasm differed from her own sexual experience, she concluded that she had not had an orgasm and set out to achieve one. That decision turned her sex life into a problem. She no longer found sex enjoyable because, in her own words, "I kept, you know, waiting for this other to happen, or at one point it was so scientific that, you know, it was like there was no pleasure." Her efforts to solve what she saw as a problem created a problematic situation.

It follows that a practical solution for this woman might involve blocking her attempts to solve the problem. Although we know that blocking a problem eradicates the need for a solution, this approach builds a view for seeing how blocking a solution eradicates the problem. Thus, problems are conceptualized as half of a more encompassing recursive complementarity that necessarily includes solutions.

The other complementarity that Watzlawick and his colleagues construct (1974) involves the relation between behavior and cognition. They use the term "frame" to speak about the way one perceives, conceptualizes, understands, and experiences a situation. Given this cognitive viewpoint, they step beyond being radical behaviorists.

One task of therapy, according to Watzlawick, Weakland, and Fisch (1974), is to change the cognitive frames that organize behavior. This change of frame is called a "reframe" and is defined by them as altering the conceptual, emotional, and/or perceptual view of a situation so that the same "facts" take on an entirely different meaning. An enormous amount of popular literature on "positive thinking" is derived from the simple idea of "reframing." "Positive thinking" involves framing a set of circumstances in a way that leads to seeing the "positive" consequences of the situation. For example, bankruptcy can be reframed as providing an opportunity for starting a new career.

MRI therapy thus attempts to construct two recursive complementarities. The first is that between problem behavior and behavioral efforts to solve the problem. The second involves the higher-order distinction between behavior and a cognitive frame of behavior, or between what Bateson (1972; 1979) loosely called simple action and punctuation of a context. Using these recursive complementarities, this strategy is able to organize patterns of systemic intervention.

Cybernetic Patterns of Intervention

To change a problem, in this perspective, requires changing the recursive relation between problems and attempted solutions. Thus the focus of treatment is a problem *plus* its attempted solutions. To change the organization of that relation requires addressing the cognitive frame that gives it meaning. MRI therapeutic interventions are therefore constructed to address the following structure:

(problem/solution) / cognitive frame

The therapist attempts to change the cognitive frame in order to break up the pattern of logic connecting a problem and its solution. When that pattern is broken, the problem-solution relation is disconnected with the practical consequence of eradicating the problem (and solution). For instance, reframing an adolescent's behavior as "disobedient" rather than "sick" interrupts the kind of solution that parents and professionals might design. In the new frame, it does not make any sense to respond to "disobedient" behavior as one would to "sick" behavior. To carry the example a step further, if the reframe involved naming the adolescent's behavior as providing some useful service to the family (rather than framing it as "sick" or "disobedient"), then all logic for trying to solve or correct the behavior becomes questionable.

It is interesting to note that the distinction between a problem and a solution arises from a particular cognitive frame. "Problems" and "solutions" are not names of simple actions but are names of categories of action. If a client complains that her problem is "anxiety," what specific actions are classified by that category of action? Can the client clearly mark when the anxiety exactly begins and ends? Our point is that when anxiety or any category of action is analyzed in behavioral terms, it is found to refer to a sequence of actions in some social context.

In general, any reference to problems and solutions indicates underlying sequences of simple action. Because these sequences are organized in a way that leads to discomfort and pain, as well as comfort and relief, they become named as "problems" and "attempted solutions." The focus of therapy, from this view, is addressing the organization of the whole sequence, not any particular part, whether that part be distinguished by simple actions, such as coughing or stuttering, or classes of action, such as problems and solutions.

Another way of viewing the distinction between problems and attempted solutions is to note that its relation is often specified in terms of a logic of negation. Having a solution means negating the problem, whereas an existing problem means the absence of a (successful) solution. Given our view of recursive complementarity, however, we can frame this either/or distinction as the right-hand side of a more encompassing distinction:

Pattern of interaction / (problem/solution)

In this reframe, problems and solutions interact in order to construct and stabilize a particular pattern of interaction. It should be no surprise that Watzlawick and Weakland (1977) have referred to their perspective as "the interactional view."

In this frame, the aim of therapy is not changing problem behavior or solution behavior but altering a pattern of interaction. This is what we meant in our earlier statement that the recursive relation of problems and attempted solutions must be addressed. Their recursive relation is a pattern of interaction.

Watzlawick, Weakland, and Fisch (1974, pp. 80–81) provide the classic example: an agoraphobic whose problem was part of a pattern of interaction that included his efforts to solve it. The man's problem intensified to the point that he could neither go to work or even get food from a grocery store. He finally decided to commit suicide by driving his car until his anxiety or a heart attack finished him. As can be guessed, his surrender provided the cure. His suicide drive, which involved stopping his problem-solving habits, left him completely free of his agoraphobia.

In cybernetic terms, attempted solutions and problems are connected through a feedback relation wherein the more one tries to solve a problem the more one maintains it. Problems and solutions express the complementary relation that defines a cybernetic system: (stability/change). Problems are stabilized by changing efforts to solve them. Again, in a troubled situation, the more one attempts to change a problem through trying all sorts of solutions, the more one stabilizes it. Our previous definition of the structure MRI therapy must address can now be seen as an analogue of our basic cybernetic definition of the communicational ingredients of therapeutic change:

(stability/change) / meaningful noise

The task of therapy is now defined as identifying the cognitive frame or meaningful noise that clients bring and using it to reorganize the way they organize themselves.

If a client complains that he is troubled by what ants are saying about mosquitoes, that communication may be accepted and utilized by the therapist as meaningful noise. The task of the therapist then becomes to manage the client's communication to provide a resource for them. Watzlawick, Weakland, and Fisch (1974, p. 104) compare this method to "judo, where the opponent's thrust is not opposed by a counterthrust of at least the same force, but rather accepted and amplified by yielding to it and going with it." Watts (1961, p. 68) similarly describes the "teacher of liberation" as one who structures a situation where the false premises of a "student" are fully utilized to demonstrate their absurdity. This strategy involves "pointing out new ways of acting upon the student's false assumptions until the student convinces himself that they are false."

In general, the presenting communications of clients are accepted and fed back to them in such a way that adaptive change may evolve. These communications are thus meaningful noise to both clients and therapists who see them, in different ways, as useful components of the therapeutic process.

The general cybernetic feedback structure of MRI therapy centers around every session assessing whether and to what extent the goal of therapy has been achieved. The advantage of a behaviorally specified therapeutic contract is that it provides a clear way of structuring feedback. No matter what is done or not done in a therapy session, the therapist (or client) can evaluate the progress in terms of a clearly specified goal.

This orientation proposes that the therapist should design his interventions to alter the client's class of attempted solutions. This may be done by offering a distinct set of new solutions or by diverting them from trying any solution (which may be seen as a different class of solution).

To change the class of solution requires addressing the client's cognitive frame of reference. As Watzlawick, Weakland, and Fisch (1974, p. 102) propose, "successful reframing must lift the problem out of the 'symptom' frame and into another frame that does not carry the implication of unchangeability." They immediately add that, "of course, not just any other frame will do, but only one that is congenial to the person's way of thinking and of categorizing reality."

One technique for creating such a useful frame for a problem has been named "positive connotation" by Selvini-Palazzoli and associates (1978). This method requires that the descriptions provided by a client's frame of reference be used to construct an alternative frame of reference that is positively connoted. An example of this is the difference between an optimist and a pessimist. As the old saying goes, an optimist describes a mug of beer as half full while the pessimist says the mug is half empty. The pattern described in each frame of reference is the same, but the connotation is different.

The connotation of a frame of reference does not necessarily have to be "positive." It is important that the connotation change to provide a difference that may transform the situation. Sometimes it may be useful to shift what a client holds as a "positive" frame toward a "negative" frame. A case of Milton H. Erickson (cited in Bateson and Brown 1975, p. 33) illustrates this approach. He was working with an alcoholic who had been a flying ace in World War I. When he came to Erickson he presented a scrapbook of photographs and newspaper clippings of his war achievements. Erickson listened to his story, picked up his scrapbook, threw it in a trash can, and declared, "It has nothing to do with you!" When asked how he starts a drinking binge, the man replied that he begins by getting two boilermakers. He then drinks one whiskey and washes it down with a beer, drinks the other whiskey and washes it down with a beer. With that information, Erickson instructed him to leave his office, proceed to the nearest bar, and order two boilermakers. When he finished the first one, he was told to say, "Here's to that bastard, Milton Erickson, may he choke on his own spit." When he picked up the second one, he was instructed to say, "Here's to that bastard, Milton Erickson, may he rot in hell." The man was then dismissed.

Erickson placed the man's drinking within the new frame of reference of a "bastard" who took his album and threw it in a wastepaper basket. The man could not take a drink without getting angry at "that bastard Milton Erickson." This anger, which arose from a negatively connoted frame of reference, short-circuited the habitual pattern organizing the man's drinking.

The MRI approach thus addresses our basic form for therapeutic change

(stability/change) / meaningful noise

in a unique way. Here, the therapist joins and stabilizes the communications that arise from the client's frame of reference and then changes their connotation. The meaningful noise modifies the client's frame of reference in a way that blocks the problematic class of solution behavior and/or enables a new class of behavior to emerge.

Watzlawick, Weakland, and Fisch (1974) have presented an interesting intervention for managing a crisis between parents and their rebellious teenagers that exemplifies how they handle the multiple communications of stability, change, and meaningful noise. They instruct the parents to perform what they call "benevolent sabotage." Rather than having them try to control their teenager's behavior in a direct fashion (for example, interrogating and scolding), they are told to announce to their adolescent that although they want him to comply with their requests, there is nothing they can do to control him. They are then to start acting in peculiar ways in response to their teenager's misbehavior. When the teenager fails to come home on time, for instance, the parents are instructed to pretend to be asleep and to wait a long time before unlocking the door. And then, in a sincere manner, apologize for their oversight. If his clothes aren't picked up, they might get "accidentally" thrown away. Every misbehavior of the adolescent is responded to in this fashion.

The structure of this intervention addresses stability in terms of the parent's continued requests for the teenager to behave appropriately. With respect to change, rather than trying one solution after another aimed at a one-up position with their adolescent, they are now instructed to try a different class of solution that requires their taking what appears as a one-down position. This new political frame of reference results in a dramatic shift. As Watzlawick, Weakland, and Fisch (1974, pp. 145–46) note, "it makes it useless and unappealing for the adolescent to rebel, since there is not much left to rebel against." By blocking the previous approach to problem solving, there is no longer an interactional structure that can support the problem behavior.

The success of this intervention rests upon how the therapist presents and explains it to the parents. Enter the meaningful noise. From the parents' language, clues can be gathered to suggest how to package and deliver the intervention. Watzlawick, Weakland, and Fisch (1974, p. 145) suggest that those parents who see life as requiring constant sacrifices can be told that the assignment will be a difficult sacrifice for them but that it is their parental duty to do this. To other parents, particularly those who are "military minded," the rationale might include the reminder that "trainees of a tough instructor will probably hate his guts, but stand an excellent chance of surviving in combat."

The intervention of "benevolent sabotage" addresses the multiple communications of stability, change, and meaningful noise as follows:

(stable requests for teenager's appropriate behavior / changing ways of introducing confusion in response to teenager's misbehavior via taking one-down position) / rationale for parents' task

The structure of MRI therapy involving the use of "benevolent sabotage" would begin with creating a therapeutic contract that specifies, in behavioral terms, the problem and intended goal. The problem might be defined as a teenager who won't come home on time and do his work. Assessing the attempted solutions in such a case might reveal that the parents try to manage their teenager by being "overtly punitive and repressive but covertly permissive and seductive" (Watzlawick, Weakland, and Fisch 1974, p. 146). The parents' own frame of reference will subsequently be disclosed by how they present and explain their situation. With this information, the therapist may design an intervention involving "benevolent sabotage" that alters the class of solution within the context of a modified frame of reference. Benevolent sabotage, to follow through with this example, creates a situation where the parents now "become overtly permissive and helpless but covertly punitive in a way against which the youngster cannot very well rebel" (Watzlawick, Weakland, and Fisch 1974, p. 146).

In any MRI therapy, feedback involves constructing reframes, with or without behavioral assignments, and then evaluating whether the contracted goal has been achieved. When the goal of therapy, usually cast in terms of problem alleviation, is achieved, the therapy is concluded. If a new contract or goal is proposed, therapy starts again. If the goal of therapy is not achieved, different interventions are designed. In such a situation, the previous session is not viewed as a failure but as a diagnostic probe that provided additional information about the troubled client's recursive relation between his problem and attempted solution. All behavioral outcomes, whether seen as connected to the client or therapist, are thus connoted in a way that constructs useful feedback.

A Case Study of John Weakland

This case was conducted by John Weakland as a demonstration for a brief therapy workshop. Paul Watzlawick was an observer of the session and occasionally offered suggestions to the therapist via an earphone. The transcript of this case has been published and analyzed by Fisch, Weakland, and Segal in their book, *The Tactics of Change* (1982, pp. 219–254). The following analysis and comments, however, are separate and distinct from their view.

The complete case involved two sessions; most of it is presented in this transcript. The identified patient is a thirty-five-year-old unmarried man under treatment at the mental health center where the workshop was conducted.

SESSION 1

THERAPIST: I appreciate your coming here today, so that the people here have an opportunity to see the way we work in our particular style, but I don't think *you* should count on getting too much from it. I rather gathered that your situation's a pretty difficult one anyway. I talked just a little with Dr. Y [the patient's therapist at the mental health center]. He filled me in a little bit, and it, well, doesn't sound like something that I'm going to change with a twist of my wrist, you know —that wouldn't be very realistic. To start with, although I know this is going to be somewhat repetitious of the things you've been talking to him about, I'm new on the scene; I only talked with him five minutes. Could you tell me, essentially as of right now, what's the problem you're concerned about, coming here about?

The therapist begins by addressing stability and change. Stability is acknowledged through the therapist's respect for the complexity of the situation ("I rather gathered that your situation's a pretty difficult one anyway"). In addition, the presupposition that some change will occur is constructed. The only questions are whether it will be perceived as earth shattering to the patient ("I don't think *you* should count on getting too much from it") and whether it will require much effort (". . . it doesn't sound like something that I'm going to change with a twist of my wrist . . ."). The most important part of the therapist's introduction is his first question to the patient, which presents the most basic distinction of MRI therapy: "What's the problem?"

PATIENT: I am a music teacher, violin, and I'm a very, very, very poor performer—to the extent that my hands shake, they sweat when I perform, which they do not do at any other time. That's it in a little nutshell.

At this point the therapist carefully explores what exactly the patient means by his problem definition. In an MRI strategy, the initial semantic frame (problem definition) must be carefully constructed for it will guide the course of subsequent questions and interventions.

THERAPIST: O.K. When you say you're a poor performer, you mean as a public performer?

PATIENT: Yes.

THERAPIST: When you're playing for yourself or giving lessons—what's it like then?

PATIENT: It's nothing like when I'm performing for even one or two people. When I have to play something from the beginning to the end, hopefully well.

THERAPIST: Uh-huh. [Pause] When you say if you have to play something from beginning to the end, have you ever been in the—isn't it always that situation in public, or have you ever tried playing part of a piece in public?

PATIENT: I don't recall ever trying to play a part of a piece.

THERAPIST: Uh-huh.

PATIENT: Except for movements of specific works. But that I would consider in itself a piece.

THERAPIST: O.K. [Pause] When you say that even one or two people—essentially that makes it public?

PATIENT: Yes.

THERAPIST: Uhh, does it progress from there? For example, is four twice as bad as two or . . .

The therapist is attempting to discern as many differences as he can with respect to the patient's problem definition: private versus public performance; part of musical score versus whole musical score; small public versus large public. If the patient presents some information that indicates how his problem may be made different (for example, "worse"), a clue may be provided for designing a therapeutic strategy.

PATIENT: No. That's not the case.

THERAPIST: So if it's one or two, it's already pretty much on the way to . . .

PATIENT: [Interrupting] Well, it certainly could. It doesn't progress geometrically.

THERAPIST: Uh-huh.

PATIENT: Certainly if it were a situation in which this hall were full, then it would be bad. Or it usually is, at any rate.

THERAPIST: Uh-huh. [Pause] Well, to tell you the truth, I feel a little the same myself. If this hall were full, I would be even more nervous than I am right now; and I still feel that people are looking over my shoulder through the camera—but I'm not meaning that that's comparable to what you're telling me about, just in the same direction. [Pause] O.K., so if there are more people, it's worse, but not in direct proportion.

PATIENT: S'correct.

THERAPIST: Uh-huh. Anything else that makes it worse?

The therapist is again searching for difference with respect to definitions of the presenting problem.

PATIENT: Yes, if there's someone whose judgment regarding my performance I really respect, or really want to impress, then it becomes seemingly progressively worse.

THERAPIST: Uh-huh.

PATIENT: Certainly my satisfaction is reduced.

The therapist, at this point, has received a sufficiently clear definition of the problem: "He has trouble performing on the violin because of nervousness" (Fisch, Weakland, and Segal, p. 220). In addition, the intensity of his problem is related to his evaluation of a listener's ability to judge his performance. With this information, the therapist can proceed to address how the patient has tried to solve the problem.

THERAPIST: Uh-huh. [Pause] Uh, how have you tried to deal with this problem up to now, both on your own and in terms of help you got from anybody else?

PATIENT: Well, I [clears throat] didn't pursue the problem recently. I have for the last couple of years, but I really haven't pursued the problem because I spent ten years in architecture school and various other activities. So I haven't really tried to attack the problem until recently, and that is—I tried to perform when I came back to . . .

THERAPIST: [Interrupting] O.K. The ten years were sort of a time out from this . . .

PATIENT: [Interrupting] Correct. I wasn't working on any music at all.

THERAPIST: Uh-huh.

PATIENT: But now when I came back, I tried to perform on several occasions, and it was dismal as I remembered it back when I was eighteen, when it made me quit to begin with, because it was so bad. And the rewards I got for performing were so small that I gave it up to begin with. And back then, I had the advice of music teachers and that was all. They suggested to perform more, perform more, but I didn't perform very much, but when I did, it was, it was very unsuccessful.

Fisch, Weakland, and Segal (p. 225) point out that the man's solution essentially involved trying harder to play better. As the therapist uncovers attempted solutions, a political frame of reference is constructed: we see who did what with respect to trying to solve the problem.

THERAPIST: O.K. So at that time they would just tell you, "You gotta just sort of plunge into it and get with it . . ."

PATIENT: [Interrupting] "Until it becomes as familiar to you as a normal ordinary event." But it never became that familiar, with me, and it's not going to become that familiar with me if I'm so bad that no one wants to hear me.

THERAPIST: [Pause] I'm sort of curious, if it was that bad that long ago . . . that you ever came back to it at all.

The therapist explores the patient's semantic frame of reference when he asks him to explain why he stuck with music.

PATIENT: Does seem peculiar.

THERAPIST: How did that come about?

PATIENT: I didn't give up. I didn't give up on my talent, I suppose.

THERAPIST: Uh-huh.

PATIENT: Would be—a brief summary of it. There are other reasons, too. I wasn't particularly satisfied with what I was doing, which was nothing, and [pause] I have to pursue some career.

The patient is providing some meaningful noise—his belief in his own talent and pursuit for a satisfying career.

THERAPIST: O.K. And—so you came back to it partly by default?

PATIENT: Yes.

THERAPIST: Uh-huh. [Pause] O.K. So way back then, they were telling you, "Well, you just gotta get with it, and get with it and eventually it will change," but it didn't.

Since you've been trying to grapple with it in the recent past, what've you been trying—how've you been trying to do that?

The therapist immediately gatekeeps the information to refocus on attempted solutions.

PATIENT: I'm trying a ps—a therapist.

THERAPIST: O.K.

PATIENT: Among other things, and trying to perform more. And I haven't been too successful in the latter direction.

THERAPIST: Uh-huh.

PATIENT: When I have, it—some people tell me it's, uh, I'm doing better, but I'm not so sure.

THERAPIST: [Pause] Well, I don't know who's telling you, but [pause] in general I would say you'd be on the safer side to be a little skeptical of positive opinions you hear unless you are quite sure either you're hearing it the same way yourself or that that person has critical standards that they're not fudging in order to try to encourage you.

"Positive opinions" may be taken as messages of "change." Since the therapist encourages the patient to be skeptical about positive messages (that is, change), he is by implication introducing a message of "stability."

PATIENT: In my field it's almost impossible to get that kind of an opinion from anybody.

THERAPIST: Well, then I guess the best thing you can do is at least be skeptical about the opinions . . .

PATIENT: [Interrupting] Granted.

THERAPIST: . . . you get.

PATIENT: I am.

THERAPIST: Because the worst thing you could do would be to get the idea that you're doing better than you are, which essentially would be a—would lead you into a bad place. It would lead you into a place where you'd be attempting too much, and you couldn't do anything but take a bad fall.

The multiple communications of encouragement and skepticism, succeeding and taking a fall, or change and stability are now being managed by the therapist in a way that addresses their *complementarity.* For example, too many reports of success are described as connected to possibly taking a bad fall. Therefore, the therapist argues, encouragement should be encountered with skepticism. These complementarities, of course, point toward the recursive relation connecting problem and solution behavior. Or, in more general terms, communications of change imply communications of stability and vice versa.

PATIENT: But I am of the opinion that most people in my field receive exactly that kind of advice. Poor advice. Overestimations of their talent, and they pursue their careers, to, incredibly enough, some satisfactory end.

THERAPIST: Huh. Well, O.K. Maybe some of them get by, even having that kind of advice and criticism, but I think there's a couple reasons why that—even if they do, that wouldn't be appropriate for you. In the first place, I think probably you're . . . Sounds like they're people that not only snow others but they're able to snow themselves, and that doesn't seem to me the way you are. You are more clear-eyed and critical about where you're at, and also you've had this problem and you don't want to get into a situation where you're overreaching yourself, because it might give you a bad fall, and if anything, set you back even further. That's why I'm saying that I think it's desirable that if somebody gives you encouraging statements that you take it with a rather skeptical reservation in your mind.

PATIENT: Well, I—I certainly think that sounds like reasonable advice, except I'm so incredibly skeptical of most everything that I'm not so sure in the field of which I am in that that's the best way to be. If I were supremely confident, regardless of how it actually was in some nebulous reality, it would be better than it certainly is.

THERAPIST: [Pause] I don't see how you're ever going to be supremely confident given your . . .

PATIENT: [Interrupting] I won't be . . .

THERAPIST: . . . actual experience in . . .

PATIENT: . . . I won't be. I agree.

THERAPIST: O.K. That's good, because if you were, I'd—I'd be scared as hell what was going to happen to you next. [Patient laughs.] Uh, O.K. So first you had advice, "Get on with it and it'll get sort of customary, and then you won't feel this way," and that wasn't any good, even a long time ago, and now you've been in therapy—what have you been trying there?

The therapist again positively underscores the patient's pessimism as resourceful skepticism by suggesting that he would be worried if the patient became supremely confident. The therapist then returns to refocusing on the patient's problem-solving efforts.

PATIENT: Uhm, I don't understand the question. I mean, I'm not sure how to respond to it.

THERAPIST: Well—the basic question is: What've you been doing to try to grapple with this problem? And when I asked you that, you said, "Well, I've gone into treatment"—O.K., what's been happening there, and how's it worked?

PATIENT: We've been discussing [sigh] my expectations and my—my actual feelings as I perform. Uh, and my history.

THERAPIST: Uh-huh.

PATIENT: Whether it's getting better or not, I'm just not sure. I'm such a—I don't know how—I don't really feel that—I feel that some start has been made.

THERAPIST: But not very much change has taken place?

PATIENT: Not—no.

THERAPIST: O.K. Are you doing anything on your own outside to grapple with it—in addition to the . . .

PATIENT: [Interrupting] Yes. I'm trying to get opportunities to perform, for better or for worse.

THERAPIST: All right. And how's that go?

PATIENT: That hasn't been too successful lately.

THERAPIST: In what way?

PATIENT: Well, I just haven't—been able to get an opportunity to perform in—very often. I have on several occasions, but not often. Other than grabbing anyone that comes into my own living room. Saying "Sit down."

THERAPIST: O.K. Uh, other than your therapist, is there anyone who in any way is trying to help you with this?

PATIENT: I have a violin teacher as I've had so many times in the past—but his efforts in this direction are nonexistent.

THERAPIST: I'm sorry, I got a little lost there—I couldn't . . .

PATIENT: I have a violin—I take violin . . .

THERAPIST: O.K.

PATIENT: . . . from a teacher, and—he's aware of my performance difficulties only too well. But other than the usual advice to perform more, which certainly may have some merit [laughs], that's about all that he can do.

THERAPIST: O.K. All he does really is about the same as your teacher told you years and years ago.

PATIENT: Years and years ago, that's correct.

THERAPIST: O.K . . .

PATIENT: [Interrupting] And I'm a teacher, and I can't give much better advice either.

THERAPIST: O.K.

PATIENT: I have a pupil myself who has—exactly seems to have the same characteristics in performing for *me* that I have in performing for other people.

THERAPIST: O.K. Any friends or other performers give you any advice, or attempt to help you in any way?

PATIENT: Other than in general what we've talked about, no.

All information confirms that the class of solution involves trying harder and performing more. The relevant social context thus far includes his teachers, past and present, his own efforts, and his therapist.

THERAPIST: [Pause] Uh-huh. [Therapist receives message through earpiece.] O.K. Uh, my colleague has something that he wants to know about, I don't really know why. Uh [pause], when you gave up your move toward a career in architecture, you said it didn't mean all that much to you. But it might have to someone else. Who was most disappointed when you gave that up?

This question enables the therapists to probe a bit more into the social context that may be contributing to problem formation, maintenance, and resolution.

PATIENT: Perhaps my parents.
THERAPIST: Both of them equally, or . . . ?
PATIENT: No—it's difficult to say. My—my mother would be most disappointed because she probably has—feels a greater stake in my success than does my father.

At this point, other therapeutic strategies might prescribe hypothesizing about family coalition patterns, hierarchy, and so forth. An MRI therapy, however, will limit its focus to seeing the relation between a problem and efforts to solve it, whether it involves other family members or not.

THERAPIST: Uh-huh. [Pause] Does your mother also feel that way about your music, or was she more inclined to architecture?
PATIENT: She'd incline to anything.
THERAPIST: She just wanted to see you make something of yourself, sort of thing?
PATIENT: Yes, and so did he, but in a, in a . . . He did regard music as a waste of time.
THERAPIST: Uh-huh.
PATIENT: Unsuited, unsuitable vocation.
THERAPIST: [Pause] But the music was all right with your mother?
PATIENT: Well, as I said, anything would be all right with her.
THERAPIST: As long as you got on with it and . . .

PATIENT: Well, even that, as long as I survived—she would be at least grateful.

THERAPIST: [Pause] She doesn't sound like she has very high expectations of you.

PATIENT: Oh, she has high expectations—very, very high expectations.

THERAPIST: But she doesn't expect them to be fulfilled?

PATIENT: Well, she's not—she's very scared about putting her viewpoint forth in front of me.

THERAPIST: Uh-huh.

PATIENT: Or if she does, having listened to my viewpoint, she —I've usually gotten my way.

THERAPIST: [Pause] Uh-huh. Um, your parents are still alive?

PATIENT: Yes.

THERAPIST: And where do they live?

PATIENT: In a small community about a hundred and ten miles north of here.

THERAPIST: Uh-huh. How much are you in touch with them?

PATIENT: Uh, I hear from them once every week or two.

THERAPIST: O.K., so they're—keep pretty much aware of where you're at on all this?

PATIENT: [Sighs] Oh well, they . . .

THERAPIST: [Interrupting] I don't necessarily mean in specific detail, but . . .

PATIENT: No—they're—yes, they—they know how I'm getting along . . .

THERAPIST: Uh-huh.

PATIENT: . . . from what I tell them.

THERAPIST: Uhh, what do they say to you about it?

PATIENT: They have no idea of the real problems involved. My father doesn't even know I have this problem—I don't think. Except if he'd talk to my mother about it, and I can't imagine that he would ever be so concerned as to talk to her about . . .

THERAPIST: O.K. But she's aware that you're . . .

PATIENT: [Interrupting] She's aware I'm nervous in performance, yes, very much so.

THERAPIST: Uh-huh. What does she say to you about it? Give you some advice, or what?

PATIENT: Not really. She says, "I know you can do it."

THERAPIST: O.K. [Pause] And she continues to know you can do it, no matter how long you have the trouble?

PATIENT: I think she would, yes.

THERAPIST: Uh-huh. Well, she has for quite a while already . . .

PATIENT: [Interrupting] Yeah, oh yes. Quite a while.

As Fisch, Weakland, and Segal (p. 232) note, these comments indicate that the parents aren't actively involved in the present problem-solving efforts although the mother takes a view similar to everyone else's. They also note that the patient's condescending view of his mother and hostile view of his father will provide resources later in the session.

THERAPIST: Uh-huh. I understand from Dr. Y that you live with a roommate. Does he pay any attention to this problem?

PATIENT: No.

THERAPIST: How can he not, so to speak? Does he . . .

PATIENT: Uh [pause], Bach is the same to him as—Nancy Wilson or Elton John.

THERAPIST: Uh-huh. [Pause] O.K., but I'm sort of wondering, doesn't he see you struggling to make arrangements to perform and coming home looking sort of whacked out by what an effort it was and that sort of thing?

Checking the roommate's *view* is a way of approaching how the patient frames it.

PATIENT: Well, he regards it as a play activity on my part. Something which I get enjoyment out of. Some form of therapy. Which it is.

THERAPIST: [Pause] Doesn't sound like fun.

PATIENT: Uh, well, it—I didn't say it was exactly fun. It's something that's—I think—I'm, you know, I enjoy doing in a way. It's not [sigh]—I enjoy the effort that comes from it. Whatever it amounts to.

Enjoyment of "the effort that comes from it" provides meaningful noise and a resource for the therapist to potentially draw upon.

THERAPIST: Well, there is an old saying that—sometimes it's better to travel hopefully than to arrive. And your mother has maybe been in a similar position for a long time. Let me shift gears a little bit and ask you about something different. Uh, how much thought have you given to the potential and probable disadvantages of licking this problem?

The patient's previous reference to partly enjoying his problem-solving efforts has provided a clue for structuring an intervention by suggesting that there may be some experience of loss or disappointment if the problem is solved (for example, "it's better to travel hopefully than to arrive"). The therapist verbally marks that he is shifting their frame of reference ("let me shift gears . . .") and then explicitly addresses the negative consequences of problem resolution.

PATIENT: [Pause] The disadvantages of licking this problem?

THERAPIST: Yeah.

PATIENT: Actually, some thought, because I—I feel I'd be possibly disappointed with myself—that I would be disappointed with the responses that I would have because—I have actually fantasized quite high expectations for myself. [Sigh] And I thought it's certainly possible that—I don't—well, it's a scary—scary proposition in a way.

THERAPIST: O.K. Am I picking you up right that part of this is—you might find out if you didn't have this problem that . . .

PATIENT: I didn't have any talent.

THERAPIST: You didn't have any talent and . . .

PATIENT: Well, I don't think that would be the case.

THERAPIST: O.K. You didn't have as much as . . .

PATIENT: As much as I would like to hope I would have.

THERAPIST: . . . as you could always hope—when this problem is in your way.

PATIENT: Correct.

THERAPIST: O.K., and . . . O.K., and since you are—I understand you have a practical interest in getting over this problem—it would help you get on with your career—maybe you'd find that it was still very tough, even if you did get over it.

The therapist and client continue constructing the view that there are negative consequences associated with solving the problem.

PATIENT: Uh, I don't think that would be the case, as far as the —the actual career as a teacher . . .

THERAPIST: O.K., maybe more that you might not . . .

PATIENT: [Interrupting] I would not be able to indulge my fantasies as much as I normally do, but as far as—I think it would be quite helpful to me in my career, where I am in this city with the colleagues and so on that I have. No doubts about that.

THERAPIST: O.K. Practically, it would be helpful, but it might be hard on your fantasies . . .

PATIENT: [Interrupting] It—it could be, but I am generally able to—face mediocrity from time to time, since it comes upon me quite frequently.

THERAPIST: Uh-huh. O.K. You thought of any other disadvantages?

PATIENT: Not really.

THERAPIST: Uh-huh. [Pause]

PATIENT: And I haven't—you know, delved into that disadvantage all that much.

THERAPIST: [Sigh] Well, I think you should. [Pause] You're . . .

PATIENT: I'd agree.

THERAPIST: You're proposing—well, I don't know how far you'll get, or how long it'll take, but you're proposing to make a change in something that's rather central to your life, and something that's been a part of your life for twenty years at least. In a sense, it was a part of your life even when you were not actively playing, because you were doing something that was a substitute in relation to this problem. So that's—an enormously sizable change you're proposing, and there's a natural tendency when somebody is trying to deal with a problem to be pretty clear on what the potential advantages are, but equally that means you're not looking at any possible disadvantages, and there is no change that's a hundred percent one way. So I think it's only a reasonable caution to devote some attention to what the disadvantages might be, and since it's particularly difficult to think of disadvantages—there's a natural tendency to think the other way—anything to counteract that inherent bias by, oh, trying to think about it in that other direction very freely, and not say, "Well, I've got to be cold, cool, calculating, and rational about it, but let me—let my imagination go, and I can always sort it out later, because the danger is not thinking enough rather than going overboard." So I really think it would be to your advantage to think some more about the potential disadvantages, maybe a little bit right now, but—be a useful thing to think about when you leave here and have some time to do it adequately.

The therapist is continuing to engage the patient to more fully address both the disadvantages and advantages of problem resolution. The therapist is using the language of "advantages" and "disadvantages" to address the multiple communications of change and stability.

PATIENT: That [sighs] it could be certainly related to the problem itself. The disadvantages.

THERAPIST: [Pause] Uh, you see, just to—this thing actually, basically, you've got to do the thinking on. But just to give you a couple of thoughts that come to my mind as to sort of the shape or extent of things. One possibility would be that there could be a disadvantage even if you were to find that, by golly, your talent is really pretty good. You might be erring in your judgment on the low side on that. And if so, what is that going to do? That's going to lead you, or at least tend to lead you, in the direction of expanding your area and scope of performance, which will lead you into larger audiences and more critical judgment. And, O.K., that won't happen unless you get over this problem basically, but this is the sort of problem—that is my impression, although I'm sure no musical expert—but it's my impression from, say working under observation myself, from dealing with people that have similar problems to this, there's a realistic core of this that a person never gets over completely. You never get over being somewhat anxious when you're in a performance situation where people are looking at you critically. For example, athletes are notoriously concerned with exactly this problem. So that you've got a core there—no matter what progress you make, there's a core of your problem that's never going to go away.

PATIENT: Well, of course, I question whether I actually have a problem sometimes, because I realize everyone is nervous, and I'm somewhat nervous now. It's [sigh] . . . But my nervousness now is not comparable to my . . . This is what makes me think there is actually a problem here [laughs], but it's not comparable to the nervousness I experience, uh, when I have to perform.

THERAPIST: Uh-huh.

PATIENT: The nervousness—I'm willing to be a little anxious, willing to be a little nervous, but I'm not—I'm concerned about it being incapacitating, *ridiculously* incapacitating.

THERAPIST: Yep, yeah, I think I understand the distinction you're making.

PATIENT: Given a 10 to 20 percent fall-off in brilliance at the violin—wouldn't be too abnormal, as a matter of fact. At all.

THERAPIST: [Receives directions from earpiece] My colleague raises a question in relation to what you were just saying—essentially a question around distinguishing between normal nervousness and a problem. He would like to know: have you failed in the sense that you were in a performance situation and you just couldn't play, or you played terribly badly?

The definition of the presenting problem is becoming more polished.

PATIENT: Oh, yes.

THERAPIST: O.K., could you give me an example of that, so that might clarify things for him?

PATIENT: [Sighs] Yes, I—I did deliver a performance, I virtually had to in my second year at the conservatory.

THERAPIST: Uh-huh.

PATIENT: Before a conscript assemblage of students, and I particularly chose a piece that was well within my capabilities musically and technically.

THERAPIST: Uh-huh.

PATIENT: And I was quite confident that I would be, would have been very confident performing it for myself, or for a person if I did not realize they were there.

THERAPIST: Uh-huh.

PATIENT: And I was—I forgot a great deal of the piece, my left hand was shaking so much that I couldn't execute a simple scale with any efficiency at all. It was very, very upsetting to me at the time.

THERAPIST: Uh-huh.

PATIENT: It was the decisive factor in making me quit.

THERAPIST: Uh-huh. Has there been a similar failure lately since you've gone back to . . .

PATIENT: No, because I have not performed in front of such an audience. But I perform in front of small audiences, just as I had performed in front of small audiences and before large audiences up until that time, and I experience the difficulties now that I remember experiencing quite well back then.

THERAPIST: Uh-huh. So you're sort of—you got part of it, and you're saying it's so similar you can extrapolate from that to what it would be like if you tried the real thing?

PATIENT: Uh, yes. Perhaps now I'm—needless to say, older, hopefully a bit more mature, so it might—I might be able to handle it a little bit better, but I question whether or not I would.

THERAPIST: Uh-huh.

PATIENT: Uh, I have actually, the only thing that made that particular performance stand out in my mind was not necessarily that I was more incapacitated at that time, but because of the size of the audience, and the fact that I had worked so hard and so carefully schemed this out, that the disappointment was greater. I've been as incapacitated since that time almost, and before that time, but that particular one does stand out in my mind, yes.

THERAPIST: O.K. Can you at this point think of, or even imagine, any other disadvantages in getting over this problem?

PATIENT: No.

THERAPIST: Uhm. [Pause] How do you think it would—getting over this problem would affect your relationship with your parents?

Fisch, Weakland, and Segal (p. 239) note that "the therapist is not asking this for information but as a way of introducing another intervention." He is working within the frame of reference called "disadvantages of improvement" as a means of constructing another intervention.

PATIENT: [Sigh] Well, by all rights, my relationship with them should improve. Uh, from my father's standpoint, I would—I would tend to be more economically successful. And I don't—I think that would be the most important thing that would matter to him. As far as my mother—I—it certainly should improve here, because she wants me to be more satisfied. Now, if I were more satisfied, and I think I would be, then she should theoretically be happier.

The patient has provided the advantages of change. The therapist shifts to addressing possible disadvantages and negative consequences.

THERAPIST: Well, theoretically.

PATIENT: I mean, I—I really earnestly don't see any reason why she shouldn't.

THERAPIST: Well, I can see a couple of reasons.

PATIENT: Yes, I can too [laughs], if you're going in that direction, but, uh, knowing our relationship over many years, the fact my mother cradles me somewhat, yes. This would be more independent, but I like to think —I would give her the benefit of the doubt in this direction.

THERAPIST: Well, O.K., let's give your mother the benefit of the doubt and turn to your father for a minute. Now, obviously, I'm just taking a guess based on somewhat minimal evidence, but that guess would be in the direction of your father, although he may come on about you oughta make something of yourself, his basic view is, essentially, you ain't gonna make anything of yourself, and you've really blown everything you ever did, and therefore, it would be one hell of a shock to your father if you licked this problem. That'd probably rattle him right to his back teeth.

The therapist has basically recycled what he already knows about the man's relationship with his father within the frame of disadvantages of problem resolution. We can view this as meaningful noise for the patient out of which he may construct punctuations that provide new resources for the session.

PATIENT: But he doesn't know about the problem. Second, I would agree with your estimate of what he feels about me, but I don't—there may be something in the sense that he would like to feel that he is more successful than I am . . .

The patient constructs a new semantic frame: problem resolution would mean that his father won't feel more successful than he is.

THERAPIST: [Interrupting] O.K.

PATIENT: And he has some reasonable basis for believing that I would—I mean, he has some reasonable basis for shock if I should overcome this problem.

THERAPIST: Well, he'd have a couple of bases. I don't know how much he knows about your—problem specifically, but certainly he knows that—you know, you aren't making anything big. If you got over the problem, what he would be likely to find out is you would be doing O.K., and not only you'd be doing O.K., you'd be doing O.K. in an area that he doesn't think much of, and that would be a rather powerful combination. Like a punch in the nose to the old man.

Again, the therapist recycles the patient's meaningful noise back to him but underscores a political implication of problem resolution. As Fisch, Weakland, and Segal (p. 241) put it, "By overcoming your problem, you can one-up your father."

PATIENT: Well, it's one, of course, I—a punch I would like to deliver.

One of the disadvantages of problem resolution, upsetting father, is now connoted as a positive consequence for the patient. We can now more clearly see that the therapist's earlier probing of the man's relationship with his parents was done with an eye on constructing this intervention.

THERAPIST: [Pause] Um. Well, maybe.

PATIENT: Oh, but I would, I . . . oh, yes.

THERAPIST: [Sighing] Well, O.K. [Pause] No way I can—no way I can dispute you except that I don't know, might shake you up more than you would think to shake your old man up.

PATIENT: Well, I've shaken him up in the past through a few failures and through a few positive things . . .

THERAPIST: [Interrupting] You—with your old man, a failure wouldn't shake him up nearly as bad as a success would [small laugh].

PATIENT: [Pause] True. But I wouldn't—I wouldn't mind just seeing him being shaken up.

THERAPIST: O.K. [Pause] Whose observation of your playing . . . well, let me back off from that to ask a preliminary first. Is it just observation you're concerned about, or do you get actual criticism when you do badly?

Back to the presenting problem.

PATIENT: Is it just observation that I'm concerned about, or actual criticism?

THERAPIST: Yeah. In other words, I'm wondering is there somebody that is laying some words on you about "My God, you're flopping there, and you oughta be able to get on with it," or is it more you know people observe when you do poorly, and you get shaky, but they're not talking about it?

PATIENT: Well, that's—this—that's it, more or less, the second time.

THERAPIST: O.K. Whose observation would you be most concerned about?

PATIENT: [Sigh] Other violin teachers.

THERAPIST: Uh-huh.

PATIENT: Other knowledgeable violin teachers. There are several in this city that I would—I would be delighted to be able to perform well in front of.

THERAPIST: Uh-huh. [Pause] Do you know how to perform badly?

PATIENT: Uh, we tried that, and I was so nervous at the time that I wasn't—I could not make up my mind whether I should try to perform badly or not. Because I was unaware of the discussion that had taken place with my therapist.

THERAPIST: O.K. I understood that—I may be wrong—but I understood from him a little bit different—that he had asked you to perform in a mediocre way.

PATIENT: Uh-huh.

THERAPIST: I'm saying something a little different. I'm saying, do you know how to perform really badly?

The therapist is constructing another intervention based on having the patient successfully achieve the task of deliberately playing badly. Purposefully constructing what he's afraid of doing spontaneously is one way of disrupting problem-solution interaction. In terms of the multiple communications of change, stability, and meaningful noise, we have:

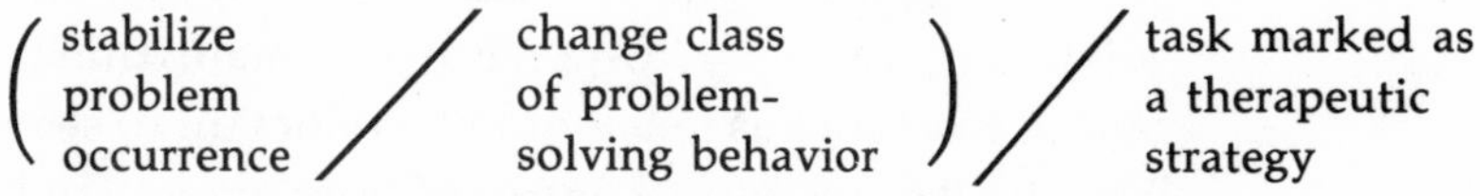

Change involves blocking the patient's habitual way of trying harder to successfully perform, while stability is connected to prescribing the problem's occurrence. With respect to meaningful noise, the therapist has marked his suggestions within the context of a therapeutic strategy. He will soon point out that the patient can "learn something" by performing badly and stops short of explaining what he can learn, suggesting that "that might be moving too fast" (that is, changing too fast).

PATIENT: No. Probably not. I certainly can perform really badly, I assume, but I'm not . . .

THERAPIST: Oh, that's an assumption.

PATIENT: Well, I have never tried to perform badly.

THERAPIST: Uh-huh.

PATIENT: Nor even mediocrely.

THERAPIST: [Pause] Well, I think you might learn something by —if you're up to making the attempt to perform actually badly, but . . . I . . . I'm hesitant to say much more about that because that might be moving too fast. I don't think you've really thought enough yet about the possible consequences of getting over this problem. And by "getting over the problem," I mean at most getting over the really out of control anxiety. I certainly don't mean getting over all the anxieties we

> were talking about a few minutes ago. And it's hard to distinguish where is that line between the real shakes and the sort of anxiety that is natural, normal, and, up to a point, even useful when one is performing. To go back to my analogy, I don't mean that violin playing is at the level, of course, of athletic performance; but, as the athletes who have dealt with this problem will point out, you've got to get a little bit anxious to get up to do what you can, and maybe something comparable to that—that some degree of anxiety is a thing that you can turn to use when you get out there ready to go. But the main thing I'm saying is—I sure as hell would be reluctant to see you learn how to get more control of your anxiety, which you might do by learning how to play badly to start with, deliberately, until you'd looked at the potential consequences a good deal more, because if you start to move in this thing, it's—it's a snowball. Snowball in the sense that an improvement leads to more improvement. It's also a snowball in a more profound sense. As you do better, your horizons as to what you might do will widen. That both has the disadvantage that the severity of pressure of observation will increase, and whether—how the two would keep pace is very hard to judge. It also has the disadvantage that widening of horizons means a lot of choices will enter into your life that aren't there now; and therefore, decisions will have to be made all over the place.

The meaningful noise gets more specific in terms of playing badly to "get more control of your anxiety." The therapist, however, warns the patient that the consequences of change should be fully considered before taking any further steps. The patient is thus caught in an interesting tangle of logic. If he wants to solve his problem, he has a strategy—play badly in order to gain control of his anxiety. At the same time, the therapist has cautioned the patient to not proceed until he has carefully examined the consequences that might arise when his problem is solved. Since the negative consequences the therapist is talking about are actually positive outcomes, a full consideration of them will more than likely lead the patient to wanting to try the strategy with even more determination. More importantly, the patient and therapist's set of choices does not include deciding whether the strategy will work but focuses on determining whether the patient really wants the consequences of change.

PATIENT: That's what you have agents for. When they're that wide.

THERAPIST: Well, O.K., but either they gotta bring some decisions back to you, or at least you've got to make the decision, "Who do I want to be my agent, and is he doing a good job?" And it gets, you know—as things expand, there just gets to be a lot larger and tougher decisions to make, and . . . we're going to have to stop shortly. Let me raise a couple of points with you while we're still here. First of all, what would be a significant but minimal improvement for you? And I mean—let me define that a little more. What, if it were to happen, would lead you to say, "Look, I'm not out of the woods, but I've made a definite first step."

PATIENT: [Pause] Uh . . .

The therapist is completing the final aspect of an MRI therapeutic contract—specifying the patient's treatment goal.

THERAPIST: And think it over, because this can be a very difficult thing to judge, and particularly to get some index that you can't just kid yourself about, you know.

PATIENT: Well, I've thought about that. It's possible a first step would not necessarily be a successful performance. A first step would be perhaps that someone was interested, other than myself, in it being a successful performance. That I had help on the problem. That I had knowledgeable help on the problem.

The patient's response is not a satisfactory definition of a treatment outcome. As Fisch, Weakland, and Segal (p. 245) note, "he is confusing means with ends." The therapist subsequently attempts to reach clarification. In this exchange, the therapist suggests a few interventions, including the patient announcing his problem to an audience before playing. Such a strategy reinforces the idea that blocking his habitual ways of trying to play better may result in problem resolution. Finally the therapist restates his question about therapeutic outcome with an emphasis on behavioral description.

THERAPIST: . . . Uh, all right, is there anything on the matter that would be a sign of a first step? Can you think of anything that would be a sort of visible sign? Or an audible sign? What, if it were to observably happen, would be an index or criterion that a first step—significant, although maybe small—has occurred?

PATIENT: That I got through an entire piece in a performance situation without a memory slip of any kind.

THERAPIST: [Pause] O.K. That makes the first step pretty nearly the same as the final step.

PATIENT: Oh, no, no, no . . .

THERAPIST: No?

PATIENT: . . . no, no, no.

THERAPIST: What would be the final step?

PATIENT: The final step is to get through it without any memory slip *well.*

THERAPIST: Oh. O.K. Let me see if I got the difference. If you got through it without any memory slip, but not necessarily well, that would be the first step?

PATIENT: Hmmm-huh.

THERAPIST: Uh-huh.

PATIENT: "Well" is a big, big field.

THERAPIST: It's too bad you can't have a different sort of memory slip.

PATIENT: [Pause] How so?

THERAPIST: Well, all—all you'd have to do is, instead of forgetting the music, would be to forget the audience.

Note the structure of this subtle intervention:

(stability	/	change)	/	meaningful noise
(stabilize forgetting	/	change what is forgotten)	/	therapist's strategy for problem solving

PATIENT: Yes [softly].

THERAPIST: But, anyway, before all of this—I think the most important thing is to seriously give some time and thought to the potential disadvantages of making this sort of improvement. I'd like to ask you, if we could arrange it in our schedule, might it be possible for you to come back once more somewhere in the next couple of days?

PATIENT: Sure.

THERAPIST: All right. I'll have to check and see about that. Either I would check with you if we manage to arrange that, or Dr. Y would call you. Meanwhile, would you take some time—a half-hour at the minimum, set it aside, and sit down and think about, and make notes on, any possible disadvantages to getting over this problem that you could think of, and when I say any, I mean to reiterate, don't make them restricted to what seems likely and logical, but even if you think it's something that seems way far out, fine. Because to deliberately attempt to think of the far out will free up, free up your vision and your imagination for anything else. There is a sort of built-in block there that I tried to describe earlier. So would you do that?

PATIENT: Of course.

THERAPIST: O.K. Fine. Then that's really all I've got in mind now, except that I again—I appreciate your coming in, because it's mainly for our benefit.

This intervention may be viewed on several levels. A focus on the consequences of problem resolution sets up the patient to focus more on choosing whether he wants to change rather than worrying about how to change. If he decides to change, several therapeutic strategies have been proposed—all of them addressing ways of blocking his habits of problem solving. In addition, the therapist has constructed the exemplary (negative) consequences of improvement to actually be those things that would benefit the patient. Finally, if the patient follows the therapist's assignment then it is possible that his attention will shift away from his habitual attempts to solve the problem thus enabling the problem to be solved.

SESSION 2

THERAPIST: I'd like to say first that I appreciate your taking the trouble to come back, particularly on short notice, and even more because it's going to have to be a rather short get-together for reasons of the way they've got this schedule arranged. They're just sort of fitting this meeting in, but I thought it would be worthwhile to do, particularly because I did want to have a chance to check back with you on the matter that I'd asked you to think about. That is, the potential disadvantages of making a change and improvement.

The therapist begins with a follow-up on the homework. For MRI therapy, the assignment is almost always the initial distinction for calibrating information in a session.

PATIENT: O.K. I've thought about it. As a matter of fact, I made a list.

THERAPIST: Uh-huh.

PATIENT: But . . .

THERAPIST: Do you have the list with you?

PATIENT: [Sighs] I confess, no.

THERAPIST: O.K. But I hope you've got it in mind.

PATIENT: I do. Would you like me in general to give you—sort of just go down [laughs], down the list in general, going that way? I had some difficulty fantasizing about disadvantages. I couldn't—in other words—I could get started on nitty gritty details of what would happen were I a good performer.

THERAPIST: Uh-huh.

PATIENT: And I'd see if I'm heading—for example, more students to take, which I don't like.

THERAPIST: Uh-huh.

PATIENT: More bad students. And . . .

THERAPIST: Yeah, I imagine they're easier to come by than good students, aren't they?

PATIENT: Much, yes. So then—I would be in a position once in a while of having to hurt people's feelings, which I really don't like to do, to their face. Of maybe sorting out good students from bad students and telling people that they ought to go back to knitting, or something else, which most of them should do.

THERAPIST: Uh-huh.

PATIENT: [Sighs] For the most part, I looked at myself, and I would have to face my own inadequacies as a performer, and I don't—I don't know really what they are yet. I know what . . .

THERAPIST: [Interrupting] That you'd be faced with finding out, and that you wouldn't even know what you . . .

PATIENT: [Interrupting] Well, I might be surprised. I might be quite surprised . . .

THERAPIST: [Interrupting] Yeah, but could it be a matter of getting in touch with what is now unknown?

PATIENT: Yes.

THERAPIST: Uh-huh.

PATIENT: Could be. Be more likely—probably be facing squarely what is known.

THERAPIST: O.K.

PATIENT: Or what I suspect, and that is that my talent is limited, and it may be more limited than I would like to suspect. [Pause] O.K. That's somewhat what I've come to in the way of a realistic fantasy. Now I can fantasize extensively about it, but that faces, you know, problems like getting an agent. [Sighs] This kind of thing which we talked about last time.

THERAPIST: Uh-huh.

PATIENT: O.K. Well, at any rate, what it made me do [clears throat] . . . I'm playing better actually. I—I'm—I'm playing better in private than I would have before.

THERAPIST: [Made a few surprised "Oh's" during the above.] O.K., but that's in private.

Fisch, Weakland, and Segal (p. 252) analyze the therapist's response as follows: "When the patient is reporting the change in his playing, the therapist is acknowledging this, but only by inexplicit 'Oh's.' Explicitly, he raises a reservation—'O.K., but that's in private.' " From our perspective, these communications address change and stability, respectively.

PATIENT: That is private.

THERAPIST: Uh-huh.

PATIENT: But—I thought about all the stuff—the other things which we discussed somewhat. Is the—what do I really recognize as the minimal first step in conquering the difficulty, or at least making it livable? And—to an extent I've done that, in that I am playing a little better. I'm a little more relaxed when I play, and I was playing something yesterday, and I think I played it with more enthusiasm than I played since I was sixteen. Which—I didn't quite account for at first.

THERAPIST: Well, I can't account for it either.

PATIENT: And that was in private.

THERAPIST: It sounds nice, and I don't want to take away from the immediate feeling of it, but don't . . .

Here the therapist addresses stability.

PATIENT: O.K. So here's what ultimately . . .

THERAPIST: . . . attach too much to that . . .

PATIENT: O.K. So when I—when I sort of thought a little bit. But here's what's—what my fantasizing has made me do.

THERAPIST: Uh-huh.

PATIENT: It's made me look at my problem as just—as the self-existence of the other side of the problem. As about the same. Advantages and disadvantages as to its self-existence I have now. Therefore, it's not, you know, Valhalla, that I play and perform well. But then, it seems like such an easy thing to do, if it's not Valhalla, just to perform well. So, therefore, what I've actually done is to think of the disadvantages; I've thought all—I had thought of the conquering of the problem as possible. And now I've put myself into a —a realistic position on the other side.

THERAPIST: Uh-huh.

PATIENT: So now, having done that, I know the disadvantages of fantasizing all the good things that come out.

THERAPIST: O.K. Let me see if I'm picking you up clear. I—I get it that, in thinking it over in this way, you moved from a picture in which the present situation is potentially very black and conquering your problem is very white, to "Well, there's not that much an opposition, a sharp difference between the two. Each one has some good and bad to it, and therefore it's not that big enormous difference that it was before"?

PATIENT: Yes.

The meaningful noise of patient and therapist are laced with complementarity: problem existence and problem eradication are now distinct *and* related. Each side of the distinction is now seen as having advantages and disadvantages, which when fully considered, may blur their distinction.

Fisch, Weakland, and Segal (p. 254), in a follow-up report, note that several years after this interview, the violinist gradually ended treatment without formal termination. He successfully went into the real estate business and gave up his professional career in music, although he played for his own enjoyment.

As we have seen, the MRI approach to constructing therapy is based upon very simple ideas regarding the nature of therapeutic change. In the above case, this orientation would not argue that correcting a defective or inappropriate family structure was the basis of the therapeutic intervention, nor would it see any experience of insight with reference to past history as having any significance for the treatment. Instead, the approach strictly attends to the recursive organization of problem and solution interaction.

Although the ideas underlying this therapy are brief and simple, it is not necessarily an easy task to construct it. Perhaps the greatest obstacle for therapists in constructing MRI therapy arises when they become distracted by formal explanatory principles.

Most traditions of psychotherapy are rooted to an assumption that the therapist must know *why* his patient is in a particular condition before an appropriate treatment can be proposed. This notion is closely related to another assumption that the client must also understand his condition as a prerequisite for change. MRI therapy not only sidesteps these assumptions but holds them as potential obstacles for achieving effective problem solving.

To successfully construct MRI therapy during the course of treatment one must disengage from efforts to primarily understand the situation. Instead, one is restricted to using the simple theoretical idea of "problem-solution interaction" to manage attempts to alleviate presenting problems. When a therapist is able to focus on this basic idea and ignore other organizing principles, MRI therapy can be constructed.

And finally, therapists who are stymied by a case while attempting to construct MRI therapy can always apply this principle of problem solving to their own strategy. In such a situation, the therapist can remember that the prescriptions and maps for an MRI approach are only guidelines that can themselves become the subject of correction. Thus, the therapist's efforts to apply the strategy of problem-solution interaction may sometimes become the sort of solution that maintains a problem. In this situation, we often respond to the old adage, "If at first you don't succeed, try, try, again."

However, the advice of Fisch, Weakland, and Segal (p. 18) further reminds us that "if you don't succeed after the second time, then try something *different.*" The core of the MRI approach is always a return to the basic insight of cybernetics. In cybernetics errors are useful: they provide information that may make a difference in what one does next.

It follows that when a therapist attempts to avoid mistakes or errors, the results could be disastrous to clients. The very basis for cybernetic self-correction, as we've noted, arises from the creation of error or difference that, in turn, governs the change of future behavior. Oscar Peterson (cited in Lyons 1978, p. 31), widely acclaimed as a jazz pianist's pianist, was once asked how he feels when he hits an occasional wrong note. He replied that since "every note can be related to a chord," there are no wrong notes. The trick is to integrate whatever note you happen to hit into one's musical arrangement.

Peterson's point applies to systemic therapy. When every action, including those called "solutions," is seen as connected to other actions, a view of interaction can be built. In this perspective, there are no problems or solutions per se. There are only patterns of interaction that people sometimes choose to chop up into pieces called "problems," "solutions," and "therapy." Nevertheless, these punctuations are real to the people who experience them and must therefore be communicated in those terms. The MRI view provides an effective way of dealing with these punctuations by reminding us that solutions, as well as problems, may be a problem (and similarly, that problems, as well as solutions, may be a solution). These double views, when specified as patterns of interaction, lead us once again toward constructing MRI therapy.

CHAPTER 4

Triadic Social Relations

> The therapist may fail to achieve his ends if he engages in pointless debate with the family about the cause of the problem, attempts to educate them about family communication, or tries to persuade them to accept "family therapy." The goal is not to teach the family about their malfunctioning system but to change the family sequences so that the presenting problems are resolved.
>
> —JAY HALEY
> *Problem-Solving Therapy* (1976)

JAY HALEY describes his book *Problem-Solving Therapy* (1976, p. x) as "offering an approach to therapy that defines the unit (of treatment) as at least a triad." Various theoreticians and clinicians, particularly Haley and Salvador Minuchin, have contributed to understanding and organizing systemic therapy in terms of triadic social relations, and although Haley and Minuchin prefer to differentiate their work in terms of "strategic" and "structural," respectively, they are, for all practical purposes, more similar than different.

The differences stem largely from the fact that Minuchin prefers sociological descriptions to articulate his work, whereas Haley's descriptions are more rooted to the tradition of communication and cybernetic ideas. In addition, Haley describes his work as different from Minuchin in that it "has an absolute focus on the symptom." He adds that Minuchin "tends to work that way when there is a life-threatening symptom like anorexia. With that, he absolutely focuses on the symptom, makes the parents make the kid eat and so on. In that there is no difference between his approach and mine" (cited in Simon 1982, p. 58).

Historically, it is important to realize that the view of triadic social relations as an organizing principle for constructing systemic family therapy was jointly developed by Braulio Montalvo, Haley, and Minuchin at the Philadelphia Child Guidance Clinic. * We have chosen to focus on Haley's theoretical work because of his efforts to articulate this approach in terms of a communicational view. We will also provide a comparison of Haley and Minuchin's strategies. In addition, two case studies will be presented. The first case, supervised by Jay Haley, demonstrates the use of therapeutic paradox; the second case, conducted by H. Charles Fishman, demonstrates a "structural approach" to family therapy.

Jay Haley's Strategy

Haley's therapy, like that of MRI, begins by establishing a clear focus on the problem to be treated. Rather than seeing that problem as half of a recursive complementarity that includes all attempted solutions, Haley prefers to see the problem as connected to a sequence of actions involving the interaction of at least three people. Since these relations usually involve family members, his therapy is often seen as "family therapy." Thus, for Haley, problems are used as "levers" to change family relationships.

It could be argued that MRI follows a more efficient approach and that it is not necessary to multiply explanatory principles beyond the idea of problem and solution interaction. If that interaction does, in fact, take place within a context of triadic social relations, then the relationship system could still be seen as more

*Other therapists, most notably Murray Bowen, have also used the notion of triadic social relations to build a view of family process. Bowen, however, has principally used the notion of "triangles" as a semantic frame of reference for giving meaning to family action and individual experience. This differs from Haley's and Minuchin's focus on using triadic social relations as a political frame for organizing the action of therapy. When we speak of triadic social relations as a strategy for organizing systemic therapy, we are limiting our analysis to this latter political view.

easily changed by restricting one's focus to problem-solution interaction.

Haley, on the other hand, could argue that the idea of triadic relations is more efficient. From this view, changing a social organization will necessarily disrupt the recursive relation between problem and solution interaction. Continuing the argument, the advantage of his approach is that a social organization can be reorganized in a specific fashion, enabling a more adaptive situation to be constructed. Watzlawick and his colleagues could counterargue, however, that if a more adaptive situation *needed* to be constructed, a new problem would appear. Problems thus become the steersmen guiding what is to be worked on. We prefer to see each of these orientations as working on both problem-solution interaction and triadic social relations. They differ only with regard to which distinction is used to primarily organize therapy.

One of the basic distinctions that Haley prescribes is identifying the problem. In the first therapy session, he suggests that the problem be articulated in a progression of different ways: first allowing it to be expressed metaphorically, then obtaining a specific behavioral description of the problem, and finally, getting a brief summary of what specific changes the therapy will work toward achieving. These distinctions serve to organize each session of therapy and help client and therapist evaluate their progress.

In addition, Haley prescribes that a therapist should construct a view that discerns triadic social relations. This, of course, is the most fundamental distinction in Haley therapy. To detect triadic social relations, a family or social group must be allowed to interact in front of the therapist. As Haley (1976, p. 38) puts it, "rather than only have a *conversation* about a problem, he [the therapist] should try at this stage to bring the problem *action* into the room." With such an enactment, the therapist can distinguish the sequential organization of their social behavior.

enactment

Consider the following brief sequence taken from a first interview (Haley 1980, pp. 127–28):

THERAPIST: O.K. Let—let me find out—let me find out what—what the fight is all about here. What's been happening in the last, uh—

FATHER: It's been a constant—constant turmoil between her and him. *(son and mother)*
SON: Me?
FATHER: Between her and him.
MOTHER: Not really.
FATHER: She can't cope, and he can't cope.
SON: Do you realize that I'm a drug addict?

Haley (p. 128) notes that this brief sequence is an illustration of the typical pattern of triadic social relations in the family. As Haley describes this pattern, the father's criticism of the mother's inability to cope suggests a disagreement between them. When this occurs, the son distracts them by presenting himself as the problem. Haley notes that this sequence also occurs in the form of the son initiating an argument with his father whenever parental conflict begins to surface. In this way parental issues are calibrated by the son's behavior.

Semantic and Political Frames

At this point we can begin noting how Haley uses his basic distinctions to construct a labyrinth of semantic and political frames of reference for therapy. He starts by addressing a semantic frame: the specification of a problem which is eventually shaped into a precise behavioral meaning. That semantic frame is then framed by a political frame of reference that attends to the social sequence that surrounds the problem: who-does-what-to-whom-when. For instance, a family may define the problem as a child's temper tantrums. After achieving a behavioral definition of what this means, the therapist could proceed to find the sequence of events that organize the problem. Following Haley's (1976, pp. 106–7) example, one might sketch the following sequence:

Step 1. *Father—incompetent:* the father behaves in an upset or depressed way
Step 2. *Child—misbehaving:* the child begins to express symptoms
Step 3. *Mother—incompetent:* the mother ineffectually deals with the child, and the father becomes involved

Step 4. *Father—competent:* the father effectively deals with the child and recovers from his state of incompetency
Step 5. *Child—behaving:* the child behaves properly and is defined as normal
Step 6. *Mother—competent:* the mother capably deals with child and father, expecting more from them
Step 1. *Father—incompetent:* the father behaves in an upset or depressed way: the cycle begins again

The most important point about this sequence is that it captures the repeating cycle of social behavior that includes the problem. As Haley (1976, p. 106) describes this particular case, in this recursive organization of triadic relations, the system involves "all participants behaving in a way to keep the sequence going. The father's state of mind was a product of his relationship with mother and child, who were also as they were because of sequences established with him and with each other." The aim of therapy is to interrupt these patterns of organization.

If a therapist were constructing an MRI view, the presenting problem would be examined with respect to what solutions had been tried. If therapy focused on the child's symptomatic behavior (step 2), then a careful examination of the mother's efforts to deal with the child (step 3) would occur. In addition, other problem-solving efforts would be explored that might reveal the father's efforts to deal with the child (steps 3 and 4). These distinctions would expose the recursive organization of the problem and efforts to solve it.

Haley broadens the therapist's view by noting that the problem-solving interactional pattern is itself part of a more encompassing social pattern. In our previous example, Haley would focus on the pattern that connects steps 1 through 6, while MRI would attend to steps 2 through 4. Again, MRI could argue that their view is more efficient and that change of the recursive organization of steps 2 through 4 will alter the more encompassing pattern of steps 1 through 6.

Haley (1976, p. 107) proposes, however, that the larger sequence must be addressed and changed in such a way that at least two behaviors are changed; and in cases involving problematic children, it is valuable to have the view that "as change occurs with the child, there will often, but not always, be conflict between the parents as one of the stages of therapy."

It is important to recognize that the sequential patterns of organization Haley is interested in are not just a serial listing of events that occur before and after a symptomatic occurrence. He is interested in those social sequences that are recursively organized in feedback fashion. The task of a family therapist, from this view, is to identify problematic recursive cycles and direct interventions at them. A therapist may work with a family's recursive cycle within the therapy room, or the focus may include cycles embracing larger systems outside the family, such as schools and hospitals.

To *explain* his position, Haley introduces what he considers one of the central ideas of his theory—the notion of hierarchy. For him the ideas of social organization and hierarchy are indistinguishable. With regard to families, people are differentiated in terms of generations, income, skills, creative talents, physical agility, intelligence, and so forth. Haley believes that hierarchy in three-generation families of grandparents, parents and children is easiest to distinguish.

To understand how this hierarchy is organized, Haley proposes that one examine the sequential organization of behavioral events in a family. With respect to our previous example of a sequence involving a father, mother, and child, Haley (1976, p. 107) analyzes it as a "malfunctioning hierarchy" where the "mother and father are not relating as peers with each other in an executive capacity."

Haley's (1976, p. 104) key point for diagnosing troubled systems is that "an organization is in trouble when coalitions occur across levels of a hierarchy, particularly when the coalitions are secret." By "coalition," he means "a process of joint action *against* a third person" (1976, p. 109). He cites the classic example of a dominating grandmother who corrects a child with a behavioral problem when the so-called irresponsible mother fails to be an effective parent. In this case, the grandmother can be seen as joining with the child to save her from the mother. Haley notes that cross-generational coalitions are not in themselves problematic but lead to trouble when they are repeated over and over again. In accounting for the occurrence of problematic coalition patterns and symptomatic experience, Haley notes that they are associated with transitional crises in the family's developmental life. These transitions or developmental states are described by Haley (1973) as: (1) the courtship period; (2) early marriage; (3) childbirth and dealing with the young; (4) middle marriage; (5) weaning parents from children; and (6) retirement and old age.

We can see now that Haley constructs additional frames of reference with his view of social hierarchy. We can trace this as follows:

S_1 = problem definition

S_2 = social hierarchy

P_1 = sequential organization of problem

P_2 = coalitions across levels of a social hierarchy

In terms of nested frames, this would appear as:

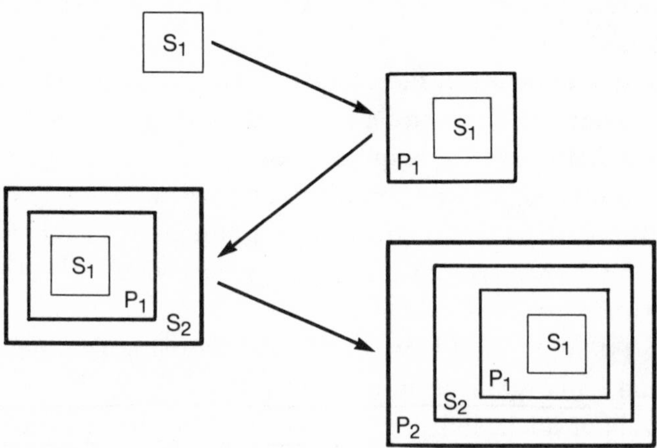

Following a definition of the problem (S_1), distinctions are drawn that discern its sequential organization (P_1). These frames are then viewed within the perspective of a social hierarchy. In other words, Haley proposes an explanatory theory or semantic frame for the organization of the sequence—his view of hierarchy. Distinctions are consequently prescribed that identify the troubled social system's hierarchy, usually in terms of different generations (S_2). This frame is then examined with respect to the political structure of coalitions (P_2). In particular, coalitions that occur across levels of the social hierarchy are underscored. And finally, all of these frames of reference are viewed within the semantic frame of family developmental stages.

Recursive Complementarities

We can now see that Haley constructs several recursive complementarities. The first involves the relation, "sequence/problem" where a problem is seen as part of a broader sequence of action in a social context. For instance, this complementarity may be seen in the form of the following description (see Haley 1976, pp. 110–11):

sequence involving action of grandmother, mother, and child	/	child's misbehavior

At this level of description, "the repeating sequence of behavior is the focus of therapy" (Haley 1976, p. 2). Here, a symptom or problem is a label, metaphor, signification, or crystallization of a particular social sequence.

Haley goes on to construct a higher-order recursive complementarity involving the relation of a sequence to coalition patterns. This complementarity actually encompasses the previous one:

coalition patterns / (sequence/problem)

For the sake of brevity we refer to the above nesting of complementary frames as simply the form "coalition patterns/sequence." For instance, this complementarity may involve the following description:

grandmother siding with child against mother	/	sequence involving action of grandmother, mother, and child

At this higher-order level of description the goal of therapy becomes reframed. As Haley (1976, p. 108) states it, the "simplest goal is to change a sequence by preventing coalitions across generation lines." Coalitions necessarily involve three people where two people jointly relate against a third. Again, this means that the sequences of action Haley is interested in are those that necessarily involve the action of at least three people. It is at this level of description that his major distinction for organizing therapy is most obviously disclosed—the recursive organization of triadic relations.

With these recursive complementarities, it makes sense that problems are used to change the sequences that surround them, which in turn alter the coalition patterns of those who participate in the sequences. With respect to the cybernetic organization of therapy, Haley uses the contracted problem and goals to evaluate and steer the therapist's (and client's) course of action. Each session evaluates the progress of therapy in terms of whether the goals set by the therapeutic contract have been fully met. Unlike the approach of Watzlawick and his colleagues, Haley goes on to assess the sequential organization of the problem and the coalition patterns of the social system. With this view, therapy may be structured in stages with different problems worked on at different times.

Cybernetic Patterns of Interaction

Haley's strategy for therapy can be seen as using different forms of intervention, or what he calls "directives." Since he is interested in knowing the present-state organization of a family, he must provoke them to act in order to see them operate. These provocations, interventions, or directives are inseparable from diagnosis and provide what Minuchin (1974, p. 131) calls "interactional diagnosis." As Haley (1971, p. 282) describes it, the family therapist is "interested in diagnosing how the family responds to his therapeutic interventions." This diagnosis has nothing to do with reifying the name of a disease, symptom, or problem as in traditional clinical diagnosis but enables the therapist to learn how a social system blocks efforts to bring about change. In more traditional clinical language, Haley wants to see how a system "resists" change in order to know how to successfully address and utilize its "resistance."

Beyond interventions to assess how the family organizes itself, Haley speaks of another class of interventions, or directives, which are consciously planned to solve the presenting problem. The purpose of these directives is to change the sequence in order to realign coalition patterns. If this is done, the problem will disappear.

These different forms of intervention can also be distinguished between those that are part of a self-corrective feedback loop that occurs within a session and those that belong to a feedback loop spanning different sessions. The term "interactional diagnosis" can be used to refer to the former while we could reserve Haley's term "directive" to be used for the latter. Although each actually attends to both intervention and diagnosis, the former is more concerned with knowing how the family stabilizes, whereas the latter is principally aimed at initiating therapeutic change.

Haley acknowledges that some directives are "paradoxical" and involve "two levels on which two messages are communicated, 'change,' and, within the framework of the message, 'don't change' " (1976, p. 68). We regard the communications of troubled systems, as well as therapeutic systems, as embodying these two different messages. Furthermore, the recursive complementarity of "stability/change" is itself a way of defining the organization of a cybernetic system. Thus, we view all of Haley's directives, including those he sees as paradoxical and nonparadoxical, as responsive to requests for both change and stability.

Haley's recommendations for designing directives follow the advice of Milton Erickson. In short, directives should be designed to utilize the way a family talks about its situation, as well as any other resource they may present. Directives thus follow our basic cybernetic pattern:

(stability/change) / meaningful noise

where here the meaningful noise refers to the way the directive is packaged in terms of metaphor, language, ideas, and tasks that arise from the family's own paradigm of communication.

Designing directives in this approach, whether they be in the form of analogies or tasks, involves addressing not only the presenting problem but the sequence that encompasses the problem, as well as the coalition patterns that enact it. As Haley (1976, p. 77) puts it, "the best task is one that uses the presenting problem to make a structural change in the family." In this recipe for therapy, clients and therapist construct different but related goals: clients want the problem to change while the therapist wants the organization to change.

Haley (1976, p. 77) provides several examples of directives that aim at achieving organizational changes in a family. In one case involving a problem child who set fires, the therapist attempted to get the mother and problem child more involved while at the same time excluding a parental child. He did this by asking the mother to set aside a time each day for teaching the problem child how to set a safe fire with matches. In another case, the problem child was afraid of dogs. The therapist calibrated the mother's overinvolvement with the child by having the father and child go out and select a puppy who was afraid of people.

In these directives, the family's communication regarding their problem is utilized in a way to create an organizational change. In terms of multiple communications, stability refers to prescribing the family's descriptions of their problem,* while change refers to how the therapist addresses modifying their family structure. The logic and rationale the therapist gives to the family for the directive provides meaningful noise. In the above example involving a firesetter, having the problem child set fires prescribes *stability* of his reality while having him do it under the guidance of his mother prescribed an organizational *change.* The *meaningful noise* in this instance involves their being assigned this task in order to teach the problem child how to set a "safe" fire.

Before proceeding, we should note that we have not introduced the metaphor of "power" in describing Haley's strategy for a therapeutic reality. We find that Haley uses that term to explain *why* families and social groups organize themselves in hierarchies and coalitions. As we have implied, it may be unnecessary to introduce the idea of power to understand or construct Haley's

*In particular, stability is addressed by using the definition of the presenting problem (S_1) as a way of maintaining a clear therapeutic contract.

basic approach to therapy. To understand how Haley comprehends his approach, however, requires reinstating the notion of power.

When Haley introduces "power," he is actually constructing an additional semantic frame to give meaning to his previously drawn distinctions. The consequences of believing in this semantic frame may, of course, lead to particular ways of organizing how one chooses to distinguish and act upon problems, sequences, social hierarchies, and coalition patterns.

Again, one can know these basic distinctions without reference to the semantic frame of power. Hierarchies and coalition patterns can be simply seen as patterns of difference and relationship without any further attribution of meaning. The historical argument between Bateson and Haley (see Rabkin 1978; Keeney 1983) thus comes down to an argument over which semantic frame (pattern or power) is to be used to explain the distinctions of hierarchy and coalitions in social contexts. We will avoid any further discussion of the different consequences that arise when power or pattern is used to frame these distinctions. That topic and issue will continue to challenge social philosophers and researchers for years to come.

The Use of Therapeutic Paradox: A Case Study Supervised by Jay Haley

The following case study is an example of the use of therapeutic paradox within systemic family therapy. Although the focus here is limited to the therapist's treatment of an individual's symptom, it's important to realize that what is presented was part of a broader treatment of the family. It may be helpful to view Haley's use of therapeutic paradox as a particular tool enabling fine focus work on symptoms to be done within his more general frame of triadic social relations and family therapy. Stated differently, the use of therapeutic paradox to change symptomatic behavior is sometimes one of his stages for working with social systems.

Jay Haley's strategy for constructing therapy may also be seen as arising from two different, but related perspectives. First, he is rooted to a "structural view" where all problematic action is seen as embodied by triadic social relations. It is this view that he originally developed with his colleagues Montalvo and Minuchin. In addition, Haley is a master at using symptomatic behavior as a means of eradicating it. This approach, which he once called a part of "uncommon therapy," largely stems from his association with Milton Erickson. To fully understand Haley's approach thus requires acknowledging his connection to a structural view as well as the techniques of symptom utilization. Haley's own case studies (see Haley 1976; 1980) usually emphasize how he constructs therapy in terms of triadic social relations. We have chosen to present a case study that emphasizes his use of symptoms and therapeutic paradox. Again, it should not be forgotten that Haley's use of therapeutic paradox is always done within the more encompassing perspective of a structural view. His pragmatic strategies for alleviating problem behavior are always seen in the context of a view of social structure.

The case that follows was conducted by John Lester, who at the time was a student of the Philadelphia Child Guidance Clinic, and was closely supervised by Jay Haley from behind a one-way mirror. The family that came for treatment included a mother, a twenty-year-old daughter and her two small children, and a ten-year-old boy. In addition, two older daughters lived outside the home. The mother had been separated from her husband for several years, and the family received public assistance.

The family came to therapy because of the ten-year-old boy's masturbation problem, which started when he was five years old. He masturbated at school and in the living room in front of other family members. His masturbation was so severe, according to his mother, that he wore holes in the crotch of his pants and at one time was hospitalized for blood in his urine. The mother also reported that he sucked his thumb and often stole from her. After a year and a half of child therapy, there had been no improvement in these symptoms.

SESSION 1

The mother, problem son, and grandchild are present with the therapist.

MOTHER: This is my son, George, and that's Richard.

THERAPIST: Hello. *(as Richard, the two-year-old grandson shakes hands with his left hand)* Good, that hand.

MOTHER: My daughter was supposed to be here today, but she got a little piece of a job. She only worked one day and they want her to work this evening.

After the family is comfortable, the therapist begins inquiring about the problem.

THERAPIST: I know it's kind of difficult for you to explain this over again, but it's very necessary. Feel free and take your time in doing it. I'd like to ask you what are some of the things that have been tried to help him.

MOTHER: Well, really the only things, the only thing we tried is the tutoring and the medicine. He's been taking Dexedrine, I think it's Dexedrine. . . .

The mother reports that problem-solving efforts by his previous therapy included an attempt to understand why he masturbated so frequently and a reward and punishment strategy. He was deprived of things when he masturbated and was rewarded with a dollar for every week he did not masturbate. Since the family was poor, the mother claimed that she began borrowing money from him. The boy also received tutoring and was given Dexedrine.

THERAPIST: Is it a thing that you discuss freely in the house? I mean is everyone in your house aware of it, or is it something that is hush-hush?

MOTHER: Oh, no, it's been something that uh—Barbara used to try to get after him and then his other sister before she went away to school she used to get after him and tell him to stop, you know, and then we started to try not to nag him about it, you know, but really it seems there was nothing concrete. The medicine seems to help him relax a little, the medicine seems to help. But, uh, trying to find the answer why he does it, you know?

Note that the only other people who have been politically part of the repeating social sequences of the boy's problem are his mother and sisters.

(Later in the interview)

THERAPIST: We won't discuss it among each other. It will be a private thing between George and myself, because he is a boy, you know. He needs—it needs to be private. I think we can discuss it better. I would appreciate it if, you know, we wouldn't discuss it any more. It will be discussed between him and myself. Alright?

MOTHER: Okay.

THERAPIST: Okay, George?

GEORGE: Uh-huh.

The therapist introduces the semantic frame that the boy's masturbation problem is a private matter for men. This consequently alters the politics of the situation: the therapist blocks other family members from communicating about the problem in therapy and thereby constructs a differentiated relationship with the boy.

The next step in this therapy investigates the boy's relationship with his mother by asking him to criticize her.

THERAPIST: You have such a good mother. You know that, don't you?

GEORGE: Uh-huh.

THERAPIST: I bet it's kind of hard for you to say anything bad about her. In fact, if somebody would say something bad about her, you'd probably be ready to fight, wouldn't you?

GEORGE: Yeah.

THERAPIST: That's good that you protect her. I just want to see something. Let me see if you can think of one small thing that's bad you can say for the sake of your mother. Just a small thing.

GEORGE: Nothing.
THERAPIST: Just think on it. Just think about it for a minute.
GEORGE: I can't think of nothing.
THERAPIST: You can't think of anything?

The boy's inability to criticize his mother may be perceived by structuralists as his being overinvolved with her. With this view, it is likely that the therapist's strategy will continue to help differentiate them. The therapist's next move is to challenge the mother by pointing out that she may possibly become upset if the boy's problems are alleviated. This semantic frame of reference puts the mother in an awkward political situation. Haley suggests that the only way she can disprove this prediction is to help her son become normal and then show that she does not get upset. This strategy politically puts the therapist in charge of helping the boy in the office, while the mother takes over in helping him at home. In this way, therapist and mother are joined in their separate efforts to help the boy.

THERAPIST: I might be able to help George with his thumb sucking and masturbating. Help him get over it. But by you being so used to having this problem with him, you know, and by some way or whatever, if it does cease, he will be a lot more difficult to be with, to live with. Due to the predicament that he is in, and after you have been subjected to this for a long time, you know, you are used to it, right? And it just stops.
MOTHER: He's going to have to have an outlet.
THERAPIST: But see, I want to know if *you* can stand it. I mean, you are going to be left there. You're going to be left there by yourself without the little things that you're doing now to prevent, you know—or whatever you do when he starts sucking his finger and masturbating, you know. You know it won't happen no more, you won't be able to do those things anymore. What will you do with yourself?

The therapist addresses stability through pointing out the possible negative consequences of problem resolution.

MOTHER: What will I do with myself? Well, I can find plenty of things to do with myself.

(Later in the interview)

THERAPIST: When he was hospitalized and the blood came into his urine, and when he would masturbate, you would have to be there. You're upset about it, and if it stops, what would you do?

MOTHER: Well, that's kind of hard. What would I do? You say he's going to turn bad, right?

THERAPIST: Not to the extent where he would be—you know, just a normal boy. He'll be hard to live with, a little difficult to live with.

MOTHER: I could, I could put up with it.

THERAPIST: You what?

MOTHER: I think I could put up with it. I could put up with it. He's got to grow up someday.

THERAPIST: But still and all *(pointing to boy on her lap),* you still have your grandson to take his place.

MOTHER: Yeah. I'll still have him.

The therapist has gently addressed the positive social contribution the boy's problem provides to the family. Namely, it allows mother to be closely involved with someone and in so doing, contributes to achieving family stability.

(Later, when therapist and boy are alone)

THERAPIST: Do you know of any place in your house where you can go and masturbate all by yourself?

GEORGE: Yeah.

This information may lead to clues as to how the political organization of the boy's masturbation habit may be altered.

THERAPIST: You know some place where nobody will see you?

GEORGE: Uh-huh.

THERAPIST: Do you ever go there now and masturbate now when you don't want to be bothered?

GEORGE: Sometimes.

THERAPIST: Tell me, how good can you write? Can you count?

GEORGE: Yeah.

THERAPIST: Can you count real good?

GEORGE: Yeah, I can count.

THERAPIST: All right, I'm going to see. *(getting a paper and pencil)* I want you to do something for me. Okay, now first of all, let me make something known to you. Now this is strictly between me and you. Right?

GEORGE: Uh-huh.

THERAPIST: Now, you have to promise me. Can I trust you?

GEORGE: Yeah.

THERAPIST: Okay. Don't let me down. All right?

GEORGE: All right.

THERAPIST: I believe in you. You got an honest face. You do—you got an honest face. Let me see now, how many days in a week?

GEORGE: Seven.

(Later they have finished filling out the list of days)

THERAPIST: Next Friday will be the seventeenth, right?

GEORGE: Uh-huh.

THERAPIST: It will be the last day that you have to mark down each day, right?

GEORGE: Uh-huh.

THERAPIST: Now you know what you have to do, right?

GEORGE: Yeah.

THERAPIST: Now you explain to me what I want you to do.

GEORGE: Every time I masturbate, I put a mark in this block.

THERAPIST: For each day, right? Every time you masturbate on . . .

GEORGE: Friday, Saturday, Sunday, Monday, Tuesday, Wednesday, Thursday, Friday.

THERAPIST: And what else? You remember to do what?

GEORGE: Don't let anybody know.

THERAPIST: Right. Don't let nobody see you, hear? Don't tell nobody about our agreement, right?

GEORGE: Right.

THERAPIST: I'll give you this. *(gives him the list)* You keep this in your pocket, okay?

GEORGE: Uh-huh.

THERAPIST: Here, I'll give you a pencil.

The therapist's intervention focuses on establishing a private relationship with the boy as a means of differentiating him from his mother. In addition, we note that his symptom is prescribed *(stability),* while the context in which it occurs is slightly altered *(change)* by having him keep track of how many times he masturbates. The rationale *(meaningful noise)* for this task involves an implicit demonstration of "trust" between the boy and his therapist.

SESSION 2

At the second interview, the therapist begins by seeing the mother and son together and then seeing the son alone. He initially asks the mother again whether she can tolerate her son's becoming normal *(consequences of change).*

THERAPIST: I just don't think that you do understand exactly. And the only way that I could ever find out if you did, is when George is cured of doing what he's doing —when he stops doing what he's doing, then you show me that you can handle it and live with it. That's the only way.

(Later the therapist sees the boy alone)

THERAPIST: Hey, remember what we talked about? Did you do it?

GEORGE: I brought the paper.

THERAPIST: You did? Let me see. I knew I could count on you, I really did.

(They look at the paper together and the therapist hands the boy his pen)

THERAPIST: Hold that for me. Do you have an ink pen?

GEORGE: No.

THERAPIST: You can have that one.

GEORGE: Thank you.
THERAPIST: You're welcome.

In each session the boy has been rewarded with a pencil or pen. This action, whether done intentionally or not, has the effect of joining this therapy with the boy's previous experience of therapy which involved a reward strategy.

GEORGE: This is how many times I masturbated.
THERAPIST: Let's see—on Friday you didn't do it at all.
GEORGE: Right.
THERAPIST: On Saturday you did it one time.
GEORGE: Uh-huh.
THERAPIST: On Sunday you did it four times.
GEORGE: Right.
THERAPIST: And then you hadn't done it Monday, you didn't do it Wednesday, you didn't do it Thursday, or Friday. Right?
GEORGE: Right.
THERAPIST: All right, well tell me, uh—you did it more Sunday than you did Saturday. Why was that? Kind of bored in the house on Sunday?

The information derived from this assignment provides clues to the therapist as to the organization of the boy's masturbation. Finding that he does it more on Sunday, the therapist searches for a semantic frame *(meaningful noise)* that the boy may use to put his behavior in context.

GEORGE: Uh-huh. Nothing to do.
THERAPIST: Do you think you can remember out of these five times which time it felt best? On Sunday or Saturday?
GEORGE: On Sunday.
THERAPIST: Felt better on Sunday, huh? The reason why I'm asking, George—you know I always like to explain things, right? I want you to know the reason for everything—you know the reason I'm asking is that, uh—it is important that you do enjoy it *all* the time, you know.

The therapist offers the meaningful noise that he is helping the boy learn how to *enjoy* masturbation.

GEORGE: Uh-huh.
THERAPIST: See this one time right here that you did it on Saturday and you didn't enjoy it. You know you're just wasting your time. You could have been what—doing something else. You know. I don't think it's fair to you. Do you understand?

The therapist implies that there may be positive consequences associated with changing his pattern of masturbating.

GEORGE: Yes.
THERAPIST: If I see you do this on Saturday and you don't enjoy it, I'm going to tell you, right? I'm gonna say, "Look, George, you're wasting your time doing it on Saturday. Do it on Sunday." I'll tell you what. Now that we decided, you know, the both of us, that Sunday is the best day, right?
GEORGE: Uh-huh.
THERAPIST: It would be better to like—now next time, see, go on from here and exclude all these weekdays and just do it on Sunday, right?
GEORGE: Uh-huh.
THERAPIST: Okay. I think that would be better, don't you?
GEORGE: Yeah.
THERAPIST: Because it felt better on Sunday, right?
GEORGE: Uh-huh.
THERAPIST: Yeah, I think that would be the best time.
GEORGE: Yeah.
THERAPIST: But I'll tell you something else, too, now that you're gonna enjoy it more, right?
GEORGE: Uh-huh.
THERAPIST: You should do it a little more. Okay? You should do it a little more 'cause you're gonna enjoy it. It wouldn't make sense to do it the rest of the days and you ain't enjoying it at all, right?
GEORGE: Uh-huh.

THERAPIST: You enjoy it more, so you do it more. Sitting around and you ain't got anything to do, shoot, you might as well go on and enjoy it more on Sunday, right?

GEORGE: Uh-huh.

THERAPIST: Okay. Let me see. I'll give you a couple more lines here. I don't even have to put no more down here because you're just gonna do it on Sunday, right?

GEORGE: Right.

THERAPIST: So here. I'll tell you what now to do. Draw a line right through Monday, Tuesday, Wednesday, Thursday, and Friday. Draw a line right through them because we don't need them no more. I want you to tell me what day you're supposed to do it.

Haley's strategy for constructing a therapy often includes asking clients to repeat part or all of their assignment.

GEORGE: Sunday.

THERAPIST: Now, what about the rest of the days?

GEORGE: Leave it alone.

THERAPIST: All of them, right?

GEORGE: Uh-huh.

THERAPIST: Got your word on that?

GEORGE: Yes.

THERAPIST: *(shakes hand)* My man. Now, here is what you do: Now you did it four times last Sunday, right?

GEORGE: Right.

THERAPIST: Now that you gonna enjoy it, you know, you might as well go ahead and do it more. Right?

GEORGE: Uh-huh.

THERAPIST: Now for me this Sunday, here's what I want you to do. I want you to do it eight times. Eight times, now. So you might have to get up a little early to start. You know?

GEORGE: Uh-huh.

The therapist has used the semantic frame of enjoying masturbation as an avenue toward prescribing a change in the sequence organizing his problem behavior. The boy is now told to masturbate only on Sunday and to increase the number of times he does it on that day. The structure of his intervention continues to be:

(stabilize masturbation behavior / change time and frequency of occurrence) / meaningful noise: learning to enjoy masturbation

At this time in the session, the therapist shifts to asking the boy about other topics outside of the masturbation problem.

THERAPIST: What kind of games do you play after school?
GEORGE: Well, let's see. I play tag.
THERAPIST: Do you run fast?
GEORGE: Yeah.
THERAPIST: Who is the fastest runner in your neighborhood?
GEORGE: Me.
THERAPIST: Yeah? I'll bet you can beat them all running. You got long legs like I got. I got long legs too. I move around pretty fast. Do you play football?
GEORGE: Uh-huh.
THERAPIST: You do? Do you play baseball?
GEORGE: Uh-huh.
THERAPIST: What sport do you like best?
GEORGE: Basketball.
THERAPIST: Basketball. You got a girlfriend?
GEORGE: Yeah.
THERAPIST: What's her name?
GEORGE: Marian.
THERAPIST: Is she pretty?
GEORGE: Uh-huh.
THERAPIST: Do y'all ever play "catch a girl, kiss a girl"?
GEORGE: No.
THERAPIST: Y'all don't play that? We used to play that.

SESSION 3

Therapy begins with the therapist and the mother alone, followed by the therapist and the boy alone

THERAPIST: Has George been masturbating in your presence or in the living room or whatever?

MOTHER: Yes.

THERAPIST: He has? Often?

MOTHER: About the same.

THERAPIST: Uh-huh.

MOTHER: But I didn't say anything to him about it. I didn't mention it.

The mother reports a change in the social pattern organizing his masturbation behavior—she hasn't said anything about it.

THERAPIST: Uh-huh. Can you give me an idea when and where? Any particular time?

MOTHER: Since he's been home I noticed it during the day. When he was looking at the television or—he hasn't been out of the house too much. Yesterday was the first time he's really been out of the house. His sister took him out.

THERAPIST: What day was this? You mean this week that they were out of school?

MOTHER: Uh-huh. I think all weekend he stayed in.

Later the therapist sees the boy alone and they look at the schedule sheet.

THERAPIST: Now explain to me, you know, exactly what you have there.

GEORGE: That's how many times I did it.

THERAPIST: How many times is it?

GEORGE: Eight.

THERAPIST: You did it eight times?

GEORGE: Uh-huh.

THERAPIST: I can't hear you with your hand up to your mouth.

GEORGE: Eight.

THERAPIST: Eight times. What time did you get up Sunday?

GEORGE: Nine o'clock. My sister got me up.

THERAPIST: She woke you up at nine o'clock. Why did she get you up so early?

GEORGE: I don't know.

THERAPIST: Did you tell her?
GEORGE: Uh-huh.
THERAPIST: You told her to wake you up early?
GEORGE: Yeah.
THERAPIST: So you could get it all in?
GEORGE: Uh-huh.
THERAPIST: Very good. Good man, good man.

Later the conversation continues.

THERAPIST: Did you do it?
GEORGE: Uh-huh.
THERAPIST: When was that?
GEORGE: On Monday.
THERAPIST: Monday?
GEORGE: Uh-huh
THERAPIST: How many times did you do it?
GEORGE: I don't know.
THERAPIST: Was you in your room?
GEORGE: Yeah.
THERAPIST: Well, I got to know. Now look, hold it up—wait a minute—you gotta tell me now. Where were you when you did it?
GEORGE: In my room.
THERAPIST: Monday?
GEORGE: Uh-huh.
THERAPIST: And any other time?
GEORGE: No.
THERAPIST: And why did you do it Monday?
GEORGE: I don't know. I couldn't help it.
THERAPIST: Mm-mmm.
GEORGE: I can't—you know, I just end up doing it.
THERAPIST: I understand. Okay.

The fact that the boy's masturbation problem has not been alleviated is not a sign that the therapist's intervention has not been successful. Each intervention is only designed to elicit new information which, in turn, enables new interventions to be shaped. Since the boy did not follow instructions and masturbated on a day when he wasn't supposed to, the therapist must consider using this outcome as a resource. In this case, Haley chose to set up the punishment of having him masturbate more on Sunday. This prescription constructs a political frame that challenges the boy to rebel against masturbation. Within this context, masturbating on days other than Sunday results in Sunday's masturbation being punishment, whereas following the instructions results in Sunday's masturbation being a reward. The boy is caught in an interesting paradox: if he does what the therapist prescribes, he is free to masturbate on Sunday. If he disobeys the therapist, he must masturbate on Sunday. Carrying this further, should he decide to rebel and not perform his punishment on Sunday, he still ends up masturbating less. Whatever he does or doesn't do, the therapeutic reality now contextualizes his masturbation in an alternative way.

THERAPIST: You said you did it on Monday, right?

GEORGE: Uh-huh.

THERAPIST: And we had an agreement that you were just supposed to do it . . .

GEORGE: On Sunday.

THERAPIST: Well, because you did it on Monday, right?

GEORGE: Uh-huh.

THERAPIST: I want you to do it next Sunday, right?

GEORGE: Right.

THERAPIST: Four more times than you did it this Sunday past. Understand?

GEORGE: Uh-huh.

THERAPIST: Let's see now what we put here. We ain't got no more room over here. Then after I fill this out, I want to explain to you exactly how—because I don't think you're doing it right. I want you to try—try my way. You know, it's just about like yours, but it's a little better, okay?

GEORGE: Okay.

Later in the interview:

THERAPIST: We have to get the right amount here.

GEORGE: One, two, three, four, five, six, seven, eight, nine, ten, eleven, twelve.

THERAPIST: Right. Now, how many times did you have to do it last Sunday?

GEORGE: Eight.

THERAPIST: Okay. Now, how many times you got to do it this Sunday?

GEORGE: Twelve.

THERAPIST: Now, why do you have to do it twelve times this Sunday? *(pause)* You forgot. So you won't forget—because you did it on Monday. Okay?

GEORGE: All right.

THERAPIST: Now, if you forget, I'll write it down here so you can see. Now, why do you have to do it twelve times on Sunday?

GEORGE: Because I did it on Monday.

THERAPIST: Right. Okay, now, how many times do you have to do it Sunday?

GEORGE: Twelve.

THERAPIST: Where at?

GEORGE: In my room.

THERAPIST: Okay. Now, let's get away from that for a minute and let me explain to you—tell you what I was talking about. Now, you said when you masturbate, you know, you take your zipper down and put your hand in your zipper.

GEORGE: Uh-huh.

THERAPIST: And you do it that way. Right?

GEORGE: Right.

THERAPIST: Or sometimes you don't. If you don't do that, you just do it without taking your zipper down. Right?

GEORGE: Right.

THERAPIST: Okay. Now, this Sunday when you do it, I want you to do it differently, okay?

The therapist is adding another change in the pattern that organizes masturbation by turning it into an ordeal.

GEORGE: Okay.

THERAPIST: Now, here's how I want you to do it. Stand up and

I'll show you. I want you to unbuckle your pants. Right?

GEORGE: Uh-huh.

THERAPIST: Take your pants all the way off, right?

GEORGE: Yeah.

THERAPIST: But you must fold them up neat. You know how to fold your pants up neat? You know, put the creases together?

GEORGE: Yeah.

THERAPIST: And lay them on your bed. Okay?

GEORGE: Uh-huh.

THERAPIST: Take off your underwear. Right?

GEORGE: Yeah.

THERAPIST: Put them up, fold them up neat and lay them right on top of your pants. Right?

GEORGE: Yeah.

THERAPIST: Now, you gotta do all that now. You just can't take them and throw them in the corner. You understand?

GEORGE: Uh-huh.

THERAPIST: Now, go ahead and tell me what I told you.

Later in the interview:

THERAPIST: Now, go through it again from the beginning. Go ahead.

GEORGE: *(with a big sigh)* Take off my pants, fold them up, put them on the side of my bed . . .

THERAPIST: Which side? This is the bed, which side?

Later in the interview:

THERAPIST: Because you're not masturbating around your mother and sister and all, you're not around your mother too much either, so I think it would be nice if you could do something nice for your mother. Do you think of anything nice that you would like to do?

This task prescribes that the boy find an alternative way of carrying out the contribution his public masturbation has previously provided to family stability.

SESSION 4

In session 4, the therapist explores the political frames that organize the mother's life. Structurally speaking, this can be seen as a way of underscoring her own autonomy. In particular, this is done by talking to her about the men in her life, her education, and the possibility of getting a job.

MOTHER: When I was working, and I liked my work very much, I was doing interviewing.

THERAPIST: Oh, yeah?

MOTHER: Uh-huh. And then you came home. Work and come home, and even though your food is cooked you got to come and heat it up, you know, take it out of the refrigerator. You come home and it's still in the refrigerator, you know.

THERAPIST: Right.

MOTHER: This isn't done and that ain't done. As old as the girls was, you know. And you would just get yourself into, you know . . .

THERAPIST: I personally should think that you would try to go ahead and get back into the thing you want to do, the working thing. I would like to—well, I know why you can't get into it: because you have the responsibility of your daughter's children. I think it would be important for you to try to do something about that also.

The last part of the session brings together the therapist and the boy. It is discovered that the boy is beginning to rebel. He didn't bring his record of masturbation to the session. The therapist now begins tying the second symptom, thumb sucking, to his masturbation behavior.

SESSION 5

This time, the sister brought the boy to therapy, and the mother did not come. The therapist began by talking with his sister alone and then worked with the boy alone. The boy did not do his assignment.

THERAPIST: You ain't gonna have to get up as early as you been doing, okay?

GEORGE: Uh-huh.

THERAPIST: I want you to do it eight times, alright?

GEORGE: Alright.

THERAPIST: This Sunday, eight times.

GEORGE: Right.

THERAPIST: Alright. Now, because you don't suck your thumb when you are playing hockey, right?

GEORGE: Uh-huh.

THERAPIST: And when you're reading comic books you don't suck your thumb. I don't think it's necessary, do you? Not for a big guy like you, you know.

GEORGE: Uh-huh.

THERAPIST: Imagine you get a girlfriend and you be sitting there and you try to kiss her—she may try to kiss you and you got your thumb in your mouth. That would blow it, wouldn't it? Sure would.

GEORGE: Uh-huh.

THERAPIST: Look, I want you—I would like, when you suck your thumb during the week, that is one more time you have to masturbate.

Later in the interview:

THERAPIST: What you do? Do it again. What you do?

GEORGE: Stand up, take my pants off, fold them up and put them on the other side of the bed. Take my underwear off, fold them up, and put them on the bed, and masturbate like this.

THERAPIST: Right. And brace your feet like this. There you go.

GEORGE: Take my underwear and put them on.

THERAPIST: Uh-huh.

GEORGE: Get my pants and put them on.

THERAPIST: Uh-huh.

GEORGE: Fasten them . . . zipper them up.

THERAPIST: How many times is that?

GEORGE: Once.

THERAPIST: Once. Right.

GEORGE: Uh-huh.

THERAPIST: Now, what did you tell me before you left last week? Huh?

GEORGE: I was gonna bring the paper.

THERAPIST: And you was gonna do it, too. Didn't you?

GEORGE: Uh-huh.

THERAPIST: How do you think that makes me feel? Huh?

GEORGE: Bad.

THERAPIST: Huh? I can't hear you.

GEORGE: Bad.

THERAPIST: How do you feel? For not doing it? Huh? Well, then why didn't you do it? George, look at me, I'm talking to you. Look at me. Well, I'll tell you what—I don't know, George, I really don't. I don't even know if I should trust you anymore. Could I trust you?

The original semantic frame of reference, "trust" is reintroduced and challenged.

GEORGE: Uh-huh.

THERAPIST: You think so? Hmm?

GEORGE: Uh-huh. *(beginning to cry)*

THERAPIST: Now this time I'm gonna tell you straight out. Now, I don't want no excuses, hear? None at all, right? Because you know what I'm telling you. I could understand if you was a little kid that didn't understand, but you understand, don't you?

GEORGE: Uh-huh.

THERAPIST: All right. Now, come on over here and wipe your eyes. *(giving him a Kleenex)* Now, this time it's gonna be different because you messed up. *(throwing pen angrily in waste basket)* My ink pen doesn't even write. I'm so disgusted with you. *(takes another pen)* Now, this Monday, right?

GEORGE: Uh-huh.

THERAPIST: Oh, by the way, do you have the paper for me?

GEORGE: I was outside and forgot it. I didn't go back upstairs.

THERAPIST: You forgot to bring it?

GEORGE: I forgot to take it outside with me.

THERAPIST: Well, did you do what I asked?

GEORGE: Uh-huh. I remember how you said to do it too.

THERAPIST: How many times were you supposed to do it? Did I tell you?

GEORGE: Twelve.

THERAPIST: How many times?

GEORGE: Twelve.

THERAPIST: How many times did you do it?

GEORGE: Six.

THERAPIST: You did it six times?

GEORGE: Uh-huh.

THERAPIST: Why didn't you do it all the times I told you? You understood what I told you when you was here, right?

GEORGE: Uh-huh.

THERAPIST: Why did you let me down? And what did I tell you about your thumb sucking?

GEORGE: Every time I suck my thumb, that counts for masturbating.

THERAPIST: Right. You didn't do that either, did you?

GEORGE: Uh-huh.

THERAPIST: Why? I want you to tell me why now. I mean, it's not fair, it's really not fair. It's not. And you forgot the paper on top of that. I'm talking to you. You forgot the paper. Now, because you didn't do it the way I asked you to do it, I want you to do one day a week, you understand? No, that's wrong, I'm wrong now. You see, boy, you really got me upset. I want you to do it Monday, one time in the living room! You understand? In the living room when your mother and sister are there. You understand? Just one time, all right? Tuesday, I want you to do it one time, in the living room. Wednesday, I want you to do it one time, in the living room. Thursday, I want you to do it one time, in the living room. Friday, one time in the living room, right? Saturday, one time in the living room. You understand?

GEORGE: Uh-huh.

THERAPIST: On Sunday, I want you to do it *eight* times. Right? Now, how many times did I say to do it?

GEORGE: Eight on Sunday.

THERAPIST: Right. Now, I'm gonna write it here because you might forget again and I'm not going for that no more. Now, when you suck your thumb, you gotta do it one more time on Sunday. You understand?

GEORGE: Uh-huh.

THERAPIST: Now, I'm not confusing you, am I?

GEORGE: No.

THERAPIST: Because I don't want no excuses when you come back, hear? Now, here's another thing. I won't see you next Wednesday, hear?

GEORGE: Uh-huh.

THERAPIST: But I'll see you the following Wednesday. Right?

GEORGE: Uh-huh.

THERAPIST: And next week just do it the same way here. Just do it the same way I showed you. All right?

GEORGE: Okay.

Later in the interview:

THERAPIST: Up until this Sunday, right? I won't see you for two weeks, but I just want you to do it up until Sunday. Hear?

GEORGE: Uh-huh.

THERAPIST: You understand now? You're supposed to do it once a day here.

GEORGE: In the living room.

THERAPIST: Right. And on Sunday, how many times?

GEORGE: Eight.

THERAPIST: Now, don't forget the paper, hear? Go ahead *(they sign the paper)* and let me sign this again. I hate to be signing my name to things and you don't. See, we're still buddies. Okay? Here, wipe your eyes now. Come on now, come on. Here's your ball.

At this point, therapy has completely turned the context of the boy's masturbation upside down. The punishment is now defined as what was originally the presenting problem—masturbating in front of his family. More specifically, the boy's masturbation has been differentiated into two categories of behavior: punishment and reward—themes that join this therapy with his previous therapy. The boy, however, is now put in charge of the outcome that determines the class of behavior contextualizing his masturbation.

SESSION 6

In this session the therapist sees the mother and son together.

MOTHER: We have to get him back on the ball again. I had to go to school for him. The teacher says he won't listen.

THERAPIST: He won't listen?

MOTHER: Yeah. And he starts playing around in the room instead of doing his work like he used to. There is another boy in his room that she says he has been following behind, so he's gonna get back on the ball again in school or else get a whippin'.

Later in the interview:

MOTHER: The teacher sent for me because she said he had changed and she knew he could do better.

THERAPIST: She said he had changed?

MOTHER: Uh-huh. She knew he could do better and uh—he had started to play around quite a bit in the room.

THERAPIST: Well, I'm sure that you will remember what I discussed with you about being able to accept a change. And I also said that I didn't think that you could accept it.

The mother's report on a change in the boy's behavior that troubles her is recycled into the semantic frame earlier established by the therapist that challenged whether the mother could handle the consequences of his improvement.

MOTHER: But uh—George can do better work than he's been doing.

Later in the interview:

THERAPIST: You are looking better and you are doing, you know, a lot better. And George, I know you'll agree that your mother is feeling better. Right?

GEORGE: Uh-huh.

THERAPIST: And she just is looking more relaxed, more at ease. You know.

GEORGE: Uh-huh.

THERAPIST: She's beginning to shine, you know. Letting all her beauty come out, you know.

GEORGE: Uh-huh.

THERAPIST: You notice that?

GEORGE: Uh-huh.

Underscoring the positive social consequences associated with George's change is a way of communicating that family stability has not been threatened.

THERAPIST: Now, even though this is happening, I'd like to see if you can say something bad about her.

GEORGE: No.

THERAPIST: Now, don't answer without thinking. Think about it. *(pause)* Something you don't like. Does she let you do everything you want to do?

GEORGE: No.

THERAPIST: What doesn't she let you do that you would like to do?

GEORGE: Well, sometimes I like to stay up late. She don't let me do that.

THERAPIST: Well, that's something bad. Something bad that you don't like. You don't like that, right?

GEORGE: Right.

THERAPIST: Think of something else that you don't like that she does.

GEORGE: Well, a lot of times I don't like to eat.

THERAPIST: And what happens?

GEORGE: I have to eat.

THERAPIST: You—maybe you'll be outside playing, or you want to go outside and play and she'll make you eat.
GEORGE: Uh-huh.

Structurally speaking, these comments suggest George is moving away from being overinvolved with his mother.

Later in the interview, the therapist is alone with the boy, looking at the paper.

THERAPIST: What did you do here?
GEORGE: I had to do it eight times on Sunday. You mean up here?
THERAPIST: Uh-huh.
GEORGE: I just put them numbers there.
THERAPIST: Mhmmmm. You just wrote those in there?
GEORGE: I like to write the numbers.
THERAPIST: Well, what happened the following week? This week that just passed?
GEORGE: I don't know.
THERAPIST: What happened? *(pause)* What did you do this week that just passed?

The therapist had left it unclear as to what the boy was to do in the second week. Haley instructed the therapist to do that in order to assess whether any change was taking place. Should the masturbation issue disappear for the boy, the therapist will drop working on it.

GEORGE: Huh?
THERAPIST: Just what did you do?
GEORGE: Well, I was doing my homework. My written homework.
THERAPIST: Did you do any masturbating?
GEORGE: Yeah.
THERAPIST: When?
GEORGE: I don't remember what day it was.
THERAPIST: You don't remember?
GEORGE: No.
THERAPIST: You don't remember none of what day it was?
GEORGE: I think I was doing some Monday. I don't know.

THERAPIST: You're not sure?

GEORGE: Uh-huh.

THERAPIST: Well, since you been—you know you been pretty good. You know that? You been doing a good job. And I've been kind of hard on you, haven't I?

GEORGE: No.

THERAPIST: I haven't?

GEORGE: No.

THERAPIST: You don't think so?

GEORGE: Not to me.

THERAPIST: Good. I think I've been kind of rough on you, though. I'm gonna give you—I'm gonna give you a break. Okay?

GEORGE: Uh-huh.

THERAPIST: I'm going to—I'm not gonna tell you to do it like I said.

GEORGE: Uh-huh.

THERAPIST: You know?

GEORGE: Yeah.

THERAPIST: I guess for a while we're just gonna forget about it, okay?

GEORGE: Right.

THERAPIST: I ain't gonna give you any more papers, okay?

GEORGE: Uh-huh.

THERAPIST: We'll just—you know—just forget about it for a little while, for about a week or two, okay?

GEORGE: Uh-huh.

THERAPIST: Then you have more time to go out and play. You won't have to be writing things down, okay?

GEORGE: Uh-huh.

THERAPIST: Let's forget about it for a little while—talk about some of the things . . .

GEORGE: I'm going to camp.

THERAPIST: You are? When?

GEORGE: I don't know what day, but I'm going to Camp William Penn.

THERAPIST: You are? That's good.

GEORGE: Uh-huh.

THERAPIST: Who got you into camp?
GEORGE: At the school.
THERAPIST: Oh. When you leaving?
GEORGE: I don't know. I'm gonna stay for two weeks.
THERAPIST: Oh, that's good. That's real good.

During the next six weeks, the therapist worked with the mother and daughter. Although the boy was present in the sessions, his masturbation was not discussed. The therapeutic focus shifted to moving the daughter out of the house. When that occurred, the therapist evaluated the mother-son relationship to see that they didn't begin getting overinvolved again due to daughter's disengagement. The therapist saw the mother alone and asked about the boy's current masturbation behavior.

MOTHER: When he's not out he just can't sit down and look at television or do something without that thumb in the mouth and the other hand *(gestures toward her lap)* and it looks like lately he's been doing it a little more openly, you know?
THERAPIST: Uh-huh.
MOTHER: And I sit there and I watch him, you know—I don't say nothing. I just sit there and watch him and watch to see how—a couple of times I said something to him, you know.
THERAPIST: What did you say?
MOTHER: Huh?
THERAPIST: What did you say? How did you deal with it?
MOTHER: I just ask him if he'd try not to. I just ask him to take his hand away . . .
THERAPIST: Exactly what would you say to him?
MOTHER: I ask him to try not to, you know . . . to try not to.
THERAPIST: Try not to do what? Now, say for instance if you caught him, what would you say exactly?
MOTHER: Well, a couple of times I just told him, I said, "Take your hand away from . . ." you know. "You been doing it, I've been sitting here watching you while you was doing it."
THERAPIST: Do you say, "Take your hand out of your pants"?

MOTHER: Yeah.

THERAPIST: Do you ever say, "Take your hands off your penis" to him?

MOTHER: No.

THERAPIST: When you would say that, what would he do?

MOTHER: Well, he'll move, he'll move his hand.

THERAPIST: What would he be doing? Would his hands be still or would he be motionless or would he be moving or what?

MOTHER: Not too much movement . . . he had like his thumb, just his thumb was in the zipper, but then he knew I was watching, you know.

Haley notes that the present problem is not masturbation, but an interactional game between mother and son. The boy would place his thumb in his belt or zipper until she told him not to. Haley and the therapist decided to ignore this behavior and to continue focusing on the daughter. Two months later the therapist did a follow-up interview with the mother and boy and checked again on the masturbation problem.

When asked if the masturbation was better, the mother said, "Oh, yes. Because when we first started, sometimes I would get up during the night and check in his room. He would have his hands in his shorts." The mother added that she hadn't noticed that happening now. When asked about the thumb sucking, she reported that it was occasional.

When the therapist asked the boy about the masturbation problem, he said it was over. His mother subsequently replied, "I think George can tell you better than I can. I haven't noticed him doing it. Have you been sticking your hands inside your pants?" The boy responded, "No."

The masturbation symptom that had been a problem for five years was resolved in eight interviews over a period of ten weeks. In a five-year follow-up, it was found that the daughter was living with her husband, and George, now fifteen years old, was doing well in school. The mother reported that he had not masturbated publicly since their therapy. George was seen alone one final time as a means of trying to determine whether he masturbated privately and whether he had pleasure. Despite the interviewer's efforts, the boy would not say whether he masturbated or not.

Comparison of Jay Haley's and Salvador Minuchin's Strategies

As we previously mentioned, the main difference between "strategic" and "structural" orientations stems largely from the former's communicational focus on problems and the latter's primary attention to the sociological structures of family systems. Minuchin's structural family therapy, like Haley's strategic therapy, constructs a view of hierarchy, where parents are supposed to be clearly in charge of their children. Minuchin has referred to an old Chinese saying to illustrate this view of a clear hierarchy:

> When the father is in truth a father, and the son a son, when the elder brother is an elder brother, and the younger brother a younger brother, the husband a husband, and the wife a wife, then the house is on the right way. When the house is set in order, the world is established on a firm course.

The sociological structure of the family system is conceived by structuralists in terms of subsystem units, such as a wife-husband, father-child, and siblings. When a family is too "enmeshed" (that is, lacking sufficient subsystem differentiation), or "disengaged" (lacking sufficient subsystem connection), pathology is predicted to occur. The purpose of structural family therapy is therefore to help differentiate and connect subsystems.

One of the primary distinctions that is used to construct a view of family organization, both within and across subsystems, is that of triadic social relations. For example, a father may be seen as encouraging his son to disrespect the mother, who, in turn, is seen as inappropriately scolding the son when she's angry at her husband. A triadic pattern emerges where the son's behavior calibrates the interaction of the mother and father. As structural family therapists describe this particular pattern, the parental conflict is "detoured" through the son.

Semantic and Political Frames

In terms of semantic and political frames of reference, Minuchin's structural approach can be loosely mapped as follows:

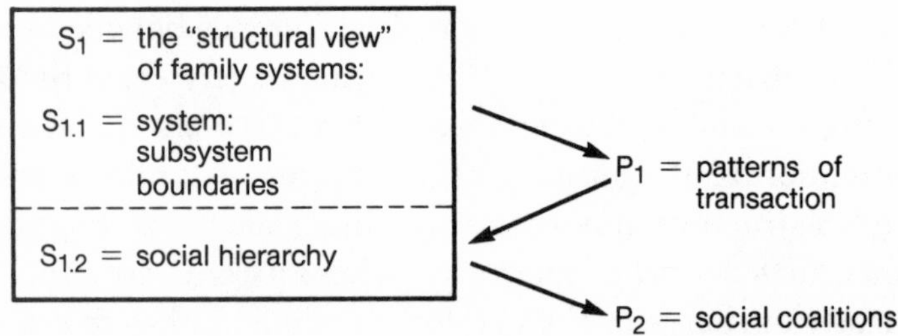

The initial semantic frame (S_1) the structural therapist constructs is always the same: it is a particular view of how family systems are organized. It involves defining whole family systems as comprised of subsystems coupled to one another through boundaries that may be described as enmeshed or disengaged ($S_{1.1}$).

All families are seen by structural therapists in this way. The specific ways in which the members enact their participation in family structures is noted by observing their redundant patterns of transaction: who-does-what-to-whom-when. This political frame of reference (P_1) is essentially the same frame that Haley constructs with respect to the sequential organization of behavior.

In addition, like Haley, structural family therapists proceed to further construct the view of social hierarchy ($S_{1.2}$) and the political frame of social coalition patterns (P_2). Again the key difference between strategic and structural family therapy revolves around their initial semantic frame: strategic therapy constructs and primarily utilizes a definition of the presenting problem which is different for each family; structural family therapy constructs and primarily utilizes a structural view of family systems which enables different families to be seen through the same lens of conceptual understanding. Although the structural therapist has the same general theoretical lens for families, Minuchin and Fishman (1981) have delineated different structural maps that are specifically applied to certain kinds of families, such as families with two people, three-generational structures, large families, stepparent families, families with fluctuating membership, and psychosomatic families.

Haley's and Minuchin's strategies can also be seen as starting in opposite directions. For Haley, the family's presenting problem leads to a view of the sequential pattern organizing it and then to the semantic and political frames of social hierarchy and coalition patterns, respectively. Haley, in effect, begins with a small slice of behavior and then builds up toward family structure. In his clinical method of working, particular problems are used as levers for changing family structures.

Minuchin, on the other hand, begins with a complete theoretical model of family structure. With this cognitive template he encounters a family and notes how his experience of his interaction with the family fits his model. It is critical to note that the structural therapist does not directly observe family subsystems and boundaries. What is observed involves action and sequences of action. These observations are then generalized or typified as categories of the structural family model.

Suppose a structural therapist tells an older child to close the door of her bedroom and then informs us that he did that as a way of structuring a boundary in a highly enmeshed family system. From the perspective of political action, the most we can say is that this intervention interrupts a sequence of action and/or alters a particular pattern of social relations. Minuchin, however, articulates this therapeutic move from a semantic frame that gives it a particular meaning. Namely, the closing of the girl's door is depicted as signifying a structural boundary.

Minuchin's strategy, in effect, lays a structural model over the presenting family communication. The therapist's task is to interact and observe how the family accommodates to this model. The therapist's structural maps, of course, are always hypothetical and only provide clues for intervention. If the therapist's interventions are not successful, then he must alter the structural map. This circular process of feedback correction is critical for constructing an effective, changing, structural therapy.

Although Minuchin does not use the presenting-problem definition as an unwavering compass for therapy, he still finds it necessary to construct a therapeutic contract. "The contract," Minuchin (1974, p. 132) claims, "holds out a promise of help for the family with the problem that has brought it into therapy." In our view, it is a way of respectfully addressing the family's request for change. For Minuchin, the contract does not have to be firmly defined. Whatever the initial contract is, the therapist must subsequently work toward broadening its focus to more and more address structural domains. For example, in the beginning the contract may immediately address the presenting problem: "I'll help you with Joe's delinquent behavior." As soon as possible, however, the contract will broaden its social focus: "I will help you in getting together on disciplining your children."

Like Haley, Minuchin's therapy is calibrated by a contract. The structural contract, however, is more encouraged to drift toward addressing social structures than constrained to follow the initial presenting complaint.

Because the structural therapist is primarily interested in changing structure, the sequence embodying the presenting problem doesn't necessarily have to be directly addressed. Other sequences, isomorphic to the problematic one, may become the therapeutic focus. The sequence attended to is less important than the structure that is believed to embody it. The therapist, in other words, works with any sequence as a means of changing family structure. From this perspective, a sequence involving a father giving his daughter a handkerchief when she cries, a mother helping her son do his chores, or a son having an asthma attack when his parents begin arguing may be seen as isomorphs arising out of the same family structure. If any of these sequences is changed in a way that involves structural transformation, it is probable that all the sequences will change in a ripplelike fashion.

Recursive Complementarity

Minuchin's strategy addresses the construction of complementarity in a most direct fashion. In fact, "complementarity" is the name of a particular category of structural technique (Minuchin and Fishman 1981, pp. 191–206). Minuchin and Fishman hold that all symptomatic behavior is linked in complementary fashion to the behavior of other family members. They introduce this view of complementarity to family systems whenever the opportunity arises. For instance, when a family member states that he or she is the problem, a structural therapist may respond, "If your problems were connected to someone else in the family, who do you think it might be?"

In this way, the view that his problematic behavior is related to other family members is being constructed. This type of construction, familiar to many family therapists, is actually the semantic frame of reference called "family therapy." The idea that an individual's experience is an intricately woven part of a more encompassing family whole is the most basic semantic frame of family therapy. In both political and semantic frames, Minuchin is always a sculptor who builds the reality of the "family as a whole organism"—a reality he constructs for his clients, as well as his students.

Minuchin, like Haley, places critical importance on a developmental frame of reference, noting that family structure must successfully change during developmental transitions or symptomatic experience may appear. Both Minuchin and Haley note that ignoring the family's developmental process is a serious error.

Cybernetic Patterns of Intervention

In the practice of therapy, structural family therapists organize themselves to address two distinct, but complementary operations: (1) joining the family; and (2) restructuring the family. "To join a family system," Minuchin (1974, p. 123) notes, "the therapist must accept the family's organization and style and blend with them." This must be done, Minuchin (p. 125) adds, because "successful restructuring often requires support of the structures that must eventually be challenged." Restructuring operations refer to all therapeutic efforts that aim at changing the family system. Minuchin (p. 140) names several categories of restructuring operations including the live performance of a family sequence of action in a session (enactment), drawing distinctions that join and/or separate family members (marking boundaries), assigning tasks, utilizing symptoms, altering social sequences through escalating intensity* and perhaps most important, directly altering coalition patterns. All of these restructuring operations involve the construction of political frames within therapy.

Structural family therapy comes alive when the operations of "joining" and "restructuring" are coupled. The structural therapist does not first join and then singularly attempt to restructure a family. Instead, joining and restructuring occur together in a rhythmic dance.

The complementary actions of joining and restructuring are Minuchin's way of addressing what we call a system's requests for stability and change. The stability of a family system is acknowledged by joining operations, whereas restructuring operations address change. Minuchin addresses this complementarity in another way when he speaks of "diagnosis" and "intervention." Diagnosis, principally concerned with understanding a system's stabilized structures, is not seen as separate from interventions, which attempt to change those family structures. To know how a family maintains stability requires seeing what it does in response to a request for change. Thus, a therapist must intervene and try to change the family structure as a means of knowing its structure. This operation, where diagnosis and intervention are intertwined, is called "interactional diagnosis." "Interactional diagnosis," Minuchin (1974, p. 131) states, "constantly changes as the family assimilates the therapist, accommodates to him, and restructures, or resists restructuring interventions."

*The restructuring operation of "escalating intensity" often involves recalibrating a transactional pattern through amplifying the affective experience typically associated with it by increasing the duration or frequency of the transactional pattern itself.

The structure of structural family therapy, from the perspective of the therapist, can now be seen as follows:

(joining operations/ restructuring operations) / the structural model of families

In this approach the therapist must recursively organize therapeutic communications that attempt to join and restructure the family. The therapist gives meaning to *his* perceptions and actions through reference to the structural model of families. These ingredients of structural family therapy correspond to the multiple communications of:

(stability/change) / meaningful noise

Again, we are speaking of these communications from the perspective of the structural family therapist. In particular, the structural model is meaningful noise for the therapist.

The structural model, as meaningful noise for therapists, begins with a conventional way of understanding individuals and families. Individuals are described as seeking a satisfactory dialectic between the experience of belonging and the experience of separateness. Families, as the context of individual experience, must therefore provide structures that facilitate the enactment of this dialectic.

In retrospect, it seems as if Minuchin deliberately set out to not limit his therapeutic strategy to simply prescribing directives for the political organization of therapy. He appears to have paid equal attention to constructing a semantic frame to which many therapists could easily join their cultural beliefs about individual experience and family life. Minuchin acknowledges that his theoretical ideas about the relations of individual experience and social context are not necessarily new to the field of psychotherapy. He correctly (1974, pp. 2–3) points out that mental health practitioners have long recognized that the boundary between the individual and his social context is artificial. Nevertheless, the practice of traditional psychotherapies tends to maintain that boundary. Therefore, although Minuchin joined a conventional semantic map of psychosocial understanding, he went further to prescribe an alternative way of addressing the politics of organizing therapy. In this way he prescribes both stability and change for those approaching the structural model of families.

With respect to the family's perspective, meaningful noise involves addressing the "cognitive schemas" the family itself sets forth. As Minuchin and Fishman (1981, p. 207) propose, "a family has not only a structure, but also a set of cognitive schemas that legitimate or validate the family organization." The therapist must accordingly "use the facts that the family recognize as true, but out of these facts she will build a new arrangement." In general, structural family therapy addresses the multiple communications of stability, change and meaningful noise as follows:

(joining/restructuring) / cognitive schema of family

These cognitive schemas of the family, also called "constructions," can be recycled to the family in an altered way by using three main categories of meaningful noise. Minuchin and Fishman (1981, p. 215) call these categories, "universal symbols," "family truths," and "expert advice." "Universal symbols" involve the therapist presenting communications that seem "supported by an institution or consensus larger than the family." This may involve appealing to common sense, moral positions the family subscribes to, tautological generalizations, and cultural traditions. "Family truths" arise from the family's own justifications of their situation and their unique worldview. Finally, "expert advice" requires that the therapist present an explanation that sounds like it arises from the wisdom of being a therapist: "I have treated similar cases that . . ."

As we have noted, restructuring operations utilize a wide variety of techniques, many of which are used by other therapeutic orientations. One of the unique contributions of structuralists to therapeutic technique stems from how they address triadic social relations. These techniques, which join them with Haley's strategy, aim at directly altering relationship patterns. The therapist may consistently affiliate with one family member, alternate his affiliation, ignore some family members, participate as a member of a coalition against one or more family member, change the sequential organization of triadic social relations through spatial rearrangements or behavioral prescriptions, and so on. In these therapeutic maneuvers, sometimes referred to as "unbalancing" operations, the goal is to change "the hierarchical relationship of the members of a subsystem" (Minuchin and Fishman 1981, p. 161). With this category of intervention, it is essentially impossible to distinguish whether the therapist is "strategic" or "structural." The therapist's identity, however, becomes clear when we see that he claims to treat problems in order to change social coalition patterns ("the strategic therapist"), or claims to treat the coalition patterns as a way of altering family structure ("the structuralist").

Structural family therapists, like strategic therapists, address family systems by realigning triadic social relations. One of Minuchin's (1974, p. 102) contributions includes his specification of different classes of triadic social relations the therapist must address. These include: (1) *triangulation,* where "each parent demands that the child side with him against the other parent"; (2) *detouring,* where "the negotiation of spouse stresses through the child serves to maintain the spouse subsystem in an illusory harmony"; and (3) *stable coalition,* where "one of the parents joins the child in a rigidly bounded cross-generational coalition against the other parent."

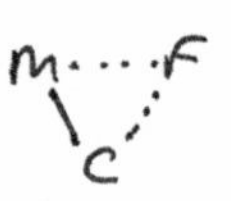

In structural family therapy, parents may be instructed to fight with each other without being interrupted by their children and disengaged family members may be given assignments that facilitate their being connected. A description of a case conducted by Minuchin (1980, p. 8) gives us a fuller view of the practice of structural family therapy.

A family presented an adolescent daughter who had anorexia nervosa. Previous problem-solving efforts by a minister, pediatrician, and child psychiatrist, among others, had failed. Minuchin scheduled the family to meet him for a lunch session. When they met, he dramatically underscored the critical importance of the parents helping their daughter eat. If she did not eat, he stated, she might die. When they tried to help her, she refused to eat and insulted them. Minuchin framed the sequence of events as an example of the daughter's strength, which could defeat her parents. He also emphasized the ways in which she insulted her parents.

In this way, Minuchin notes, the family reality was changed. The parents had previously triangulated their daughter as a way of handling their own conflicts and were thus overinvolved with her. Minuchin, by pointing out how they had been insulted and defeated by her, joined them as a marital subsystem and helped them create some distance from their daughter. The daughter, on the other hand, was now viewed as "stubborn, strong, and competent" and in a position to "monitor her own body."

The structure of this intervention can be mapped as follows:

$$\left(\frac{\text{stabilize seriousness of problem definition}}{\text{change triadic social relations}} \right) \Big/ \text{alternative construction (reframe) of situation}$$

Stability in this case is addressed by accepting the family's definition of the seriousness of the problem to be treated. The therapist simply announces that the daughter must eat to survive. The therapist then recycles descriptions of what happens in the session as meaningful noise enabling him to explain the daughter's refusal to eat as a measure of her "strength" and as an "insulting" behavior to her parents. This enables change to be addressed by shifting the triadic pattern where the parent's conflicts are calibrated by the daughter's symptom toward a triadic pattern where both parents are clearly joined in their relationship with their daughter.

In this case, the therapist is primarily aiming to change a "structural problem" rather than what the family or other therapists may view as a practical problem. Whenever a family presents a life-threatening situation, such as anorexia or diabetic coma, the practice of structural and strategic approaches are often indistinguishable to an outside observer. This similarity is demonstrated in Minuchin's previous case study. In the case that follows, however, we see a structural approach to treating an anorectic woman that primarily focuses on reorganizing the family through de-emphasizing the presenting problem.

A Structural Family Therapy Case Study of H. Charles Fishman

This clinical case was conducted by H. Charles Fishman while he was director of the Family Therapy Training Center at the Philadelphia Child Guidance Clinic. Dr. Fishman has been closely associated with Minuchin, Haley, and Montalvo, and the case provides an opportunity to view the utilization of triadic social relations in constructing structural family therapy.

The case presentation involves excerpts from the treatment of a three-generation family, in which the identified patient is a woman in her forties who has been anorectic for twenty-five years. The case material was previously edited and analyzed by Braulio Montalvo, Rich Bergman, and H. Charles Fishman, and some of their comments will be interspersed throughout the discussion.

The initial excerpt is from the first session of treatment, which involves the symptomatic woman with her parents and husband.

SESSION 1

THERAPIST: Are there ways in which you would like to change things? We don't have a whole lot of time. Are there ways in which you want to change things between you and your parents in terms of your relationship? I hear you're a very good girl. . . .

WOMAN: Yes, I would like to be able to have my cake and eat it too. *(to parents)* I would like to be able to see you when I want to see you and not see you when I don't want to see you. How do you like that for starters?

By asking how she would like to change her relationship with her parents, the therapist immediately shifts the problem definition away from the woman's anorectic behavior and moves toward addressing a particular social organizational pattern. Her response may be seen by some structurally oriented observers as metaphorical requests to be both connected and separated from her parents.

MOTHER: Does that happen now? Does that happen now?
WOMAN: How's that for starters?
MOTHER: Does that happen now?
WOMAN: No. Do you want to know why? *(therapist stands up, goes over to the woman and shakes her hand to congratulate and calm her)*
THERAPIST: Very good, what you just said there, that's great.

The sequence of behavior between mother and daughter is contextualized by the therapist's political act of shaking the woman's hand. Cybernetically speaking, we could say that the escalation between the mother and daughter is calibrated by the therapist's action. Structural family therapists, however, add the semantic frame that the therapist has "joined" the woman.

WOMAN: Can I do that now? No, because in my heart I know I won't be the good girl if I don't call or if I don't see you, so therefore I keep perpetuating that behavior.

Montalvo, in analyzing these interactions, describes the therapist's task at this point as trying to "help free the woman from ongoing patterns of enmeshment with her family of origin." The term "enmeshment" arises from structural family therapy (see Minuchin 1974) and is a semantic frame about political relationship systems. In this case, the sequences of action are semantically framed as a woman who has difficulty achieving experiences of separation and individual autonomy. The therapist will aim for a specific political change in this family organization that begins with changing the woman's position in her family of origin.

FATHER: We love Billy as much as we love you—Billy doesn't call me on the phone every night. He lives down in Jersey; he lives his life.
WOMAN: I would like to be able to see you when I want to see you. . . .
MOTHER: Good. *(nodding her head)*
WOMAN: . . . And not see you when I don't want to see you.
MOTHER: Good—it would be great.
WOMAN: And not to feel guilty and lie about it or make any excuse, like I'm going here or I'm going there or I did this or I did that, just so I don't have to see you.

MOTHER: Why do I call you on a Sunday and say, "Are you gonna be home, are you doing anything?"

WOMAN: Can't I just say "no"? Can I just say, "I don't feel like seeing you today"?

MOTHER: Yes, but those times you should just say, "Mother, not today." Why do you have to make stories up like, "We're going here or there, we won't be home"? *(mother sitting up in her chair raising her hands)* Why can't you come out and say, "No, Mother . . ."

WOMAN: Because that would hurt you.

MOTHER: *(excited)* No, it wouldn't!

FATHER: No, it wouldn't. Just say, "Look we have something to do."

The father can be seen as supporting his daughter's view. When the mother tells her to tell the truth (for example, say "Mother, not today . . ."), the father tells her to construct a story ("Look, we have something to do"). This sequence may point to a triadic relation revolving around the father's and mother's contradictory suggestions to their daughter. Structural family therapists may add the semantic frame that this triadic pattern means parental conflict is being channeled through the daughter.

MOTHER: We know you are doing . . .

WOMAN: *(interrupting)* But suppose I don't have something to do? Suppose I just don't feel like seeing anybody that day?

FATHER: Believe me, we're not going to sit in the closet waiting for you to tell me to come up.

WOMAN: Suppose, worse than that, I just don't feel like seeing you?

MOTHER: *(raising her hands)* Say it!

FATHER: Then you say, "I don't feel like seeing you." Why do you think your mother calls?

MOTHER: Do you think you're pulling something over on me when you do it?

WOMAN: *(nodding)* Yes.

MOTHER: You're not. I always say, "Why does she always have to make these stories up when I call?"

A vicious circle emerges where the more the mother requests that daughter tell the truth, the more the daughter acts as if she is not given a choice to tell the truth. As she previously stated, to not see or not call her parents for whatever reason—truthful or not—means she isn't "the good girl." Whatever political action occurs, the daughter is caught in the same semantic frame of "trying to be the good girl." Structural family therapists would view that semantic frame as further evidence that she is "enmeshed." In addition, they would construct the view of a confused hierarchy of "the good girl" who is a middle-aged woman with a husband and two adolescent children.

WOMAN: Why the hell didn't we talk about this before?

THERAPIST: Why don't you just talk about it now?

MOTHER: That fear to upset you again, that you're not going to eat again—this is why we didn't talk about it and you know how it would end if we were discussing this at home.

The sequence of interaction in this session has been marked by the woman as having included some new information. The therapist immediately addresses change by asking why they don't talk about it now. The mother indicates that fear of her daughter's not eating has played a part in calibrating their interaction.

WOMAN: Why is that I eat of primary importance?

MOTHER: I like you to be nourished.

FATHER: *(to daughter)* I don't know. . . . It's not my problem.

THERAPIST: I agree; that's your problem.

FATHER: Yes, that's your problem.

THERAPIST: And it's not even a problem, it's a habit.

The therapist connects with the father's suggestion that the problem belongs to the daughter. This can be semantically framed by structuralists as underscoring the woman's move toward disengagement and autonomy. Note that the therapist modifies his comment by saying that her problem is not really a problem, but a habit. This shift in term may suggest a more probable likelihood for change. In addition, we can generalize that the mother's messages to daughter ("tell the truth," "you should eat") are messages of engagement and stability while the father's messages to daughter ("make up a story," "eating is your problem") are messages of disengagement and change. These different messages when taken as mutually exclusive and simultaneous place the daughter in an impossible situation. This pattern is sometimes called "double bind." The resolution of this relationship knot requires transforming the relation of the parents' different messages into complementarity rather than negation. This therapeutic goal is semantically framed by structuralists as enabling the family members to achieve both separateness and togetherness.

SESSION 2

As Montalvo has pointed out, the purpose of the first session was to begin disengagement of the anorectic woman from her family of origin *(a specific political change).* The second session of treatment subsequently addresses the second-generational family with the mother (the identified patient), father, fifteen-year-old son, and thirteen-year-old daughter. The therapist will construct the view that the family embodies a confused hierarchy in which the children act more like the parents of their mother with their father in a more peripheral position.

THERAPIST: You're there to keep an eye on your mom, right?
DAUGHTER: *(shrugs)* Keep her company.
MOTHER: I didn't know that.
DAUGHTER: What? You, you know that I always ask you, "Do you want me to keep you company?" *(imitating mother)* "No, no, no, no."
MOTHER: And I always tell you, "No, go, I don't want any company."
THERAPIST: *(to daughter)* But you know that she doesn't really mean that?
MOTHER: I do mean that.

This is almost the same conversation and sequence of interaction that took place in the first session with the identified patient and her mother. The therapist will similarly encourage them to continue performing this pattern of interaction so that he will be able to utilize it as a resource.

THERAPIST: *(pointing to mother and daughter)* Talk to her about that.

MOTHER: *(to daughter)* I *do* mean it.

DAUGHTER: Well, I know I really wouldn't want to be alone.

MOTHER: No, I really do mean it, you really don't understand that that doesn't bother me at all. I'd rather see you with your friends. I always tell you or your brother I'd always rather see you with your friends.

DAUGHTER: Well, I don't always want to be with my friends. Sometimes I just feel like staying in.

MOTHER: As long as you feel like staying home just to stay home; because you feel like it.

SON: *(interjecting)* You stick around for Mom.

DAUGHTER: Well, today I stayed home with you. I didn't feel like going anywhere. I felt like staying here.

MOTHER: I know. I asked you a couple of times about that and you said that you wanted to stay home and that's okay, but I don't want you to stay home because you think you have to stay home with me. Because I'm always doing something and . . .

DAUGHTER: I know.

THERAPIST: *(to daughter)* But . . . she needs you to take care of her, doesn't she?

The therapist begins underscoring the children's parental role. A new semantic frame of reference is being constructed.

DAUGHTER: *(laughing)* Yeah.

MOTHER: *(putting her hand on daughter's lap and saying gently)* No, I don't.

SON: I always feel guilty about the time you got real sick and I was out—the first time.

DAUGHTER: I was there.

SON: She was there but I wasn't.

MOTHER: *You* feel guilty about *that?*

SON: Yeah, 'cause she was there but I wasn't and you got really sick and all and I don't know if you went to the hospital or not.

DAUGHTER: I didn't know what to do.

THERAPIST: So one of the two of you is always there with her.

DAUGHTER: Um-huh.

SON: Chances are if you came to our house at any time, one of us would be there, or the both of us.

THERAPIST: To take care of her.

SON: No, just there. I don't know . . .

THERAPIST: But you kind of want to keep an eye on her. *(to daughter)* How old are you?

The absurdity of this reverse hierarchy is gently introduced.

DAUGHTER: Thirteen.

THERAPIST: *(repeating)* Thirteen. *(to son)* And you're what, fifteen?

SON: *(nods)*

DAUGHTER: Well, it happened again. I walked in the door from school and I see Mom on the sofa screaming her lungs out. She goes, "Call Mrs. Tartman, get her here." So I called her up and if I wasn't home, I don't know what she would have done. I mean . . .

SON: Yeah, because you couldn't get up, right? *(to mother)*

DAUGHTER: You couldn't move.

SON: See if one of us wasn't there you might have died.

MOTHER: Oh, well, no. That happened so long ago; I mean we're talking six years ago.

DAUGHTER: Six years?

MOTHER: Yes, six years.

SON: It was a long time ago, but not six years though.

MOTHER: It was a long, long time.

SON: Four or five.

DAUGHTER: It was more like two years ago.

MOTHER: No it wasn't . . .

SON: *(sarcastically)* Well, there have been five of them so . . . how do you know?

MOTHER: *(nodding)* It's been a long time ago. And I made you a promise when I was in here. I said that that will never happen again. And I told you that it will never happen again.

DAUGHTER: *(agreeing with mother)* That's right.

THERAPIST: *(to daughter)* But you don't believe it, do you?

MOTHER: They don't and they have no reason to believe it yet.

The therapist now has the children report on their mother's eating, as if they were her parents. Montalvo points out that this intervention is aimed at mobilizing the mother and further highlighting the absurdity of the children's parental roles.

THERAPIST: *(to daughter)* See that? Your mother just disqualified you, see that.

DAUGHTER: I believe it . . .

THERAPIST: . . . Because these kids are missing their adolescence.

MOTHER: *(to daughter)* I can tell you. All I have to do is eat and it doesn't happen.

DAUGHTER: But you won't.

SON: Did you eat today?

MOTHER: Yes, I ate today.

DAUGHTER: Yes, she did. I was there.

THERAPIST: Did you feed her?

DAUGHTER: *(laughing)* No.

SON: But you were there to watch.

MOTHER: I mean there is always someone. . . .

THERAPIST: Were you beside her?

SON: No, I wasn't.

DAUGHTER: I was.

SON: I didn't get up in time to see you eat at breakfast. I was up by ten.

MOTHER: And my husband watched me while we were on vacation. I did a lot better. I have a lot of room for improvement.

THERAPIST: This is really nice. *(to daughter)* So, at age thirteen, instead of being out with your friends . . .

MOTHER: She's home watching whether her mother eats or not.

The therapist begins pointing out the cost to the children of taking on a parental role. He will use this information to construct an alternative semantic frame of reference which shifts the problem from anorexia to that of children missing their adolescence.

THERAPIST: *(repeating)* You're home watching your mother.

DAUGHTER: Well, I want to make sure she eats. . . . A lot of times I'll see what she's eating . . .

THERAPIST: *(to daughter)* So . . . how much time a week do you spend with your mother?

DAUGHTER: *(looking at her mother)* How much? Like a lot? *(questioningly)* Yeah, three-quarters of the time.

THERAPIST: Three-quarters of the time. Do you get a chance to go out with your girlfriends?

DAUGHTER: Oh, yeah.

THERAPIST: *(repeating)* Oh yeah, how much?

DAUGHTER: Whenever I want.

THERAPIST: Well, how much is that?

DAUGHTER: *(looking at mother)* How much?

MOTHER: It's how ever much *you* want. In other words, it's always your choice.

THERAPIST: See, you can't even remember. You have to ask your mother. When was the last time you went out with your girlfriends?

DAUGHTER: Out? Like out somewhere?

THERAPIST: Like did something . . . going to the mall . . .

DAUGHTER: *(looks at her mother and laughs nervously)*

THERAPIST: I mean, thirteen-year-old girls like going to the mall.

DAUGHTER: I don't like to shop that much. Um.

MOTHER: Were you at Rachel's yesterday?

DAUGHTER: Yeah.

MOTHER: *(nods to therapist)*

THERAPIST: Well, who was home with your mom?

SON AND DAUGHTER: *(answering together)* Dad.

MOTHER: *(turns her head slightly and laughs)*

FATHER: And her mother and father.

MOTHER: *(laughing)* Well, that's another story.

SON: Was she there yesterday?

MOTHER: Yeah.

DAUGHTER: *(to her brother)* Where were you yesterday?

SON: I was out.

MOTHER: He played golf yesterday.

THERAPIST: *(to mother)* What can you do so that these kids stop this?

MOTHER: I would like to know . . .

THERAPIST: . . . Because this is all upside down.

MOTHER: I would like to know how I can get them out of the house. I really mean that. I don't want to get rid of them, but I want them out.

THERAPIST: Why don't you tell them?

The recursive organization of this family can be described as involving parental children who are overly watchful and protective of their mother. That behavior, in turn, maintains the mother as incompetent which reinforces the children to be more parental. When the children step outside the house, mother's parents step in to maintain her role in the family system. Seen from this perspective, the children, husband, and grandparents are inappropriately joined in coalitions against the mother. These cross-generational coalition patterns thus become the focus of therapy.

FATHER: *(to his wife)* . . . If you would have something to eat . . .

THERAPIST: *(interrupting)* No, the question now is how to get the kids out of the house. You have tried for twenty years to get your wife to eat. Don't try it now.

FATHER: Yeah, but isn't that why the kids won't leave the house?

THERAPIST: No. The kids are in the house because there is somehow an inappropriate job in your house.

SON: What do you want to do?

DAUGHTER: I'm having fun with what I'm doing.

THERAPIST: See, they don't even know what fun they are missing.

FATHER: Well . . .

DAUGHTER: I'm not missing anything.

FATHER: Well, they're not in any trouble. *(laughs)*

THERAPIST: Yes, they are, because they are missing a lot of important experiences in adolescence that will help them to grow up. In other words, there are a lot of important kinds of growth experiences that a thirteen-year-old girl has with her girlfriends and things like that that they are not having. Instead, you have a couple of practical nurses. *(pointing to the children)*

MOTHER: *(to children)* . . . I can't answer for you . . . I think inside you're both kind of, you know, poo-pooing this whole idea. You're saying, "I really do like this."

THERAPIST: *(to mother)* . . . I don't want you to handle it. In other words, they don't have to agree because both think that you are absolutely irresponsible.

MOTHER: I know that.

THERAPIST: *(confirming)* That they think that.

MOTHER: I know that.

THERAPIST: So how can you make it so that they stop being your mother and father? See, when we started therapy we had your mother and father come in.

MOTHER: Right.

THERAPIST: I think I might have had the wrong ones. This is your father *(pointing to son)* and this is your mother. *(pointing to daughter)*

MOTHER: How can I get them to stop doing this? By not being an adolescent myself and taking some control over my life.

THERAPIST: Umm. That's probably unlikely though.

MOTHER: You know, I tried last year and I pooped out—I tried to go to work and it wasn't fitting in with everybody's schedule and it just kind of faded by and I . . .

THERAPIST: OK, . . . OK, I know about that. Do something with the kids right now. Because they shouldn't be there to be your mother and father. It's just not right. Do you agree?

MOTHER: Yes, but I just don't know what to do.

At this point, the therapist attempts to alter the parental behavior of the children as a means of realigning what he perceives as the social hierarchy. He does this by blocking communication about anorexia and reinforcing concern about the children missing their adolescence. Montalvo notes that the therapist observes "Mother's reported difficulties in changing without her husband's support." Accordingly, the therapist shifts gears and aims at the father becoming a more active participant. This alternative reality gives the father responsibility for stopping the children from acting like his wife's parents.

THERAPIST: . . . Right now your family is upside down. The kids are mothering mother . . . and I don't see her as changing it. I don't think she wants to. I think she likes having the kids like this.

MOTHER: I don't want to.

THERAPIST: Otherwise she'd just kick them out.

MOTHER: I just don't know how to do it.

THERAPIST: *(to father)* So I'm gonna look to you to change it. I think you are the only one who can.

FATHER: Yeah, but I don't know how to do that.

THERAPIST: I don't know how either, but I think you need to because your wife says all the time, "Well, you know, I'm just a poor, poor wet noodle and I can't be responsible." And you're a man of the world, so you can do that . . . In other words, I think you have the means to achieve that. I'm certain.

FATHER: *(shrugs and laughs)* Well, I guess I'll have to take the kids out of the house myself.

THERAPIST: All right, or order them out. I see it as real serious and I see your wife as absolutely not motivated to change it. She even talks about eating as if it's the second coming, and it isn't, and all she has to do is eat. And so she's not motivated at all. You're the only one who is. Your kids are bright kids and really nice kids but they don't have the maturity of judgment. So you're the only one who can. I mean I'm talking to you as straight as I can.

FATHER: Yeah, I'm hearing you but I'm trying to think about what to do about it but I don't know how . . .

THERAPIST: Well, you're the captain of the ship.

MOTHER: Can I ask a question?

THERAPIST: No, I'd rather not.

MOTHER: Okay.

THERAPIST: You're the captain of the ship. *(father nods)* And it really needs to change and your wife isn't gonna budge—and the kids are too concerned in this crazy upside down family that you have.

FATHER: Well, we'll have to start thinking of ways to alter that relationship.

THERAPIST: Don't start thinking about it—do something. In other words, maybe you want to talk with your wife about it, whatever, but I think it should change as of today.

The cybernetic organization of this intervention can be seen as follows:

(stability of presenting problem's contribution to the family / change of family structure) / therapist's alternative frame of reference

Stability is addressed by implicitly prescribing the symptom. When the therapist blocks the family's request to address the woman's anorectic behavior, he avoids contributing to any problem-solving effort that might help maintain it. By not prescribing that the anorectic behavior change he implicitly acknowledges its *contribution* to stabilizing the whole family and offers an alternative structure to achieve that stability. In this way, he *joins* with the family's intent to maintain itself as a stable organization. Change is addressed in this intervention by offering an alternative family structure with the children and parents assuming their appropriate roles in the family hierarchy. The therapist's alternative frame of reference, one that explains how the children are missing their adolescence by nursing their mother, provides meaningful noise. The therapist continues challenging the father to immediately correct his children's role in the family.

THERAPIST: Go ahead, what are you gonna do? Because it really needs to be done.

FATHER: *(to daughter)* Well, you're going one place or the other, right?

DAUGHTER: Bonnie's, if I'm invited.

FATHER: Well, we'll get you invited. *(to therapist)* Okay, that takes care of her.

THERAPIST: For how long?

DAUGHTER: For a week.

FATHER: We can't pan her off for more than a week.

THERAPIST: Well, what happens when she comes home? I mean you can't send her to join the Foreign Legion. You're going to have to . . .

MOTHER: No.

THERAPIST: You're going to have to do something.

DAUGHTER: I don't want to go anywhere.

THERAPIST: See that, she doesn't want to go anywhere. She doesn't have good judgment to know that she's gotta not stay home and be her mother's mother.

As the father and therapist propose change, the children propose stability.

DAUGHTER: But I only want to use the swimming pool. I mean, why would I want to leave? We have everything I need at home.

FATHER: Yeah, but you'd like to spend a couple days with Bonnie?

DAUGHTER: Um-huh.

FATHER: Yeah, well that will work out.

THERAPIST: Okay, well that's a start. *(points to son)* How about him?

MOTHER: He has been home very little this summer. I'm gonna be honest. He really has been gone a lot.

THERAPIST: Do you know what's gonna happen?

FATHER: He's gonna take over for me.

THERAPIST: You bet. See, you're reading me. We're on the same wave length. *(points to son)*

SON: Yeah, but sometimes I . . .

THERAPIST: But he's home for every meal, I bet.

SON: Oh, yeah.

THERAPIST: Aren't you watching your mother?

SON: I'm not home for every meal . . . dinner definitely.

THERAPIST: Watching her?

DAUGHTER: *(interjecting)* Breakfast.

SON: Yeah, yeah, at dinner I watch her.
THERAPIST: Watching every one of her bites.
SON: Well, yeah. I watch her.
THERAPIST: How does it make you feel when she takes a bite?
SON: I think the few times we look at her while she is eating she says, "Why are you looking at me?"
THERAPIST: Yeah, well, that makes sense.
SON: *(imitating mother)* "Do I eat any different from anyone else?"
THERAPIST: So you watch every one of her bites.
SON: No, but I see how much she takes all the time.
DAUGHTER: Yeah, I do.
SON: And it's only this small piece of meat and all these vegetables and lettuce. . . . Not that there's anything wrong with that—if you feel like being skinny.
THERAPIST: He sounds like a Jewish mother.

We now get a closer look at the absurd lengths to which the children go to monitor their mother's eating behavior. In the sequence that follows, mother attempts to reintroduce the primary distinction of anorexia. As Montalvo notes, "As the therapist is working through father, mother pulls him back to the anorexia and in order to get back to father, the therapist further exposes the inappropriateness of the children's function."

MOTHER: *(almost angrily to therapist)* Why won't I?
THERAPIST: It is futile to ask this question while the kids spend day after day, Saturday after Saturday watching her.
MOTHER: Would they stop watching me if I ate more?
THERAPIST: You better ask them. I don't know.
SON: I would.
MOTHER: *(to son)* Let me ask you this.
SON: If you ate and you were perfectly normal, don't think I'd care a hill of beans.
MOTHER: *(to daughter)* Would you feel better about leaving if I ate more? Not if I ate more, if I weighed fifteen pounds more?
DAUGHTER: I don't.
SON: Twenty.

DAUGHTER: *(pointing to mother's arm)* You're bleeding. . . .

THERAPIST: Look at how they watch you. He says twenty, and she says you're bleeding. They're just like your parents.

DAUGHTER: Well, look at her arm.

THERAPIST: Who carries the Kleenex? Does one of you carry Kleenex in case your mother starts to cry?

SON: No, she carries like a whole box of them.

THERAPIST: *(to father)* Did you see that? She says she's bleeding as though she is not competent enough to know when her own body is bleeding.

SON: I swear to God. She doesn't even know when she's bleeding.

THERAPIST: And he says gain twenty pounds instead of fifteen.

SON: Yeah, but she never knows when she's hurt, so.

THERAPIST: *(to father)* And this has got to change. You see they play this game. She says, "If I gain a few pounds," and they say, "Please gain a few pounds," and this has gone around for years already.

FATHER: It has gotten worse and she has gotten thinner.

THERAPIST: *(shrugs his shoulders)*

MOTHER: I want to stop this.

THERAPIST: And she says that she wants to stop it but don't believe it for a minute. She loves having these kids—these are nice kids.

DAUGHTER: *(laughs)*

THERAPIST: If you like them now, wait until they are old enough to be in college.

MOTHER: I want to stop it.

DAUGHTER: No, you don't.

MOTHER: Yes, I really *do.*

DAUGHTER: I believe you.

THERAPIST: *(tofather)* You're the one who has got to change it. . . . You just got to do it by fiat. You just got to take control.

One way of looking at the multiple communications of this intervention is that the mother is told to not change, father is instructed to change, while the interpretation of children's behavior provides meaningful noise.

Note, too, that an MRI-oriented therapist would probably focus on the problem-solving behavior that the children have now prescribed and come up with a strategy to block it. The perspective of triadic social relations developed by Montalvo, Haley, and Minuchin, however, is interested in larger sequences of interaction that sometimes involve other generations of a family. As we've seen in this therapeutic reality, grandparents and grandchildren are joined in their efforts to monitor and worry over the mother's eating behavior and the mother's relationship with her own family of origin is isomorphic to how her children relate to her.

SESSION 3

This session begins with the therapist being surprised by the husband and wife coming without their children.

THERAPIST: *(gets up and goes to father)* I want to shake your hand.
FATHER: I really didn't have that much to do with it.
MOTHER: He didn't do a thing.
THERAPIST: I was so impressed when I walked out. I was expecting to see the kids.
MOTHER: He didn't do anything. Our son is . . . has just been out of the house every day, all day long.
FATHER: He's been playing golf.
MOTHER: But he's at a tournament today competing.
THERAPIST: No kidding? Is he good enough to do that?
FATHER: Well, it's a junior type thing.
THERAPIST: Yeah, but even so?
FATHER: Yeah. *(to mother)* They played with sixty people last year.
MOTHER: He's very serious.
FATHER: Last week he came in sixth.
THERAPIST: Wow!
MOTHER: He's very serious.
THERAPIST: Very good. That's really to both your credit that he is so skillful in some ways.

FATHER: *(laughing)* I'm glad he has some skills. The country club playboy.

THERAPIST: Yeah, but that's more than just a nurse. And your daughter is where?

MOTHER: She left this morning for the lake with her friend, and last week she went to Ocean City. So I got her away twice.

THERAPIST: Real good.

MOTHER: Because I think she needs it a lot more than our son does because she's the less vocal. I mean he can express his disgust but she doesn't and . . . it isn't easy to get her away. I mean I have to be firm with her. . . .

THERAPIST: Because she is so worried about you.

MOTHER: And deliver her, kiss her goodbye, and say, "See you."

THERAPIST: Because she is so much your mother.

MOTHER: Is she really? Oh yes! Yes, she really is.

THERAPIST: She really is.

The therapeutic perspective(s) developed by Montalvo, Haley, Minuchin, and Fishman, among others, predicts that realigning the children to assume their appropriate place in a family hierarchy often results in marital conflict. In this particular case, when the therapy began, the couple's conflicts were calibrated by how the family responded to the mother's anorectic behavior. Montalvo points out that the following excerpt involves the therapist raising the couple's conflict "well above the threshold where they would normally diffuse and detour their issues without resolutions." The therapist attempts to facilitate a new resolution by putting "each partner on equal footing." Balancing their relationship initially requires the therapist supporting the wife.

MOTHER: *(to father)* But whenever there's an argument you say, "Shut up, you're a screaming witch, shut up." And that's all you ever say.

FATHER: Well you make no sense.

MOTHER: Well, you know, I can't. I guess that's just the way I am.

THERAPIST: *(to mother)* What that is, is your husband supporting your kids.

MOTHER: He really is.

THERAPIST: *(leaning toward mother)* You know you're doing great, go ahead.

MOTHER: *(to father)* You do it every time. Every time something occurs you always support them against me. Always, you jump in and no matter what our son and I are doing between us, you jump in and you tell me to shut up and they sit there and he beams.

FATHER: Yeah, but you're arguing with a little kid and you're taking the fourteen-year-old's side. . . .

MOTHER: Yes, and you told me, "I'm disgusted with you; you argue with him as if you were a teenager. Grow up!" And I agree with you because if I were going to argue with him it should have been on a different level. It should have been as a mother arguing with him, and I was trying to reason with him on his level and that was a mistake on my part.

FATHER: Well why do you think . . . Well then, I wouldn't side with him or tell you to shut up.

MOTHER: But, I think that no matter what I do, because I'm the mother that you ought to support me because I always support you as the father. . . . I told you I lost my credibility because you call me crazy, you make screwy signs in back of my head all of the time and the children pick that up.

FATHER: *(laughs and looks at therapist)*

MOTHER: And they do the same thing to me. You know our son says, "What are you gonna do when you have a crazy mother?" And he does say things like that because you stand there and laugh and you go *(makes circles around her head, implying that she is crazy)* . . . "You know, your crazy mother." And that's the end.

FATHER: I never do that in any seriousness and you know that.

MOTHER: Well, maybe you just do that once too often and they pick it up. And everytime . . . I know what you do because I see you all the time.

FATHER: No, when you are having an argument with our son . . .

MOTHER: You always jump in and say, "Shut up. I can't stand your mouth. Stop screaming. I can't stand people that scream and yell. Stop it." Even if I don't even start to scream, I'm thinking about it. . . . You tell me that I can't do it, I can't argue because with you, you just don't listen, you walk out and close the door and that's it, and I don't see you. . . . There's no arguing with you because I can never even get anywhere, you walk away, so I don't bother any more.

THERAPIST: *(moves to chair beside mother)* You know it's interesting, you end up as the one who's wrong.

MOTHER: I always do. Always, always I am the one that is wrong.

THERAPIST: That's not right. Do you think?

MOTHER: No, because I can't be wrong all of the time.

THERAPIST: In other words, your husband needs to support you. He needs to support you.

MOTHER: I would think out of *(turns to husband)* . . .

FATHER: I do support you when you are right.

MOTHER: But I still think you ought to support me because I am your wife, whether I am right or not. Because I can't always be right.

THERAPIST: *(takes mother's hand)* That is very smart, that's good. Go ahead.

FATHER: How can I support you when you are completely wrong?

MOTHER: Then don't say anything, and keep your nose out of it.

FATHER: *(laughs)* All right, if that's what you want.

MOTHER: Butt out.

FATHER: All right, I will.

Later in the session:

THERAPIST: The question is whether your husband is supporting you enough.

MOTHER: I feel with the kids no; I feel no.

THERAPIST: The more he puts you down, the more the kids hover around you.

MOTHER: Oh, yeah.

THERAPIST: Because they see you as an invalid, which, of course, you're not.

MOTHER: Or some sort of mental midget. I mean really.

FATHER: *(laughing)* I never called you dumb.

MOTHER: Well, I feel like it. I am not capable of making a rational decision—"because everyone knows your mother is crazy and sick. Why else would she be going to a psychiatrist?"

FATHER: Look, I never mentioned that part of it.

MOTHER: *(laughing)* You don't have to a lot of times. When you go like this *(making circles around her head, indicating she is crazy)* people begin to get the picture.

FATHER: I went like this *(repeats gesture)* a few times when you got in the car and drove over something like . . .

MOTHER: No, no that's not it.

THERAPIST: You know, he "gas lights" you a lot.

MOTHER: What's that mean?

THERAPIST: It's a movie or a play where a guy is trying to get his wife committed so he can take her money . . .

FATHER: *(laughs)*

THERAPIST: *(continues)* And he kept turning down the gas ever so little.

MOTHER: Uh-huh.

THERAPIST: And she kept saying, "It's getting darker in here." And he kept saying, "No, dear, it's your eyes"—until she was convinced she was crazy.

MOTHER: Actually, other people think I am very sane, except when they look at me.

THERAPIST: Of course, you are sane.

MOTHER: Especially, in the summertime, when I wear a bathing suit, they ask me, "Is there a problem?" But in the wintertime you can't tell because I wear a lot of clothes.

THERAPIST: You're very sane. A little scrawny, but you are sane.

FATHER: I thought you were gonna say, "Screwy."

MOTHER: Basically I am really fairly together in my mind.

FATHER: I thought you were gonna say, "Screwy." *(laughing)*

THERAPIST: Your husband just did it right there.

MOTHER: What?

THERAPIST: Talk with him *(pointing to father)* about it. He is "gas lighting" you.

FATHER: I'm not after your money, I can guarantee that. *(laughing)* I got that long ago.

MOTHER: *(laughing)* I know, my vast wealth. *(jokingly)*

FATHER: *(laughing)* Five grand; I guess we spent that pretty quick.

MOTHER: Well yes, but you took it, didn't you? *(laughing)*

THERAPIST: He is "gas lighting" you and you're cooperating.

The therapist has pointed out how both the father and mother (as well as the children) actively participate in constructing the view that she is crazy. By enacting the social construction of that view in the session, the therapist is able to interrupt and challenge it.

MOTHER: How do I not cooperate with something like that?

THERAPIST: You go right on doing what you are doing right now. You're saying, "Cut it out." You're saying, "Cut it out."

MOTHER: Well, he won't cut it out.

THERAPIST: You have to see that he does. You have to use your powers as a person. You see anybody that can fast the way that you fast has tremendous willpower.

MOTHER: Oh, you'd better believe it! *(laughing)*

The woman's anorectic behavior is now framed as indicating a positive resource.

THERAPIST: And what you need to do is to use that for constructive purposes, that same willpower, and not let him "gas light" you. Because it keeps . . .

MOTHER: *(interrupting)* Why don't I think it's worth it?

THERAPIST: He's not worth it. . . .

MOTHER: Then why am I starving myself?

THERAPIST: Maybe you would do better separated. Do you want to separate from him?

MOTHER: I don't think that that's the answer to my problem.

THERAPIST: Well, then you need to change him. He's a well-meaning guy; he is just blocking your self-image.

Later in the session, the contribution of the woman's anorexia to stabilizing the marriage is presented.

THERAPIST: But is he standing by you now?

MOTHER: No, because I am a lot more independent now and I don't want to have to get sick again to hang on to you and only get you through sickness. You know, I don't only want to keep you that way. And it seems like, when I get more my own obnoxious self, the further away you move.

FATHER: No, that's not so.

MOTHER: No, but before I got sick; before I got sick I was never really good enough. And I knew it. I was never enough for you.

FATHER: That's all in your mind.

MOTHER: No, it isn't. It is not all in my mind. It absolutely isn't. You used to get very angry with me. When I was at parties, oh, my God, you would get so mad at me and drag me home and I would say, "How come you are making me go home, just when I'm starting to have a good time?"

FATHER: Yeah, well, when you had a lampshade on your head.

MOTHER: Now, I never did have a lampshade on my head, ever. I mean I've seen people in really bad shape at a lot of those things.

FATHER: . . . I saved you from all . . . *(laughing)*

MOTHER: That's what you were doing, "I'm getting her out of here." I never really felt that I was doing anything bad. I was with all of your friends.

FATHER: Yeah, well, isn't three o'clock in the morning time to go home for something?

MOTHER: Not when everyone else is there and I'm having a good time.

FATHER: Doesn't it ever occur to you that sometimes we were the only ones left?

MOTHER: But you know, you loved me when I had to go to bed at ten o'clock every night and couldn't even . . . when we were on the cruise and I couldn't even stagger.

FATHER: Well, I couldn't not be kind to you.

MOTHER: That's why I'm indebted to you. I really am because you hung in there. But every time I get to be my own self again, I feel that I am losing you.

FATHER: No, that's all in your mind.

MOTHER: I know it is.

THERAPIST: No, it's not, he just did it to you again. There go the "gas lights."

The therapist again calibrates the social construction of "craziness."

FATHER: What, "It's all in your mind"?

THERAPIST: "It's all in your mind."

MOTHER: But it isn't in my mind.

FATHER: I really am not doing that to her.

THERAPIST: *(to mother)* But you see what you did? You accepted it. You said, "I know it is."

MOTHER: I know, I know.

THERAPIST: Change him. The question is, Can you be you? Can you be a robust person, a full person?

The therapist recycles the wife's previously constructed semantic frame as meaningful noise and prescribes change in terms of changing her husband. More specifically, an association is built between her being a full person *(a change)* and her husband making a change. In other words, the therapist is beginning to prescribe a double view of change that points toward a change in their relationship.

THERAPIST: Can you be a full person and have him love you?

MOTHER: You know when I did this I told you what I was doing. I told you because I made a conscious decision at that time. I knew that I could do it and I knew that would be a way of turning myself off from you. And I told you at the time and you said, "You don't mean it, you don't mean it," and I said, "Yes, I do mean it."

THERAPIST: When you did what?

MOTHER: I decided purposely to get thin like this and I told him ten years ago when it happened.

THERAPIST: Talk to him.

MOTHER: *(turning to father)* . . . And you wouldn't listen to me. Do you remember?

FATHER: You've said it a few times, yeah.

MOTHER: Well, I did tell you at the time, but I had to . . . I really had to. You never paid any attention to me. You really never did.

FATHER: If you die, I can't pay much attention to you either.

MOTHER: I know, but you pay attention to me when I am sick. You were so busy, so busy with your job and your house and you never talked about us. There was always, "Did you get the cement block? Did you order this?"—The house, the house, the house—"Did you go to the antique course today?" . . . so that I could learn more to be what you wanted me to be. And I couldn't function, because I needed you and you were never really there. You really were never there, ever.

FATHER: Well, I guess that was my fault.

MOTHER: So I decided . . . I told you at the time, rather than stay the way I was and go to somebody else, I told you what I was doing. I said I really want to keep this marriage because I want the children and I want to be a good mother and that's what I want more than needing somebody. But I think that I fight against getting out of it because I'm afraid there won't be anything there when I come out and what do I do then? I mean what happens if I come out of all this and get better and there's nothing there anymore?

FATHER: Anybody that has gone through all this crap could have left you long ago. *(laughs)*

Later in the session:

THERAPIST: *(to father)* You see, I see you as very committed to this relationship.

The therapist, having previously supported the wife, will now shift to positively connoting the husband's contribution to the marital relationship. In this way their marriage is politically framed in terms of complementarity.

MOTHER: He really is.

THERAPIST: Don't speak for him. *(mother laughs)* Because it is not fair. He needs to speak for himself. *(again to father)* I see you as very committed to her. But somehow she doesn't hear it. So what can you do to help? Do you feel committed to her?

FATHER: Yes, very much so and I think she knows that. We wouldn't be here.

THERAPIST: No, she doesn't. Because she just said she doesn't. Tell her.

FATHER: *(to mother)* Why the hell do you think we are here? Why do you think I leave work every time to come here? Do you think because I want you to pour your soul out in front of the TV cameras? I guess it would have been much easier to go and get a new wife. . . .

Later in the session:

THERAPIST: The question is, will your husband take you, not only in sickness . . .

FATHER: *(finishing)* . . . but in health. I will take you well and in health this time.

MOTHER: Okay, but up until now, I have been afraid to take the chance. I don't want to risk that. Do you want to know why I don't want to risk that?

FATHER: *(laughs)*

THERAPIST: He's daring you.

MOTHER: Do you remember when . . .

THERAPIST: *(to mother)* Hold on a second, he is daring you. He is saying that you are not really going to change.

MOTHER: He said, "I have seen it before."

THERAPIST: I think you are.

FATHER: Well, I am waiting.

MOTHER: Do you know what I really want to say to you? I am gonna change whether you wind up in the picture or not. . . .

FATHER: Well good. That is what I want to hear.

MOTHER: I am not quite ready to do that. I mean I can't really bring myself to that thinking. But right now that is what I want to do.

The therapist ends the session by returning the couple to resolving their conflict.

THERAPIST: What about from now on? What do you want?

MOTHER: Exactly what he has.

FATHER: What I said before, come out of this thing and whatever your personality is . . .

MOTHER: I don't think you could handle me. Honest to goodness, I don't think you could.

FATHER: If I can't, I can't.

MOTHER: But are you gonna make me feel like some sort of inferior creep, like a streetwalker? Are you gonna make me feel like somebody, in quotes, "common"? I don't want to be "common," because I am not, really.

FATHER: I never said you were.

MOTHER: *(raising eyes)* I don't believe you. I don't believe you.

THERAPIST: See, she thinks you are weak. She thinks you are very weak. The only way she can support you as a husband is by being weaker, and I don't think you are weak. I think you can have a strong wife. Because you will be more alive than you have ever been.

The therapist constructs a frame where the wife's weakness is a sign of the husband's weakness. The implication is that the husband must become strong (that is, change) in order for the wife to become strong. Each spouse must change for the relationship to change the way it remains stable.

FATHER: I think I can, too.

THERAPIST: You better tell her. I think you will be ten times more alive than you were a year ago, when you have a strong wife.

FATHER: *(to mother)* I want you to come out of this and be a strong personality or whatever it takes.

MOTHER: If you are willing to take the chance.

FATHER: I'll take the chance. Is it a deal? *(puts out hand)*

THERAPIST: Shake on it.

MOTHER: Hey, I can't take the humiliation again, you know that.

FATHER: There will be no humiliation.

MOTHER: You know I can't face that.

FATHER: There will be no humiliation. Shake. *(extends hand)*

MOTHER: *(shakes his hand)* I will have to think whether it is worth it.

FATHER: It's worth it.

THERAPIST: The fact is you don't have a choice. Because if you don't do it, you will die, either physically or emotionally.

In a one-year follow-up phone call by Dr. Fishman, the wife reported that they were happier than they've ever been. She stated that her son had spent the summer in Europe, while her daughter was vacationing in Bermuda. She had stabilized her weight at around 115 pounds and had a job teaching an exercise class. In addition, her husband had recently invited her to go on a vacation to Florida and after some hesitation due to her house and work commitments she said, "What the hell, let's go." When asked what was different since therapy she responded that two things had changed: (1) she could never get anorectic again because the kids had blossomed so well; and (2) she had learned to stay out of her parents' marriage.

CHAPTER 5

Contextual Meaning

> Therapeutic interventions in the family, as we have gradually devised, applied, and critically examined them, appear to be, at a certain point, no more than a learning process acquired by the therapists through trial and error.
>
> —Mara Selvini-Palazzoli, Luigi Boscolo, Gianfranco Cecchin, and Giuliana Prata (1978, p. 47)

The Milan Strategy

The contribution of Mara Selvini-Palazzoli, Luigi Boscolo, Gianfranco Cecchin, and Giuliana Prata (hereafter referred to as Milan) to designing family therapy has a most interesting history. The Milan members are psychiatrists with psychoanalytic training who in the late 1960s and 1970s decided to learn how to work with whole families. They constructed a context for learning family therapy that involved working as a team and studying the theoretical writings of Haley, as well as Watzlawick, Jackson, and Beavin. They later were influenced by the ideas of Gregory Bateson and in 1975 published their book *Paradox and Counterparadox.* Since that time they have received wide attention in the field of family therapy and are acknowledged as having contributed a unique strategy for organizing therapeutic change.

It is not surprising that their theoretical statements include many notions connected to the ideas of Haley and MRI. They often point out that all behavior is communication and that families organize themselves in terms of coalition patterns. However, the Milan approach to conducting family therapy is markedly different from both Haley and MRI.

Semantic and Political Frames

The difference stems from the fact that the Milan approach principally organizes itself from the perspective of a semantic frame of reference. They begin with the question, Why is this family presenting for therapy in this way at this time? (see Tomm 1982, p. 19). In effect, they violate one of the principal rules of Watzlawick, Weakland, and Fisch by asking a "why" question.* In other words, they are *principally* concerned with semantics rather than politics. They orient themselves to discover possible meanings of what is going on with a family.

The Milan approach is not primarily a symptom or problem-focused therapy, although it addresses these communications. Its emphasis is on the context of meaning that frames and organizes symptoms. The aim is to discover a pattern of contextual meaning for use in helping the troubled system reorganize itself. As we will see, this process involves triggering the family to generate its own solution.

Thus, the principle distinction for a Milan strategy for therapy revolves around constructing a hypothesis about a family system, modifying it in response to additional information from the family, and sometimes presenting the hypothesis as an intervention to the family.†

The construction of a hypothesis begins even before they see a family, on the basis of the information given to them by the referral source or phone contact. For instance, they once were invited to see a family consisting of a divorced mother of thirty-seven years and her fifteen-year-old son. The only information they had was that "the mother had called several months before on the eve of the summer holidays requesting a consultation

half of the complementary recursion!?

*As Watzlawick, Weakland, and Fisch (1974, p. 83) state, "We can take the situation as it exists here and now, without ever understanding why it got to be that way and in spite of our ignorance of its origin and evolution we can do something with (or about) it." In effect, they prescribe the rule, "Thou shalt not ask 'why' questions; thou shalt be restricted to asking 'how' and 'what' questions."

†Our view of the Milan strategy is based largely on the recent work of Luigi Boscolo and Gianfranco Cecchin.

concerning her son, who, in her words, was difficult to control, rebellious, rude, and prone to delinquent behavior (he had stolen change from her purse)" (1980, p. 4). With that information, they formulated the following hypothesis: the behavior of the boy could be a way of trying to get the father back to the family.

Milan therapy begins when such a hypothesis is constructed. This hypothesis is a semantic frame of reference, specifying why the family is operating, acting, communicating, or presenting itself in a particular manner. It also aims at being systemic by trying to connect the communications of all family members in a way that is isomorphic to the pattern that is assumed to organize the whole family. In actuality, the beginning hypotheses usually only address parts of the family system. We call these hypotheses "partial arc hypotheses" as a means of indicating that they're not fully systemic. As the session unfolds, these partial arc hypotheses become connected in a way that addresses the participation and contribution of all family members. This larger pattern of connection constitutes the fully developed "systemic hypothesis."

Given an initial hypothesis, or semantic frame of reference, the Milan group constructs other frames that include information about the sequential organization of problem (and other relevant) behavior, present family coalitions, referring contexts and people who have been involved in trying to solve the problem, and past and future views of coalition patterns, particularly with respect to the onset of symptomatic behavior. All of these categories of information address political frames of reference:

P_1 = Sequential organization of problem and other relevant behavior
P_2 = Present family coalition patterns
P_3 = Patterns of relationship with referring contexts
P_4 = Past and future views of coalition patterns, particularly in association with onset of problem

Recursive Complementarities

Although Milan does not specify how these different political frames of reference are nested, they do acknowledge that they are intertwined and connected. With respect to political frames, their approach implies a nesting of recursive complementarities:

$P_4/[P_3/(P_2/P_1)]$

Thus, the sequential organization of problem behavior is part of the present family coalition patterns which are themselves organized within referral contexts. These complementarities clearly join them with Haley's view. However, they go on to propose that all of these nested levels of process are organized by the family's own temporal perspectives with respect to historical accounts and future predictions. Haley, as well as MRI, usually does not emphasize the construction of temporal frames of reference outside of present-state descriptions.

It is important to note that the Milan approach does not focus on asking questions that require semantic interpretations by family members, although they are responsive to the family's construction of semantic frames. Their questions primarily attempt to address political frames of reference in terms of "specific interactive behavior in specific circumstances," "differences in behavior," "ranking of specific behavior or interaction," "change in behavior or relationship before and after a precise event," and so forth (Selvini-Palazzoli et al. 1980, pp. 9–11). The major semantic frame of reference in this therapy is the therapists' hypothesis. They do, however, at times ask family members to report how they understand, make sense, or explain their situation. These semantic frames provided by family members (S_f) often provide clues about what political frames need to be addressed.

The cybernetic organization of Milan therapy involves changing one's hypothesis to fit the information derived from the above-mentioned frames of reference. This process is sketched as follows:

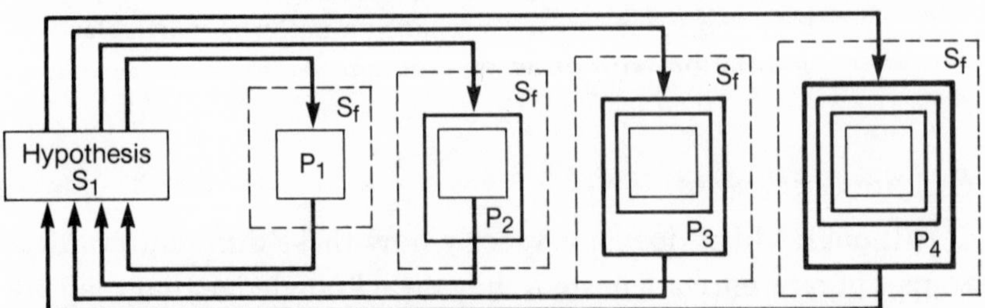

Contextual Meaning

The hypothesis of the therapist organizes the selection of questions in each of these political frames of reference. For instance, in our previous case example, the Milan team used their hypothesis to avoid questions about the boy's misbehavior and instead addressed questions about his relationship with the absent father. In this case, the initial hypothesis was quickly disproved, that is, the derived information did not fit their explanation of what was going on. As a consequence, the Milan team constructed a second hypothesis that the son's behavior was a jealous expression of his mother's involvement with "another man." This hypothesis, incidentally, fit the situation.

The feedback organization of this strategy begins with the hypothesis calibrating what political frame of reference needs to be addressed, as well as the specific content to be examined within that frame. In addition, the therapist may ask family members what any of these political frames mean to them. The semantic frames of the family (S_f) provide clues to the connection of the organization of the family's thinking to the organization of their behavior. The information derived from these different levels of inquiry subsequently enables the hypothesis to be corrected: it will either be scrapped, partially modified, or fine tuned.

The Milan approach differs from that of Haley and MRI in another respect. Namely, it avoids certain ways of interacting with a family. Some observers might even propose that they often avoid interventions that dramatically reveal how the family organizes itself and "resists" change. Others might say that there are no directives that are purposefully aimed at directly mobilizing change within a session nor are there provocative actions by the therapist that purposefully precipitate a crisis. In our opinion, however, the Milan approach involves a very subtle way of gathering information about how a family is organized.

Triadic Questions

This approach involves what they call "the triadic modality of investigation of relationships" (Selvini-Palazzoli et al. 1980, p. 9).

These so-called triadic questions sometimes involve asking a family member to comment on the dyadic relationship of two other members. For instance, a mother may be asked about the interaction between the father and son or a problem adolescent may be asked to comment on the mother and father's relationship. Triadic questions may also address more complex patterns of interaction. A child may be asked, "When your mother and father fight, which of your brothers and sisters gets most (or least) involved?"

Careful management of this approach enables coalition patterns to emerge, not only in the self-reported perceptions of the respondent but, more importantly, in the reactions precipitated in others whether it be a frown, sharp glance, smile, or shift in body posture. When appropriately used, these questions initiate reactions to other family members as opposed to the therapist. Whereas the therapeutic strategies of Haley and Minuchin often construct coalition patterns in which they become part of a triadic relation, the Milan group structures the family to enact their own coalitions. This enables the therapist to more easily avoid taking sides with a particular family member or getting trapped in a coalition for or against someone. The position of the therapist in this approach is not surprisingly called "neutrality."

By inviting a family member to comment on the relation of two (or more) other members, a reaction from another family member to his comment usually occurs. This reaction to a reaction subsequently provides an opportunity for the therapist to shape another triadic question. Thus, various political frames of reference are constructed in relation to the ongoing feedback generated by asking questions. The Milan team uses the term "circularity" to refer to "the capacity of the therapist to conduct his investigation on the basis of feedback from the family in response to the information he solicits about relationships. . . ." (Selvini-Palazzoli et al. 1980, p. 8).

The feedback organization of questions in therapy is of critical importance in a Milan strategy. This is often overlooked by therapists who only ask a progression of triadic questions in a habitual way without allowing the reactions of the family to play a part in shaping each specific question. It may be that the organization of these questions, rather than other techniques, such as the prescribed rituals and positive connotations, is the most relevant pattern of an effective Milan intervention.

The way in which questions organize a Milan session can be seen in the following case excerpt. It is the beginning of a consultation interview with a family and their therapist. The interviewing consultant is Gianfranco Cecchin, and Luigi Boscolo observes from behind a one-way mirror.

CONSULTANT: Dr. Smith [the therapist] was describing to us that he has been seeing your family for the last three years.

MOTHER: Yes.

CONSULTANT: . . . He told us that at this moment he feels that something is not moving very well. Do you agree with that?

MOTHER: I do.

CONSULTANT: Can you explain the way you feel that you didn't go far enough?

MOTHER: We've yet to achieve consistent cooperative attitudes, and there is still an awful lot of hostility that surfaces. A lot of anger and a lot of teasing and mockery . . . I'm not satisfied with where I am: I still find myself inadequately able to stay with a consistent effort to accomplish and achieve, and I find that when I fall out of my "Okay Self" then troubles are created in the family again because I can't consistently hold on to that way of being. And I feel that the kids also don't persevere. . . . They seem to be inadequately directed in any one direction. . . . They don't seem to be able to make an adequate effort. . . .

CONSULTANT: *(to husband)* Do you agree with what your wife is saying?

Note that the consultant completely ignores the specific content of what mother said and instead asks a question that requires the father to react to mother's view of the therapist's view.

FATHER: About the children? Yes.

CONSULTANT: No. About the therapy at this moment.

FATHER: Oh. Well, she was talking about how she felt about herself. I don't know what she feels about herself, but—you mean about the success of the therapy?

CONSULTANT: Yes.

FATHER: That's right. I don't think it's been successful altogether. I guess some things have been successful.

CONSULTANT: Now, at this moment, these last few months, let's say, how is it going?

FATHER: I don't think it's different than any of the other months.

CONSULTANT: Always the same.

FATHER: Back and forth.

CONSULTANT: There were some moments which were going well, and sometimes it's not going so well. How is now, today? Low point? High point?

FATHER: I don't think it's low. Something in between.

CONSULTANT: Something in between.

FATHER: Yeah.

CONSULTANT: Brigitte [the daughter], do you agree with what your parents say?

DAUGHTER: *(laughing)*

CONSULTANT: She wants to be called Brigitte Bardot?

MOTHER: Right.

CONSULTANT: *(long pause)* Do you hear my question?

DAUGHTER: I'm thinking about it. I would have to say, I agree.

CONSULTANT: So, let's say, in the whole family, who got less out of therapy in the last three years?

This question enables the therapist to recycle the same theme —evaluation of therapy—and as can be predicted, the therapist will attempt to elicit the views and reactions of each family member to other members' views and reactions.

FATHER: Least.

CONSULTANT: Least.

FATHER: That's what you mean? The least?

CONSULTANT: Yes.
MOTHER: Of the four of us?
CONSULTANT: Of the four of you.
DAUGHTER: That's hard to say because each of us get out of therapy something different, and that's probably one of the big problems. . . . So I could say I got the least, my mom got the least, my father got the least and my brother got the least. . . .
CONSULTANT: So, in the whole family, who is the one who is more for therapy at this moment? Is it your daughter?

The therapist again recycles the same theme, but from the opposite direction by asking who gets *more* from therapy.

FATHER: That's right. Well, she, her sister, and mother.
CONSULTANT: So, you can make a list of who believes more?
FATHER: Mother.
CONSULTANT: Mother believes in therapy.
FATHER: Right.
CONSULTANT: And the second one?
FATHER: She's way out in front and the second one is . . .
CONSULTANT: . . . The second one is . . .
DAUGHTER: Brigitte Bardot.
FATHER: Maybe her sister and I are bunched together.
CONSULTANT: And the last one?
FATHER: I guess it's Tom [the son]. He's the only one left.
DAUGHTER: *(laughing)* The dog.
CONSULTANT: If we were making numbers, zero to ten, let's say, your wife would be ten, right?
FATHER: Yes.
CONSULTANT: You would be at what level, you and your daughter?
FATHER: Four-and-a-half.
CONSULTANT: Your son?
MOTHER: Minus ten. *(family laughs)*
FATHER: I don't know if he'd be minus ten.
CONSULTANT: Dr. Smith, where do you think he is?
FATHER: Eleven.

In this style of questioning, the Milan strategy elicits information that enables inferences (that is, hypotheses) to be made about family structure and possible coalition patterns. Later in this same session, the consultant checks some of these hypotheses when the family starts talking about the possibility of the daughter's leaving home. The consultant utilizes the family's new theme as follows:

CONSULTANT: Who do you think in the family would miss you the most when you leave?

The consultant will use the theme of "leaving home" in the same way he used the theme of "evaluating therapy." Namely, he will ask questions about the theme that elicit views and reactions from family members about other members' views and reactions. In this therapeutic reality, the themes and content are always less important than the pattern that organizes the questions about them.

DAUGHTER: My dog.
CONSULTANT: Your dog. Your dog first, then second? Why don't you take the dog with you?
DAUGHTER: Um . . .
FATHER: I hope she does.
DAUGHTER: You want me to?
MOTHER: Take him, please.
DAUGHTER: All right.
FATHER: Take the cat, too.
DAUGHTER: No.
CONSULTANT: Who will miss you most after you are there on the West Coast? After the dog.
DAUGHTER: After the dog? Um . . . I would say my mom and my dad would be equal at first and then they would kind of like it that I wasn't there; they'd get used to it.
CONSULTANT: Both of them would suffer a little bit, huh?
DAUGHTER: Yeah.
CONSULTANT: How long do you think it would take them to recover from the loss of their daughter?

DAUGHTER: A while.
CONSULTANT: A while. Who would take longer?
DAUGHTER: My mother.
CONSULTANT: Your mother. Your father would start to forget a little bit?
DAUGHTER: Probably.
CONSULTANT: You think?
DAUGHTER: Yeah.
CONSULTANT: Do you also see your brother somewhere in the future planning to do the same thing as you do?
DAUGHTER: Oh, yeah.
CONSULTANT: Following you to California?
DAUGHTER: Well, it may not be to California, but it will probably be easier because he's the second child. I'm the first one, I had to train them. You think this was easy?
CONSULTANT: Did you succeed?
DAUGHTER: To train them?
CONSULTANT: Yeah.
DAUGHTER: I would say I was successful in some ways. Yes.
CONSULTANT: So your brother finds the job already prepared?
DAUGHTER: Well, he has the perfect example of what not to do.
CONSULTANT: I see. Who would miss your brother most?
DAUGHTER: I really don't know at this point. Um . . . possibly my father. . . .

Over and over again the Milan strategy uses themes the family presents as a way of exploring difference, relationship, and family organization. This method of asking questions may be in itself the most important ingredient for successfully constructing a Milan therapeutic reality. In addition, it should not be forgotten that the Milan associates view questions as prescriptions or "instructions," to use their term. Thus the pattern that organizes questions in Milan therapy is not only a pattern that connects questions. It is a pattern that attempts to connect and correct.

Thus, the particular class of political frame of reference to be addressed is determined by the therapists' hypothesis. Through the reactions of different family members to triadic questions that explore differences in family issues, relationship configurations, time, and behavioral sequences, among other classes of information, a pattern is organized.

Cybernetic Patterns of Intervention

At a certain stage in the course of a session the team of Milan-oriented therapists consult with one another to note whether and how the pattern that emerged in the process of asking questions confirmed or corrected the working hypothesis. This discussion often leads to the hypothesis being reconstructed in order to fit all the known information. Again, the hypothesis attempts to be systemic: since a whole family is treated, it is argued that the hypothesis necessarily must address how each member contributes to the present organization of the family.

In a way, Milan therapy is simply a dialectic between the therapists' hypotheses and the family's responses to questions. The pattern that organizes the sequence of questions in a session is actually shaped by the coalition patterns of the family's present organization. When this pattern is discerned, it will either confirm, modify, or reject the hypothesis.

Near the end of a session, the Milan team sometimes decides to construct a different order of intervention, primarily aimed at *positively connoting* "the homeostatic tendency of the system" (1978, p. 58). This occurs by announcing to the family the logic underlying the therapists' systemic hypothesis of what is going on in their situation and how the family's present dilemma fits into the whole family organization.

Hoffman has compared Milan therapy to the idea of Watzlawick, Weakland, and Fisch that the "solution" to a problem becomes the problem. In Milan work, she argues (1983, p. 41), "the family's 'solution' may not work precisely because, in some other sense, the problem is an even better 'solution.'" In this view, prescribing the logic of the therapists' hypothesis has to do with specifying how they see the family's particular problem as a solution to their unique predicament.

This logic is stated in a way that underscores the positive contribution of each member to organizing the whole system. In

Milan therapy, this announcement to the family often appears to involve prescribing that the family system should remain the same. Actually the logic implies how the family is stabilizing itself—what the Milan team calls the family homeostasis.

In terms of our cybernetic definition of therapeutic change:

(stability/change) / meaningful noise

Milan therapy positively connotes the logic underlying how a problem system remains stable by suggesting that their problem is actually a solution. This leads to the possibility that other (more adaptive) solutions won't threaten the stability of their system. In addition, the Milan approach suggests that the family requires a source of new information. This is usually addressed by the way the therapists request stability and change. Many Milan prescriptions, for example, make reference to historical events and connections that, from our perspective, provide a source of meaningful noise.

For instance, Selvini-Palazzoli and her colleagues (1978, pp. 77–82) describe a session with a ten-year-old boy, Ernesto, who talked and acted like a very old man. Ernesto spoke as if his words "came from an early nineteenth-century novel," and he refused to go out with his father because he hallucinated they were being followed by a "thin, bearded man." His parents noted that the boy's strange behavior began after the death of his grandfather and intensified four years later when an aunt visited the family.

This and other information led the therapists to hypothesize that Ernesto was miming his grandfather. They then had the boy show how his grandfather spoke to both his mother and father. Those demonstrations led to constructing the additional hypothesis that the boy was "caught in the middle of an unreconcilable couple" and "to strengthen the homeostasis, Ernesto had resuscitated his grandfather, the only one who had been able to control his mother, to keep her in place."

The therapists subsequently delivered the following message to the family (1978, p. 81):

> We are closing the first session with a message to you, Ernesto. You're doing a good thing. We understand that you considered your grandfather to be the central pillar of your family *(the hand of the therapist moved in a vertical direction as if tracing an imaginary pillar);* he kept it together, maintaining a certain balance. *(the therapist extended both hands in front of him palms down, both at the same level)* Without your grandfather's presence, you were afraid something would change, so you thought of assuming his role, perhaps because of this fear that the balance in the family would change. *(the therapist lowered his right hand, which corresponded to the side where the father was seated)* For now you should continue in this role that you've assumed spontaneously. You shouldn't change anything until the next session, which will be January 21, five weeks from now.

The therapist's prescription for the boy to continue assuming grandfather's role as a means of maintaining family "balance" addresses *stability*, while the scheduling of another session suggests *change.* In addition, the shift from a negative to a positive connotation of the boy's behavior is itself a change in the family's experimential reality. The rationale for these prescriptions of stability and change arises from the meaningful noise of family history, particularly with reference to the grandfather's death.

This type of intervention is often given at the end of a session with great care to avoid too much discussion (if any), as well as any introduction of new questions that might be distracting. The announcement is dropped on the family and the therapists quickly terminate the session. The next session is usually scheduled for a month or more later. This allows enough time for relevant sequences of action to occur and be calibrated by the intervention. Each new session then begins in the same fashion: hypothesis—questions—intervention.*

We believe that since the Milan group has developed a unique strategy for working with families, their work can't be adequately described through the frames of reference that other strategies of therapy prescribe. Efforts to describe their work through those

*Tomm (1982, p. 16) notes that Milan interventions may take many forms including "a systemic opinion (with or without a prescription for change), a reframing of family beliefs, a prescription to carry out a detailed ritual, a declaration of therapeutic impotence, an analogic enactment, etc." We have limited our discussion to focus on their best-known form of intervention that involves a formal announcement to the family that systemically addresses their situation and provides a suggestion for them to remain stable, while at the same time often scheduling another session to work with them *(implicit prescription of change).*

strategies often obscure the most basic distinctions that organize it. For instance, Boscolo and Cecchin note (pers. com. 1983) that in the beginning years of their work, most of their sessions ended with a prescription to the family. That part of their work was similar to the structure of Haley and MRI strategies. As Boscolo and Cecchin began a serious study of Bateson, their emphasis on giving "prescriptions" declined. Instead, their work shifted more and more to simply asking questions. This followed from an effort to avoid separating the prescription from what took place in the rest of the session.

Boscolo and Cecchin's occasional choice to not give prescriptions at the end of a session can be explained by noting that the prescription has already been presented in the session. Namely, the pattern that organizes their questions is isomorphic to the one they wish the family to encounter in a prescription (whether interpretations or assignments). Repackaging that pattern into a final prescription allows the family to more easily engage in a symmetrical relationship with the therapist around the issue of the intervention's "truth" or "practical relevance." In addition, giving a prescription marks the interviewer as a "therapist," which is a potential problem when the intent is to provide consultation to a system that already has a therapist.

Another way of looking at Milan sessions that do not purposefully give prescriptions is to see these sessions as providing "invisible prescriptions." Recall that a question is more than a request for description. It is also a prescription for constructing a particular experiential reality. This latter constructivist view enables the therapist to speak of his questions as "informative questions" (Boscolo and Cecchin, pers. com. 1983). If a therapist asks a daughter whether she thinks therapy is more useful to her father or mother, a particular therapeutic reality is put in motion —one that underscores relationship and difference.

Extending this view a step further, the pattern connecting a Milan therapeutic session is itself an "informative pattern" to the family. This pattern is spelled out during the entire session by the family's responses to the therapist's questions. In the early Milan approach, the therapists attempted to review the session and find a way of re-articulating the pattern connecting the family's communications in a fashion that enabled the family members to consciously attend to it. Sessions that do not include this form of final prescription, however, may be seen as presenting the same pattern, at an unconscious level, to the family. Since the therapist's hypothesis is isomorphic to the pattern that organizes questions in a session, the experience of a session necessarily includes an encounter on an unconscious level of the same pattern that organizes the therapist's hypothesis. Seen this way, we can again say that the therapist utilized an "invisible prescription."

We should note that it has been suggested that Milan therapy is not as purposefully "strategic" as other approaches that claim to be connected to cybernetic and communication ideas. In general, we believe that all therapies are organized by underlying strategies that propose particular distinctions and patterns. Even a therapy that sets out to be "not strategic" can be seen as constructing a strategy to achieve that goal.

All therapies, by the distinctions they propose, set constraints on what information will not be attended to. Along these lines, a therapist is always an information gatekeeper. Therapies can be seen in terms of how certain forms of information, questions, frames of reference, structures, patterns, and distinctions are controlled. In Milan therapy, for instance, the control of information by the therapists is seen as one of the most, if not the most, important characteristic of successful treatment. They propose that such technicalities as managing the length between sessions and blocking lengthy phone conversations with clients are ways in which information must be controlled in order to construct a useful therapy.

We believe that the critical idea needed to understand and construct Milan therapy involves the recursive organization of contextual meaning. By constructing, correcting, and reconstructing a semantic frame of reference or hypothesis, the therapy is constantly calibrated and recalibrated. The hypothesis calibrates the questions while the reactions to those questions recalibrate the hypothesis.

Given that feedback process, interventions may be constructed that involve the packaging of a hypothesis in a way that prescribes its logic and reframes its connotation to being positive with regard to the contribution of all members to organizing the whole system. The position of a therapist in this approach, as we've mentioned, is one of neutrality.

The organizing principle of neutrality follows their respect for the resourcefulness and self-corrective capacity of the families they treat. Following Bateson, they acknowledge the danger of hubris, or arrogant pride, that a therapist may adopt if he fails to fully recognize that his action is always a limited part of a self-corrective circuit connecting him to his clients. It is this awareness that sometimes distinguishes their approach from other strategies of systemic therapy—a difference that Hoffman (1983) has underscored. It naturally follows that the Milan approach to a therapeutic reality cultivates a respect for the families they treat, as well as a humility regarding their own work.

A Case Study of Luigi Boscolo and Gianfranco Cecchin

The following session was conducted by Luigi Boscolo and Gianfranco Cecchin as consultants to a family already in treatment. The family and their therapist presented a daughter, Mary, who had a history of epileptic seizures, hallucinations, and temper fits. The therapist reported that Mary had recently tried to live in her own apartment, but it didn't work out and she returned home. In addition, he noted that Mary hadn't shown up for some of her sessions. Dr. Boscolo interviewed the father, mother, daughter, and their therapist while Dr. Cecchin observed and consulted from behind a one-way mirror.

CONSULTANT: I would like to start by asking you, "How do you think therapy is doing?"

FATHER: Are you asking me, Doctor? Okay. We have been going to parental therapy, in a group meeting, and I think it's helped us a whole lot.

CONSULTANT: And who do you think got the most out of therapy, you or your wife?

The father, by talking about "parental therapy," indicates a political frame of reference that includes him and his wife. The consultant immediately addresses the political frame by asking a question that attempts to reveal a difference between its members, that is, husband and wife.

FATHER: It's hard to tell.

CONSULTANT: Let me ask your wife.

FATHER: Sure.

CONSULTANT: How do you think therapy is going?

MOTHER: Well, I wouldn't call the group we go to a therapy group in so much as it's a support group. Um—as far as Mary's therapy—it hasn't moved along as well as I think it should. There again, I don't know . . . where the trouble lies. I'm beginning to question whether as much has been done as should be done, from the medical viewpoint. Why the medication does not hold at certain times, I . . .

Mother shifts the political frame to Mary's treatment. In addition, she adds the semantic frame that Mary's problem is "medical." At this point the consultant explores how her "problem" has been handled. The consultant subsequently asks the family how long Mary has been in therapy.

MOTHER: . . . Two interviews, I think.

CONSULTANT: Two interviews. Do you get the impression that those two interviews you had would help you?

MOTHER: Yes, in the sense that we've learned to evaluate the therapist's capabilities with handling Mary as a professional person and felt that she had an understanding of the problem. As I say, my questioning has been aroused as to what should be done with medical evaluation.

Mother again contextualizes the problem as Mary's medical condition. When the consultant turns to gathering information about the girl's symptomatic behavior, it is discovered that from the age of ten to eighteen, her epilepsy had been successfully controlled by medication.

CONSULTANT: So, from the age of ten to the age of eighteen—eight years . . .

MOTHER: Right.

CONSULTANT: . . . This epilepsy didn't give you much trouble.

MOTHER: No, no.

CONSULTANT: Because it was controlled with medication.

MOTHER: Right, right.

CONSULTANT: Once in a while she would have what? Can you describe what?

MOTHER: Um . . .

CONSULTANT: Did she sometimes have some . . .

MOTHER: I would say that as a child she was unusually emotional.

CONSULTANT: No. I'm talking about when she had the petit mal. How many times, from the age of ten to the age of eighteen?

MOTHER: Never saw it.

CONSULTANT: Ahh—Never saw it.

MOTHER: Never.

CONSULTANT: So she stayed on medication from the age of ten to eighteen without having a seizure.

MOTHER: And there was no more indication of her having it during that time.

CONSULTANT: Well, still she kept taking medication. So you figured out that it was the medication that was keeping away the petit mal.

MOTHER: Right . . . that was controlling . . .

Having discovered that the girl's problem was believed to have been calibrated by medication from age ten to eighteen, the consultant now investigates the semantic frame mother provided with respect to the girl being "unusually emotional." The consultant asks the parents for specific descriptions of what they saw as "unusually emotional" behavior.

MOTHER: . . . Sensitive, crying spells . . . and often she would try to look for blame for herself.

CONSULTANT: Looking for blame for herself.

The consultant repeats the phrase, "looking for blame for herself" as a request for further amplification. The term "blame" may be a clue that would indicate coalition patterns.

MOTHER: Putting herself down, regardless of how we would offer support, encouragement, and creating an atmosphere of love and concern.

CONSULTANT: Whom was she most attached to until the age of eighteen?

This question reveals a partial arc hypothesis. The consultant is beginning to test the idea that the parents' efforts to offer help may involve a coalition pattern centering around one of the parents and their daughter.

MOTHER: Uh . . . uh . . .

CONSULTANT: *(looks to father for his response)*

FATHER: Well, I think probably her mother, because her mother has an office at home. She spent most of the time there when she was home from school in the afternoons. Due to my business, I traveled for some time and was away for weeks at a time, but then I quit. So during most of the period in the last six or seven years I was at home in the evenings, but Mary would be doing her studies.

CONSULTANT: You were on business. Often you were away. So when Mary was between the age of ten and eighteen, you were not very often home, so she . . .

FATHER: Oh, I was at home, yes, during a lot of that period. However, not during the day when she would need certain things. Her mother would take her in the car and . . .

CONSULTANT: You said that your wife was saying she was a very sensitive child. I'm talking about before the age of eighteen. She was sensitive, she was attached to her mother, you said.

Note that the consultant actually reframes mother's description of her daughter as "emotional" to that of "sensitive." The consultant's hypothesis can now be seen as linking mother's attachment to daughter with the description of daughter as "sensitive" and finally to the fact that father was away from home a lot. The consultant could now formulate the hypothesis that daughter's behavior keeps her mother from being lonely while father is away on business trips.

FATHER: I was aware of this, yes.

CONSULTANT: You were aware. But do you feel it was a problem? That it was too much attachment? Did you have some impression that this was too much?

Asking whether her attachment to mother was a problem plants the seeds for constructing the view that it may have been a problem—an example of an "informational question." This question also maintains the therapeutic focus of exploring the political frame involving possible coalition patterns.

FATHER: Well, no. In fact, she was seeing her pediatrician at the time, so this apparently was part of the medical problem, see.

CONSULTANT: I see.

FATHER: They were dosing her apparently about as much as . . .

CONSULTANT: Has your wife ever told you, for instance, "I'm a little bit worried about Mary. She is too attached to me"? Has she ever talked to you that way?

The consultant gatekeeps the information that will be talked about: attention to the medical frame is sidestepped in favor of examining the daughter's attachment to the mother.

FATHER: Oh, no. I don't think that ever came up.

CONSULTANT: Never came up.

FATHER: No. Of course, she always showed a lot of affection for me. I guess, being the only male of the family.

CONSULTANT: Who had more?

FATHER: Mary had . . .

CONSULTANT: Mary . . .

FATHER: Yes.

CONSULTANT: Yes?

FATHER: Well, certainly. I mean, she loved us both. She showed a lot of affection. Of course, when I came home, I had my share of it, too.

CONSULTANT: Your share.

FATHER: Oh, yeah.

CONSULTANT: So she would be with you when you came home.

FATHER: Oh, yeah, as much as possible.

CONSULTANT: As much as possible. Was your wife pleased?

FATHER: Oh, I'm sure she was. Yes. We never had any . . .

CONSULTANT: Also in that period, until the age of eighteen, was Mary attached to relatives?

The consultant begins addressing the political frame of reference that points toward other family members who may be part of the problem context.

MOTHER: No, we don't have any family that lives close. We have always been away from the family. My husband's mother, when she was alive, would come to visit us frequently when we were in Florida and she was in Carolina. She would stay with us and those were nice times, but we've never lived close to either side of the family.

FATHER: We're about six hundred miles from the nearest one, huh?

MOTHER: So there hasn't been close contact there.

This exploration showed that no other relatives are part of the immediate political organization of the family. However, a clue suggests that the husband's mother may have been a relevant part of the organization in the past. At this time the consultant does not directly investigate that clue. Instead he turns to a semantic frame of reference the mother presented to describe herself. Earlier in the session, in a segment not transcribed here, she characterized herself as "introverted." The mother's "introversion" fits the hypothesis that she needs her daughter at home to keep her from getting lonely (if she were extroverted, she might go out and find friends while her husband was away). The consultant now attempts to construct the complementary view that father is "extroverted."

CONSULTANT: Your mother says she's kind of introverted while your father is extroverted. No? He's always had friends. Do you remember, over the years, having had an impression that father wished that mother would be more extroverted? And father would wish that mother would go more out with him. No? Do you have the impression that he kind of felt left out a little bit over the years?

The relationship of the mother and father, now discussed in terms of introversion-extroversion, is semantically framed by the consultant as "father feeling left out." The consultant is beginning to expand his initial partial arc hypothesis toward being more systemic: the daughter's behavior can now be seen as helping both the mother and father avoid feeling left out and lonely.

DAUGHTER: Yeah, I got that impression sometimes and sometimes I got the impression—well, I wish I were more like my father than like my mother.

In this discussion of introversion-extroversion, the daughter identifies herself with wanting to be like father, that is, more extroverted. The consultant immediately grabs this political frame and works with it.

CONSULTANT: I see.

DAUGHTER: *(crying)* But I'm really sorry about my death phobia and everything. If I had everything to go back and live over again—I'm saying this with great pain—I don't ever think I'd do the same again because the way I did it, it was just so foolish. My life is just so foolish.

CONSULTANT: Listen. Let me ask this, Mary. You said, "I wish I'd been extroverted like my father—to be more like . . ." *(gatekeeping of information)*

DAUGHTER: *(crying)* I wish I would have had all the friends in the world. I wish I wouldn't have had a death phobia.

CONSULTANT: Yeah—but listen to my question now. Hm? When you say, "I wish I would be like my father. . . ." *(more gatekeeping)*

DAUGHTER: *(crying)* The way you talked about me—I just feel ruined.

CONSULTANT: What did you say?

DAUGHTER: *(sobbing)* I said, the way you talk about me, it reminds me about all the bad things in my life. It just makes me feel ruined.

CONSULTANT: Well, let me ask this question again. Listen to me. When you said, "I wish I would have been like my father, more extroverted," did you sometimes have inside yourself the feeling that if I am extroverted like my father and like to have friends, maybe even like to go out with my father—Do you feel—that mother would have been left out because mother is introverted? She might feel kind of out if you became like your father? Or if you would have liked to have gone with your father? Do you feel this sometimes? That if I become too sociable, too extroverted, I might get into such a good relationship with my father that my mother would be left out?

The consultant offers a way of talking about the possible consequences of change. Namely, if the daughter and father were both extroverted and joined together, mother, the introvert, would feel left out.

DAUGHTER: Well, no I don't feel that my mother would feel left out at all. I feel that she feels that she wants to do what she wants to do. And I just feel that I want to do what I want to do, that's all. It's just very plain and simple.

CONSULTANT: Then, suppose—suppose, Mary, that you become extroverted like your father, all right? You would have friends and maybe you would like to be a sportsman like your father. He likes sports, maybe you would have gotten involved with sports, and then your mother would have felt kind of left out, wouldn't she?

The consultant constructs an example of what he previously proposed with respect to the consequences of a changed relationship structure.

DAUGHTER: Well, no, I don't think she'd feel left out because it's her personality—she's an introvert. I don't think she'd feel left out.

CONSULTANT: I see.

DAUGHTER: Not at all.

CONSULTANT: Do you have the impression, over the years for instance, that somehow there was some sadness inside mother?

DAUGHTER: There is what?

CONSULTANT: There was some sadness in your mother—you know she was introverted. Didn't you sometimes think that. . . .

The consultant connects experiences of "sadness" with "introversion" and being "left out." Again, these informational questions address possible consequences of a changed relationship structure.

DAUGHTER: No, not at all.

CONSULTANT: Hm?

DAUGHTER: Not at all.

CONSULTANT: Do you think . . .

DAUGHTER: *(agitated)* Not at all.

CONSULTANT: Do you sometimes think, for instance, that if you would have gone out with your friends, somehow your mother would have felt kind of alone?

DAUGHTER: No.

CONSULTANT: Have you ever had a close relationship with a boy? A sexual relationship?

The ingredients for the consultant's hypothesis now include the semantic frames of attachment, introversion and extroversion, and consequences of change in terms of possible sadness and feeling left out. The consultant scans the daughter's relationships with people outside her family as a way of reinforcing or modifying the view he is building.

DAUGHTER: Sometimes . . .
CONSULTANT: Have you ever had sexual relationships?
DAUGHTER: Like what? You mean kissing and stuff like that?
CONSULTANT: Even more than that.
DAUGHTER: No, I never went past the kissing stage.

The consultant now has some information for reinforcing the view that the daughter is not seriously attached to anyone outside the family.

CONSULTANT: Do you talk to your mother, for instance, when you doubt whether to pass the kissing stage? Do you talk with her?
DAUGHTER: Yeah, I asked her like at what age I should really kiss a boy, and at what age I should go out on dates.
CONSULTANT: What advice did your mother . . .
DAUGHTER: What age I should accept a marriage proposal.
CONSULTANT: So you asked your mother what to do.
DAUGHTER: What?
CONSULTANT: You would often ask advice of your mother? You confide in your mother about your boyfriends?
DAUGHTER: Oh, yeah. Sure. I did all the time.
CONSULTANT: Was she good at advising you?
DAUGHTER: She was normally pretty good.
CONSULTANT: Yeah—What advice would she give about boys? What would she tell you? You should go slow or fast?
DAUGHTER: She advised me to take things very slowly in the relationship I had. Not to push the boy into anything he didn't want, and not to let him push anything in—me into anything I didn't want to do.

The discussion of the daughter's relationships with boys has been shaped into being an exploration about the relationship of mother and daughter. At this point, all therapeutic information supports the consultant's hypothesis that daughter's behavior provides a way of saving her parents from feeling "left out," "lonely," and "sad." The theme of introversion refers to the behavior of mother and daughter that keeps them in their home, while extroversion refers to father's life outside the family—something daughter aspires toward. The consultant at this time shifts to addressing the parent's marital relationship, looking for descriptions that can be tied to the themes of the hypothesis being constructed. For instance, when mother claims she was "outgoing" during the beginning of their marriage, the consultant immediately underscores its importance.

CONSULTANT: *(to mother)* You said that at the beginning of the marriage was a period in which you were outgoing. You were with your husband. It was a period that . . .

MOTHER: More of a social period of our lives, which I think is perhaps normal in most marriages.

CONSULTANT: Did you enjoy that period?

MOTHER: Yes. It was a very pleasant time in establishing a social group, or becoming established in one, perhaps as a married couple instead of a dating couple.

When the consultant subsequently asks the daughter to comment on her parents, she talks about how she's concerned about their future and expresses the hope that they will be able to enjoy trips together.

DAUGHTER: Well, I feel that both my parents are now kind of closing in on their retirement age and I don't want them to work as hard as they used to. . . . I don't want to see them unhappy in old age—wondering what they're going to do for the rest of their life. . . .

CONSULTANT: You are worried about them?

DAUGHTER: Well, yeah. I'm concerned about what their retirement age is going to be like.

CONSULTANT: But when you said that you would like them to take trips without you, did you say that because you feel otherwise they will be unhappy? Do you feel they are unhappy?

DAUGHTER: Well, not necessarily unhappy, but it just gives them something to do together.

CONSULTANT: Because they do not do much together?

DAUGHTER: My parents haven't been together in a social life for really a long, long time, and *(crying)* before they die I want them to see and be a part of the world they live in. And, you see, that's very important to me.

CONSULTANT: Who do you think needs this more, your father or your mother?

DAUGHTER: I think they both equally need it.

CONSULTANT: But, for instance, what do you think if you were not alive, for instance, if you were not here, if your parents did not have any child . . .

DAUGHTER: Yeah . . .

CONSULTANT: . . . Do you think it would be easier for their future, or more difficult? How do you see their future without you?

The consultant is addressing the political frame of reference that involves relationship patterns in the future. The daughter's description of her parents' lack of a social life and her concern for their happiness continues to support the consultant's hypothesis.

DAUGHTER: I don't know.

CONSULTANT: If they did not have any children, how would you see their relationship in the future, hm?

DAUGHTER: I don't know. I really couldn't answer that question.

CONSULTANT: Let me ask your mother. How do you think your life with your husband would have been without children? Without your daughter?

MOTHER: My life and my relationship with my husband, I think, would have been the same.

CONSULTANT: You said you worked. As a mother it was not satisfying?

MOTHER: Yes, yes.

CONSULTANT: It was not satisfying for you?

MOTHER: Yes, it was.

CONSULTANT: It was.

MOTHER: I always have said that my daughter was a delightful part of my life. . . .

CONSULTANT: I would like to ask you, "How would you have spent your life with your wife without your daughter?" How do you think it would have gone—your life with your wife?

FATHER: With just my wife?

CONSULTANT: Yes. You and your wife, without a daughter.

FATHER: Oh, I imagine that knowing my wife, we probably would have settled down about the same way. Maybe we wouldn't have been in the same location, I don't know, but I think that life itself would have been approximately the same.

CONSULTANT: Approximately the same.

The future frame of reference did not provide any additional information that the consultant could use. When seen as informational questions, however, the family has been given a frame of reference that implies that daughter has a part in calibrating her parents' behavior and experience. At this time the consultant begins exploring the past.

CONSULTANT: I would like to ask you, Mrs. Brown, "Do you have brothers and sisters?"

MOTHER: I have a sister.

CONSULTANT: You have a sister. Older or younger?

MOTHER: Older sister.

CONSULTANT: She is married?

MOTHER: I have no idea. I haven't had any contact with her since I was eighteen years old.

CONSULTANT: Where is she?

MOTHER: I have no idea.

CONSULTANT: You don't have any idea? You had a fight? Or you broke up?

MOTHER: No. At the time we were both living at home, and then she moved away from home and cut off contact with the family through her own choice due to a disagreement she had with my father. . . . We weren't raised together. My parents were divorced when I was very young. . . . She lived with my father, I lived with my mother.

CONSULTANT: Ah—you lived with your mother, she with your father. I see.

MOTHER: Until I was thirteen.

CONSULTANT: Thirteen. How was your life with your mother?

MOTHER: Very good.

CONSULTANT: Didn't your mother miss your sister?

Historical information is being organized by the themes of who is attached to whom and who is left out. In the transcript that follows, these family coalition patterns will be made more explicit by asking questions that involve comparing who is closer to whom in the family.

MOTHER: Yes, she did. I know that she would have liked the two of us together.

DAUGHTER: . . . I'm not really that interested in my mother's side of the family because she let me know that her sister wasn't interested in her . . .

CONSULTANT: She doesn't talk much about her first life?

DAUGHTER: . . . you know.

CONSULTANT: You're more interested in your father's, you say?

DAUGHTER: Yeah.

CONSULTANT: You are interested in your father's side of the family. I see. Also, your mother is more interested in your father's family than hers?

MOTHER: Um-hum.

CONSULTANT: I'm asking you, "Is your mother more interested in your father's family than her own?"

DAUGHTER: I'd say, yes.

CONSULTANT: Yes. Whom is your mother more attached to in your father's family?

DAUGHTER: She was very attached to my Grandma Elsie, before my grandmother died.

CONSULTANT: She was very attached to your paternal grandmother.

DAUGHTER: That was the only one I know that she was attached to.

Recall that the father's mother had been mentioned earlier in the session. The consultant will now address her involvement in the family and see if that information can further shape the hypothesis.

CONSULTANT: I see. When did your grandmother die?

DAUGHTER: About ten or eleven years ago.

CONSULTANT: She was very attached to your mother?

DAUGHTER: Yeah.

CONSULTANT: You were attached too?

DAUGHTER: Oh, yeah, I was attached to Grandma Elsie, too.

CONSULTANT: Yeah? When you think about her, do you think—"old"?

DAUGHTER: I think about an old lady standing somewhere in a hat. *(family laughs)* That's what I think about. Grandma Elsie always wore a hat.

MOTHER: She was famous for her hats.

CONSULTANT: Was she close to you? I mean, did you have a good relationship?

DAUGHTER: Oh, yeah, very close.

CONSULTANT: Very close. I see.

DAUGHTER: She always used to come visit me.

CONSULTANT: I see. So you lost a sister, I mean, you don't know anything.

MOTHER: No, there is no contact.

CONSULTANT: Your mother died seven years ago. Do you have contact with your father? Or not much?

By underscoring the mother's loss of her sister, mother-in-law, and other family members, the consultant suggests the hypothesis that the mother does not want to be left alone.

MOTHER: Oh, I had lived with my father from the time I was thirteen . . .

CONSULTANT: Yes . . .

MOTHER: . . . then until I was nineteen.

CONSULTANT: During those years you lived with your father? Your sister was also there?

MOTHER: Yes, for part of that time.

CONSULTANT: How did you get along with your sister for part of the time? How did you get along?

MOTHER: All right.

CONSULTANT: There was no closeness. . . .

MOTHER: No, there was conflict between she and my stepmother, but not between my sister and I.

The consultant has enough information about the mother's family of origin to further support and polish the hypothesis. He now turns to asking questions about the father's family.

CONSULTANT: *(to father)* Your sister is closer to you or to your brother?

FATHER: I guess to me.

CONSULTANT: Do you call her sometimes? Do you see her?

FATHER: Oh, yes, yes. We talk and we write letters.

CONSULTANT: Letters. And then sometimes do you go to see her? When you are on trips, or . . .

FATHER: Well, when we go anywhere near the Carolinas, we'll stop there.

CONSULTANT: Oh, so when you go for your trips, you stop there.

FATHER: Yes. Sure.

CONSULTANT: Is that often that you go?

FATHER: Well, every two or three years. Maybe four years. Yes, we'll go.

CONSULTANT: That pleases them, they look forward to that then.

FATHER: Oh, yes.

CONSULTANT: Yes? How about your parents?

FATHER: My father and mother are both deceased.

CONSULTANT: When did your father die?

FATHER: My father died in nineteen-forty-six.

CONSULTANT: And your mother?

FATHER: My mother? Um. . . .

DAUGHTER: About ten or eleven years ago.

FATHER: No, honey. It was, yeah, I guess it was about twelve years ago.

MOTHER: Mary was eight and she's twenty-three now, so how many years ago is that?

FATHER: Thirteen years. Now wait a minute . . .

DAUGHTER: I'm twenty-two now.
MOTHER: Twenty-two.
CONSULTANT: Excuse me, Mrs. Thomas, your mother-in-law, whom was she most attached to of the children?
MOTHER: Her children?
CONSULTANT: Of her children.
MOTHER: Oh, definitely her son.
FATHER: I was the baby.
MOTHER: . . . We enjoyed each other. I would look forward to her coming for a visit.
CONSULTANT: So it was a deep blow for you when she died.

The consultant continues to zoom in on the father's mother. By repeating questions about her death and loss, her importance to the present situation is being constructed. The therapist's hypothesis can now include the date of grandmother's death as an important piece of data, particularly its association with the onset of granddaughter's symptomatic behavior.

MOTHER: Yeah. . . .
CONSULTANT: Big blow.
MOTHER: Um-hm.
CONSULTANT: I see, very big. *(to mother)* And did you also enjoy your sister-in-law?
MOTHER: Well, I'm not really that well acquainted with them over the period of years. You see, I see them when they come to visit us or when we go there, but over the period of years I was most attached to my mother-in-law, and I suppose that had a lot to do with Mary because Mary is the only girl grandchild. . . .
CONSULTANT: I see.
MOTHER: And so we would write long letters and she would call and she always wanted to come down and visit and we sent pictures every week, you know, the weekly development . . .
CONSULTANT: How old was Mary when Mother died? She was eleven, hm?
MOTHER: No, no she was about seven because we were

in Downingtown. You were seven or eight years old.

CONSULTANT: When did she die? What year?

MOTHER: *(sighs)* What year were we in Downingtown? I can't remember.

DAUGHTER: About nineteen-sixty-five, I think.

CONSULTANT: Sixty-five? Fifteen years ago.

FATHER: Sixty-five, sixty-six.

MOTHER: About that.

CONSULTANT: I see.

MOTHER: It's hard to remember.

CONSULTANT: It was a loss. Did you feel you had almost a better relationship with your mother-in-law than with your own mother?

The consultant recycles his questions about the father's mother thus increasing her importance in the family system even more. Again note that her death occurred when Mary was seven or eight years old, while Mary began symptomatic behavior when she was around ten years old.

MOTHER: No. There were so many years in between that I couldn't compare the two. You see, the two were not part of my life at the same time.

CONSULTANT: I understand, but there was some warmth that developed. No?

MOTHER: Uh. . . .

CONSULTANT: Did you enjoy the relationship?

MOTHER: I enjoyed her.

CONSULTANT: You enjoyed her.

MOTHER: We enjoyed each other, I think. She used to like to come to our house.

CONSULTANT: Is there any other woman ever since that's taken her place in your life? I mean, any other relationship?

This question plants the seed that another relationship, perhaps her relationship with her daughter, has taken the place of her closeness with father's mother.

MOTHER: No—no—no, I think I probably felt that way about her because of her interest in Mary as a grandchild . . .

CONSULTANT: I see.

MOTHER: . . . and knowing that I'd married her favorite son. You know, that's . . .

CONSULTANT: So you married her favorite son. . . .

MOTHER: Right.

CONSULTANT: And she was a girl, which was important for her because she had all male grandchildren. . . .

MOTHER: All male grandchildren. She was delighted when we had a girl.

The consultant has now constructed a view of this family's history, particularly with respect to attachments and dates of departure. The mother's history of being left by significant others and the importance of her close relationship with her mother-in-law provide solid information for that part of the hypothesis that suggests the daughter's behavior somehow helps the mother not feel left out. At this time the consultant addresses various semantic and political frames in order to check if information can be found supporting the view that the daughter is "helping" her parents. He begins by readdressing the parents' participation in "parental therapy" and semantically frames it as helping Mary.

CONSULTANT: It is your impression, Mary, that since they have been going to this group, this group of parents, that they are helping you?

DAUGHTER: They are what?

CONSULTANT: Since they have been attending this parents' group.

DAUGHTER: I'd say they've been pretty happy over me.

MOTHER: Helping.

DAUGHTER: Oh, helping?

CONSULTANT: Do you think they are helping you at all?

DAUGHTER: Oh, helping me. Yeah.

CONSULTANT: How about you? You have been in therapy, no? Do you think you are helping your parents, too?

DAUGHTER: Helping my parents?

CONSULTANT: Um.

DAUGHTER: Yeah.

CONSULTANT: As in what—what problem do you see in your parents?

DAUGHTER: I don't know, I don't know. It's all very fuzzy to me. I don't really know what you're referring to.

CONSULTANT: You don't?

DAUGHTER: No. I don't know how I could possibly help my parents. I know that they're the ones that help me.

When the semantic frame proposing that her parents have a problem is introduced, Mary changes her previous position and negates the possibility that her therapy helps them.

CONSULTANT: But do you see a problem in your parents?

DAUGHTER: No, I don't see any problem with my parents.

CONSULTANT: You don't see any problem.

DAUGHTER: No. It's not that I'm trying to be ignorant or anything.

CONSULTANT: Is the problem the future that worries you with your parents? How will their life be in the future?

The daughter has offered two apparently contradictory messages: (1) "I'm helping my parents"; and (2) "I'm not helping my parents." The consultant, as if following a view of multiple communication, provides a temporal shift, suggesting that the daughter may be helping her parents address the problem of the future —something she stated earlier in the session. This temporal shift enables her to also state that she is not helping her parents with respect to the immediate present.

DAUGHTER: What problem? I don't—I don't know what you're talking about.

CONSULTANT: I'll stop here. I'll now have a discussion with my colleague, and I'll come back with our conclusion.

The consultant takes a consultation break. Upon re-entering the room, he provides the following announcement to the family, which is a repackaging of their systemic hypothesis. The three family members and their therapist sit in a trancelike posture while the consultant talks. There are only a few times when this posture shifts. These shifts, which will be identified in the transcript, most often involve the mother and daughter dramatically staring at one another.

CONSULTANT: My colleague and I have reached the conclusion that I now give to you. What impressed us a lot is the life of the parents. We are very much impressed with the life of Mother. It was a life, before getting married, that was somehow solitude. She had a sister, but somehow she couldn't have a meaningful relationship with the sister. She had a mother, but she was separated by the father and sister. Then she separated when she was thirteen years old from the mother and went to Father with the older sister. And then the sister left. So we are very impressed with your life, Mrs. Thomas, before you got married. We feel a lot of solitude in your life.

Information about the mother's history of relationships prior to her marriage *(meaningful noise)* is recycled back to the family in a way that enables it to be seen as a life of "solitude." Rather than using the previous semantic frames of "being left out" or "introversion," the consultant chooses the more general category, "solitude."

MOTHER: Maybe I didn't realize it.

CONSULTANT: From what you told us, really, we felt you could not have a, how do you say, a "warm relationship." Your family was all broken up somehow and we think that when you got married, there was a period when you said you were very happy.

MOTHER: Umm.

CONSULTANT: . . . Where you felt satisfied on all levels. And then we are also very impressed about Father and his solitude, after he lost his mother. His mother died when Mary was about nine years old. And in those first nine years of Mary's life, somehow, the parents—Mother and Father—had a life, maybe for the first time. *(mother nods in agreement)* Especially for

Mother, a life—a relationship—not the solitude that you had before getting married. And in those nine years your mother-in-law was very important. You could make contact. It was a very meaningful relationship also for your husband. He was in a very intense relationship with his mother, and the family was maybe in the best period of your life.

The father is put in the same frame as mother—having experienced solitude. The grandmother's presence in the family system is marked as the best period of their life, a description they previously presented.

MOTHER: Um-hm.

CONSULTANT: Mary was coming out, it was going well—was going well. But then Mary, at a certain point when her grandmother died, deeply felt that her parents were left with an emptiness. Mother had lost a very important person: mother-in-law. Daddy had lost a very important person: his own mother. So Mary somehow started to think and deeply started to constrain her tendency towards independence. Other boys and girls start slowly to become more independent: they get more and more involved in an outside life. Mary, however, started to say, "I've got to do something for my parents," and somehow she took the position of the grandmother. She developed all kinds of behaviors—ways of looking, rotating the eyes, fidgetiness, and withdrawing. She avoided relationships, particularly intense relationships with boys typical of girls her age. At the maximum, she would give a kiss, but she wouldn't get very involved because she deeply felt that "I have to fill the life of both my mother and my father, who have become empty after the death of grandmother." *(daughter turns and stares at mother)* So, somehow she took this role, as she has been doing for you all these years, by developing all these kinds of behavior. By developing all these kinds of behavior, she has both Mother and Father thinking about her all the time. By doing this she gives them the opportunity to parent her around-the-clock every day. And by doing this, their life is filled and is not void.

We are very impressed, Mary, by what you have been doing for your parents. And your parents have the opportunity, thanks to what you are doing for them, to have a life less lonely than they would have if you would not have taken on this task after your grandmother died. Did you feel, "My grandmother, when she died left a tremendous emptiness," so you decided to fill it? You are doing a great work for them by giving them the opportunity to continue being parents for you.

Now, lately, you have somehow introduced the idea of separating a little bit by deciding to go out and live in your own apartment. This is also a good thing in that it tests how your parents could do without you. You're also very sensitive in calling them and coming back when you feel it is too premature to leave them. Now, we think you are doing well and for the moment we think you should continue like this. Furthermore, we think the therapy that you have been doing is doing well in the sense that the therapy keeps things as they are for Mary. We would be alarmed if Mary suddenly started to change and become more independent—because she would leave unfinished work. Then her parents might go back to their loneliness where there might come out some emptiness. So I think, for the meanwhile, therapy with Mary is doing well in the sense that change at this point would be kind of risky.

You *(to therapist)* told us that Mary doesn't come to the appointments regularly when she comes. This is good because if she came regularly to the

> appointments she might get too involved with you *(to therapist).* If she got too involved, she may think she has to leave the parents. So meanwhile, it is too premature. We think that the therapy should go on like it is going on now.
>
> We also think it is very positive that the parents are going to continue to go to this group that they are attending with other parents. This may help the parents develop some kind of relationship for the future. Mary may even feel that now there is somebody else who can fill the void of the parents. Mary will decide this herself in the future. We think this is very good. If your parents go to these groups you may see them find their life: maybe the groups will substitute for your grandmother.
>
> You have been taking the place of your grandmother since the age of nine to help keep the life of your parents, as I said before, not lonely and not empty, and allowing them to be continuously good parents for you. And now with these groups they are attending, they might find some meaning that enables them to take away the constraints on your own independence. So in the future you might try, like all the other girls your age in adolescence, to find your own life. For the moment we think you should continue because your parents are not ready yet. You understand, Mary, what I am saying?

Mary's symptomatic behavior is now positively connoted as having provided a solution for her mother's and father's "emptiness" when grandmother died. She does this by providing opportunities, "around-the-clock," for them to parent her. Mary's recent efforts to separate from the family were also reframed as tests of whether her parents can do well without her. Consequently, the consultants prescribe that she continue being cautious about a premature departure *(prescription of stability).* In addition, they praise their therapist for keeping things from changing too fast. The consequences of too sudden of a change are spelled out in terms of her parents' possible return to loneliness and emptiness. Note, however, that *change* is prescribed when the consultants say that the parents' attendance in the parental group provides a way of their developing satisfactory outside relationships and thereby creating a substitute for "grandmother." The consequence of such a change, as they point out, implies another change: namely that Mary can become an adolescent and find her own life. In effect, all information the family has presented that can be connected to the theme of taking care of the parents' emptiness is now woven together and positively framed.

In terms of multiple communications, the intervention is structured as:

stabilize importance of present solution behavior	/	change the way in which "grandmother's" contribution has been substituted	/	meaningful noise: use of family history to explain its present operation

DAUGHTER: I think I do.

CONSULTANT: Anyway, if you don't understand very well, maybe your mother or your father will explain what I told you when you go home. . . . *(to therapist)* So, meanwhile, we think things are in equilibrium and that you should be very sensible that change doesn't occur for the moment because Mary has taken that task upon herself for her parents. We want to add that we saw Mary crying before when she said she was worried for her parents' future: "What will happen to my parents, and their retirement plans? I would like very much that they would enjoy. . . ." These are things the grandmother would have thought about.

(to Mary) So we think that you, Mary, should continue like this until you feel in the future that maybe your parents have started to feel less lonely, less empty with you starting to make your life. Do you understand? Your life becoming more inde-

pendent like the girls of your age. Meanwhile, we think that the behaviors, the attacks, are very important because it keeps your parents helping you, trying to do things for you—this fills up their life.

(to parents) I'd like to say something about the point made in the beginning of the session when you said, "How about the medical problem?" Hm? You asked me, "What do you think about the medical problem, the medicine, the diagnosis?" We would like to give an answer. We have a lot of experience with these situations; many situations similar to this. We think the problem of epilepsy is an organic problem. We think that in your situation, most likely it's not organic, but it's not possible in our experience to clearly say that it is not organic. We are more inclined to think that it's not a brain—

First of all, telling the daughter to ask her mother and father to explain the situation sets up a structure where the mother and father are joined together as experts in relation to their daughter. At the same time, the parents are put in the position of having to demonstrate that they won't be lonely and empty should Mary take steps toward independence. Until that is done, Mary is to continue her role in stabilizing the system. And finally, the consultants begin introducing the possibility that the girl's epilepsy is not medical, but is behavior that fits their explanation of how the family works.

DAUGHTER: . . . tumor?

CONSULTANT: Not a tumor or brain lesion. But we are not certain because you can never be certain. We are more inclined to think that there is not a brain lesion. Anyhow, we think even if we are more on the side that there are not brain problems, all the behavior that Mary has is behavior for her parents—in the sense that we were saying before. This behavior helps the parents in not having a void, by giving some meaning to their life by being parents. In this sense we think you should continue to take the medicine and tests the doctors prescribe. By doing these tests, she keeps going along with the task she has taken upon herself since she was nine years old in helping the parents have a life that is not alone, not empty. So maybe in the future—as I said—Mary may feel that the parents can live without her, maybe with the help of the group therapy they're following, maybe in time to see herself as not needing medical tests or medicine. For the moment, however, we think things shouldn't change.

Even the medical frame of reference is positively connoted for its contribution to stabilizing the family system. Hence, medical tests and consultations are prescribed as a means of helping the parents not be empty.

MOTHER: I agree that the anticonvulsant medicine is controlling the epilepsy, but what I'm concerned about is the depth of the hallucinations that she still has, the violent behavior that she exhibited in the past year that was never part of her life before.

CONSULTANT: You see, this violent behavior—even if there is an epilepsy—though we doubt it very much—we don't say there isn't, you understand what I mean? But we doubt very much that there is an epilepsy. Even if there were an epilepsy, which means a lesion of the brain—which we doubt very much—even with respect to what you describe in the last years as being more violent we understand why she exhibits this behavior.

When mother reinstates the reality of a medical problem, the consultant takes both sides of what could be a stalemated disagreement: he claims there might be epilepsy and there might not. After underscoring his doubt, he concludes that "we understand why she exhibits this behavior." In other words, independent of the source of her behavior, the consultant is pointing to how that behavior logically fits into the way the family is organized. It provides a solution for the problem of the mother's and father's potential emptiness.

MOTHER: I don't. I don't and Mary doesn't.

CONSULTANT: We understand. See, she has been exhibiting this behavior over the past years because somehow as she grows the push toward *independency,* particularly *independency* in leaving the home is more powerful. Understand what I mean, leaving the home? I mean a regular relationship outside like the girls of her age. So she must constrain herself more in order to continue to be worried for her parents. "How can I have them continue to be parents?" "How can I have them not feeling alone?" She has to make more efforts. That's why it comes out with more of this kind of odd behavior.

MOTHER: You mean that explains the behavior of her beating her head against the wall, and her wanting to kill herself, and attempting suicide?

CONSULTANT: Well, even this one—beating her head against the wall—is more difficult for her. We understand it is more difficult for her in the period when she is twenty-one or twenty-two years old because she is growing. It's more difficult to constrain the physiological, natural impulse that everybody has at her age toward making a relationship outside, or starting to think of making her own life. I understand it's very hard for you to understand because on the one hand she has this full-time work she has been doing for the parents since the grandmother died. Now, simultaneously, as she is twenty-one or twenty-two years old, there is also a strong physiological force that strives to make her have the life that all the other girls of her age . . .

The medical or physiological reality of the girl is now accepted but reframed as the force that is trying to change her toward independence. It is therefore the girl's resistance to this "natural change" that leads to her behavior coming out in an odd fashion.

DAUGHTER: I don't agree with that.

CONSULTANT: . . . And so it takes more the effort in this period. The idea of death or the idea of beating her head against the wall is also because it is really tough for her in this period. But when she feels in the future that she deeply starts to perceive that both her parents will be able to have a life between themselves, then she will diminish this work she's been doing. Then she'll have the possibility of finding her own life.

DAUGHTER: I don't agree with that.

CONSULTANT: As a matter of fact she cried before. By crying, Mary said, "I'm so worried about my parents. About their retirement plans. I would like them to travel around to enjoy . . ." *(daughter turns around and stares at mother)* Somehow, this is the worry for you. When she perceives in the future that there are no more reasons to worry, she will see the parents as able to have a satisfied life without solitude. The constraint will go away and she will follow the physiological forces that an adolescent girl has toward making relationships. *(knock on door, consultant leaves)*

Again, the parents are put in the position of telling their daughter when she may safely proceed in changing while the daughter is put in the position of being responsive to these messages from her parents. At that point, change, being a natural, spontaneous event, arising from her own "physiological forces," will take place. This view turns the family's meaning of their problem-solving efforts upside down. Where they had previously seen themselves as purposefully trying to achieve change, the consultants now reframe their efforts as the purposeful achievement of stability. Change is now framed as that which the girl has been resisting in order to help her parents. When she sees that her parents are fulfilled, she can stop resisting change, and her adolescence will naturally take place.

CONSULTANT: *(enters room)* My colleague says he thinks that maybe the parents have lately started to not have the feeling of loneliness—the idea of being alone without their daughter—and they might be in a position for feeling well. Also, Mary is very prudent—she goes slow. All this year she has done this work for you and so she has not developed during the year, that is, developed outside relationships with girlfriends or boyfriends. She doesn't yet get much training from the outside. At the same time, her parents may be more ready at this point to think that if our daughter goes out, maybe even gets married and makes her own life, we will be able to have our life: not an empty life, but a meaningful life. Mary, you see, at this moment it is very important to say, "go slow"—Anyway, that's our conclusion and now we will turn you over to your therapist and add that we think the therapy should be continued like it has been continuing. Okay?

The consultant introduces the view that the parents are presently changing and that Mary has been wisely prudent in not changing too fast. The consultant again constructs the complementarity that they had woven throughout the consultation: if you find change, then go slow so as to not threaten stability; whereas if you find stability, it is then safe to change.

MOTHER: Thank you.

DAUGHTER: Thank you.

FATHER: Thank you.

CONSULTANT: Eventually, if Mary has some doubts—if there's something that you don't understand very well about what I said, eventually Daddy or Mother will explain it to her.

FATHER: Hopefully we'll be able to.

MOTHER: Okay.

The task of providing meaningful noise is turned over to the parents.

Afterword

IN COMPARING the MRI and Haley strategies, we noted that each approach could, in its own way, argue that it was more efficient than the other. Similarly, one could argue that the Milan strategy more effectively deals with the political frames of triadic social relations and problem-solution interaction by its manner of addressing contextual meaning. Haley and MRI, however, could counterargue that if the political frames they address are changed, then the meanings the family attributes to their experience will subsequently change. They might add that because political frames are more accessible to observation, they are more easily managed than the slippery semantic world of contextual meaning.

While all these approaches address the politics of problem-solution interaction and social triadic relations, as well as the semantics of contextual meaning, they differ with regard to which frame of reference is primarily used to organize the other frames. In an MRI therapy, the political frame of problem-solution interaction is used to organize patterns of social interaction and contextual meaning. Haley's and Minuchin's therapies principally use triadic social relations to alter problem-solution interaction and contextual meaning. And finally, the Milan strategy differs from both Haley and MRI through its primary use of a semantic frame to change family politics.

Occasionally a therapist will ask what particular approach to systemic family therapy works best or is most effective. From the perspective we've presented, such a question is easily misleading. Rather than search for a utopian clinical method, we believe that therapists should search for what must be done in order to achieve success with any particular approach.

This view presupposes that all the diverse approaches to systemic family therapy presented in this book lead to productive results when they are appropriately constructed. If a clinician does not achieve the intended results with a particular strategy, it is probably useful for him to first assume that he is not correctly constructing and organizing the distinctions the strategy prescribes. With this assumption, feedback can be structured so that the clinician systematically alters and evaluates his own behavior until the desired therapy is achieved.

Each strategy, in fact, prescribes a particular way of viewing feedback in therapy, as well as suggests a unique way of participating in its calibration. The cybernetic feedback organization of a system is specified by the principal recursive compementarity of a therapeutic strategy. For instance, an MRI therapeutic reality underscores the recursive relation of problem behavior and attempted solutions, while Haley notes how problem behavior is organized by repeating social sequences. And finally, Milan points to the recursive coupling of semantics and family politics as a way of approaching the cybernetic organization of a system. All these views of how feedback is organized in a therapeutic system—what we earlier called "mind in therapy"—illustrate the perspective of what has been called "simple-order cybernetics" or "first-order cybernetics" (see Keeney 1983).

The therapist, however, needs more than a view of the simple cybernetic organization of a troubled system. To help transform a troubled system into a more adaptive pattern of organization requires direction for calibrating its feedback. Each of the therapeutic strategies we have presented therefore prescribes a way of constructing "feedback of feedback." This refers to the higher-order cybernetic pattern that must be constructed to alter or calibrate lower-order feedback that stabilizes problem behavior. It is this higher-order pattern that prescribes how the therapist is to participate in therapy.

In an MRI view, the therapist addresses higher-order change by attempting to alter the class of solution behavior while stabilizing the semantic specification of the presenting problem (the therapeutic contract). Haley also stabilizes the semantic frame that defines the intent of therapy but addresses change of the coalition structure and social sequence embodying the problem behavior. A Milan therapeutic reality moves from stabilizing the client's semantic definition of the situation to stabilizing the therapist's semantic frame or "systemic hypothesis" while prescribing a change in how so-called problems are viewed. Specifically, they often change the connotation of problematic behavior by pointing out its positive political contribution to family stability.

Each strategy thus prescribes the therapist's participation by how it specifies a pattern of higher-order feedback. This change in emphasis, from feedback to feedback of feedback, marks the shift from the perspective of simple cybernetics to what has been called "cybernetics of cybernetics" or "second-order cybernetics" (see Keeney 1983). The following table illustrates how the three major strategies for constructing systemic therapeutic realities address these different cybernetic perspectives.

Note that the view of simple cybernetics points to the principal recursive complementarity that each therapeutic strategy prescribes. We have implied that each of these complementarities can be seen as nested one within the other. As we suggested, the MRI view of problem/solution interaction is subsumed by

Name of Therapeutic Strategy	*Simple Cybernetics*	*Cybernetics of Cybernetics*
MRI	problem/solution	(stabilize problem definition / change class of solution) / presenting semantics
Haley	repeating social sequence / problem	(stabilize problem definition / change social structure) / family semantics
Milan	therapist's semantic hypothesis / family politics	(stabilize hypothesis / change connotation of problem behavior) / family semantics (often emphasizing history)

Haley's view of repeating social sequences that involve the participation of at least three people. Similarly, Haley's view of family politics can be seen as subsumed by the recursive complementarity prescribed by Milan. The shift to a Milan view, however, moves us toward principally addressing a semantic frame of reference—the therapist's hypothesis.

It is important to realize that the particular descriptions of a hypothesis are less important than the pattern that organizes these descriptions. As we have argued, it is assumed that the pattern organizing a therapist's semantic hypothesis is isomorphic to the pattern organizing family politics. From the perspective of the Milan strategy, there is no way to avoid having such a hypothesis. From this view, MRI is seen as always using the same class of hypothesis—specifying how so-called attempted solutions stabilize so-called problem-behavior. Similarly, Haley and Minuchin consistently utilize structural hypotheses. We should also point out that a close examination of Milan-style hypotheses reveals that they often include both structural and interactional classes of hypothesis. This should be no surprise since they originally began their work by studying these therapeutic strategies and ideas.

In any approach to systemic therapy, it is most critical in the construction of a therapeutic reality that these semantic hypotheses not be seen as anything other than a vehicle for access to the political organization of the presenting system. The hypotheses, whether called interactional, structural, contextual, or systemic, are not seen as "truth" or as a form of understanding that therapist and/or client must achieve as a prerequisite for therapeutic change. They simply provide a way of getting at basic political patterns organizing a system.

Each of the perspectives of simple cybernetics indicated in the table specifies a particular way of viewing the basic cybernetic organization (that is, politics) of a presenting system. Here we see how a therapist constructs a view of the pattern that connects the problem behavior of one individual with the behavior of others (including, and sometimes limited to, other behavior of the identified patient). The shift to the perspective of cybernetics of cybernetics specifically outlines how a therapist's interventions are to be organized. As the table summarizes this, MRI and Haley both stabilize the semantic definition of the presenting problem as a rudder that steers and stabilizes the course of therapy. MRI then attempts to change the class of solution by recycling the system's semantic frames *(meaningful noise)* in such a way that it blocks previous attempted solutions or introduces an alternative class of solution behavior. Haley, on the other hand, often recycles family semantics *(meaningful noise)* as a means of persuading the family to follow a task that secretly (as far as the family is concerned) aims at creating a change in family coalition structure.* And lastly, Milan recycles family semantics *(meaningful noise)* in such a way that a systemic hypothesis is held onto that enables the connotation of problem behavior to be changed and thereby often prescribed.

A simple cybernetic perspective thus appears to have more to do with how a therapist assesses or knows a system, while cybernetics of cybernetics prescribes a way of intervening or participating in that system. As many therapists know, it is sometimes an advantage to ignore his participation in what he observes and treats. However, should he decide to question his actions in a therapeutic system, he may shift to observing his participation in constructing what he observes. At this order of observing, the distinction between himself and the system he treats is blurred. He can always choose to momentarily ignore his participation in constructing what he observes and return to seeing himself as an "outsider." The shift from being an observer of systems to an observer of one's observing systems again constitutes the difference between simple cybernetics and cybernetics of cybernetics. Neither perspective is complete: they are complementary views that connect.

Systemic approaches to family therapy are sometimes depicted as too manipulative or distant from the people they are attempting to help. Rather than emphasize spending a lot of time getting inside a system, Watzlawick, Jackson, and Beavin (1967, p. 236) propose "that the therapist has a rather limited period of grace" in which to achieve therapeutic change because "the new system

*As we noted, Minuchin's strategy more generally prescribes stability and change in terms of joining and restructuring operations, respectively.

itself consolidates to the point where the therapist is almost inextricably caught in it and from then on is much less able to produce change." Similarly, Haley (1976, p. 218) suggests that the therapist should be a gatekeeper of information, clearly in charge of organizing what happens in therapy. And more dramatically, the Milan group has proposed (Selvini-Palazzoli, et al. 1978, p. 125) that therapists must practice their craft "in as detached a manner as possible, as they would in a chess tournament in which little or nothing is known about their adversaries."

We propose that systemic therapies share an understanding of the paradoxical relations inherent in the cybernetic structure of social systems. Bateson (1972; 1979) has generally articulated this insight in the following way: whatever is the case at one level of a system is reversed at another level. For instance, an adapted species such as cattle may be so favored by consumers that overgrazing leads to destruction of its ecological niche (and possibly contributes to the destruction of the consumer's ecology).

In the context of therapy, we have referred to two different levels of organization previously discussed in terms of simple cybernetics and cybernetics of cybernetics. Following Bateson, we could hypothesize that a shift from one level to the other carries with it some sort of reversal. In particular, we suggest that the strategy for a therapist effectively being part of a system (which is constructed from the perspective of cybernetics of cybernetics) appears paradoxical from the level of observing the simple cybernetic organization of that system (seen through the perspective of simple cybernetics). In short, to effectively get inside a system may require positioning oneself outside the system. Or, as Selvini-Palazzoli and her colleagues (1978, p. 127) put it, "the only way to love one's patients is by not loving them."

A view of mind in therapy returns us time and time again to a view of multiple descriptions and prescriptions. To know (and utilize) cybernetics requires understanding two different perspectives: simple cybernetics and cybernetics of cybernetics. Going on, recognizing and successfully responding to the organization of a cybernetic system requires addressing both stability and change. In addition, to organize and appreciate the contribution of a systemic therapist requires prescribing and discerning his participation both inside and outside the system being treated. And finally, perceiving and knowing a particular therapeutic reality requires that a therapist act in accordance with the distinctions it prescribes.

In general, all systems of punctuation, including the punctuation of punctuation, are self-verifying. As we've implied, one establishes the validity of a particular approach to systemic family therapy only by constructing it in the appropriate way. We close with a story that underscores how all outcomes may be taken as verification of some reality—in this case, proof of the existence of "psychic possession."

There was once a famous Brazilian psychic who claimed to be a medium for the master painter Monet. When he demonstrated his skill at a well-known human growth center located at Big Sur, California, he went into deep trance and used his rapidly moving feet and hands supposedly guided by the spirit of Monet to paint a picture.

The very next day, a four-year-old girl took a Magic Marker and scribbled on the painting. Needless to say, when the elders were unsuccessful in washing it off, a great sadness was felt throughout the community.

An old philosopher heard about this event and wrote a letter suggesting that the little girl's scribbling was the only part of the painting that was an authentic Monet. He explained that Monet had been awakened from his comfortable slumber in Hell by news about an imposter who claimed to be a Brazilian psychic. "Monet possessed the little girl," the philosopher said, "to deface the painting and thereby distinguish that it was not the real thing."

Thus, we see that all outcomes are grists for some mill. The girl's scribblings could be framed as being as valuable (and perhaps more reliable) an indication of Monet's presence as the psychic's painting. For clinicians, all outcomes in therapy can be similarly utilized to construct a particular therapeutic reality. Doing so, in fact, is the very art of practicing systemic family therapy.

REFERENCES
INDEX

References

Ashby, W. R. *Introduction to Cybernetics.* New York: John Wiley and Sons, 1956.

Bateson, G. [1951] 1968. Information and codification: A philosophical approach. In J. Ruesch and G. Bateson, *Communication: The social matrix of psychiatry.* New York: W. W. Norton.

———. 1972. *Steps to an ecology of mind.* New York: Ballantine.

———. 1979. *Mind and nature: A necessary unity.* New York: E. P. Dutton.

Bateson, G., and Brown, J. 1975. Caring and clarity. *CoEvolution Quarterly* 7: 32–47.

Feyerabend, P. 1970. Against method. *Minnesota Studies for the Philosophy of Science* 4:17–130.

Fisch, R., Weakland, J., and Segal, L. 1982. *The tactics of change.* San Francisco: Jossey-Bass. 1971.

Haley, J. 1971. Family therapy: A radical change. In ed. J. Haley, pp. 272–84, *Changing families:* New York: Grune and Stratton.

———. 1973. *Uncommon therapy.* New York: W. W. Norton.

———. 1976. *Problem-solving therapy.* San Francisco: Jossey-Bass.

———. 1980. *Leaving home: The therapy of disturbed young people.* New York: McGraw-Hill.

Hoffman, L. 1983. A co-evolutionary framework for systemic family therapy. In ed. B. Keeney, pp. 35–61, *Diagnosis and assessment in family therapy,* Rockville, Md: Aspen Systems.

Keeney, B. 1981. Pragmatics of family therapy. *Journal of Strategic and Systemic Therapies* 1: 44–53.

———. 1983. *Aesthetics of change.* New York: The Guilford Press.

Keeney, B. and Ross, J. 1983. Cybernetics of brief family therapy. *Journal of Marital and Family Therapy* 9:375–182.

Keeney, B., Ross, J., and Silverstein, O. 1983. Mind in bodies: The treatment of a family that presented a migraine headache. *Family Systems Medicine* 1: 61–77.

Lyons, I. 1978. Interview with Oscar Peterson. *Contemporary Keyboard,* March, pp. 30–33.

McCulloch, W. 1965. *Embodiments of mind.* Cambridge, Mass.: MIT Press.

Mihram, D., Mihram, G., and Nowakowska, M. 1977. The modern origins of the term "cybernetics." In *ACTES Proceedings of the 8th International Congress on Cybernetics.* Namur, Belgium: Association Internationale de Cybernetique.

Minuchin, S. 1974. *Families and family therapy.* Cambridge, Mass.: Harvard University Press.

———. 1980. Structural family therapy. *The American Family,* Report 3. Philadelphia: Smith Kline and French Laboratories.

Minuchin, S. and Fishman, C. 1981. *Family therapy techniques.* Cambridge, Mass.: Harvard University Press.

Naess, A. 1972. *The pluralist and possibilist aspect of the scientific enterprise.* Universitetsforlaget, Oslo: Allen and Unwin.

Rabkin, R. 1978. Who plays the pipes? *Family Process* 17: 485–88.

Richards, J. and von Glaserfeld, E. 1979. The control of perception and the construction of reality. *Dialectica* 33: 37–58.

Selvini-Palazzoli, M., Cecchin, G., Prata, G., and Boscolo, L. 1978. *Paradox and counterparadox.* New York: Jason Aronson.

———. 1980. Hypothesizing-circularity-neutrality. *Family Process* 19: 3–12.

Simon, R. 1982. Behind the one-way mirror: An interview with Jay Haley. *The Family Therapy Networker* 6: 18–59.

Slater, P. 1974. *Earthwalk.* New York: Bantam Books.

Spencer-Brown, G. 1973. *Laws of form.* New York: Bantam.

Tomm, K. 1982. The Milan approach to family therapy: A tentative report. In *Treating Families with Special Needs,* D. Freeman and B. Trate, eds. Ottawa, Canada: The Canadian Association of Social Workers.

Varela, F. 1979. *Principles of biological autonomy.* New York: Elsevier North Holland.

Von Foerster, H. 1981*a.* Foreword to *Rigor and imagination,* eds. C. Wilder-Mott and J. Weakland. New York: Praeger.

Von Foerster, H. 1981*b. Observing systems.* Seaside, California: Intersystems Publications.

Watts, A. 1961. *Psychotherapy east and west.* New York: Ballantine.

Watzlawick, P. 1964. *An anthology of human communication.* Palo Alto: Science and Behavior Books.

Watzlawick, P., Jackson, D., and Beavin, J. 1967. *Pragmatics of human communication.* New York: W. W. Norton.

Watzlawick, P. and Weakland, J., eds. 1977. *The interactional view.* New York: W. W. Norton.

Watzlawick, P., Weakland, J., and Fisch, R. 1974. *Change: Principles of problem formation and problem resolution.* New York: W. W. Norton.

Whitaker, C. 1979. On family therapy (interview with Bruce Howe). *Pilgrimage: The Journal of Existential Psychology* 7: 107–114.

Index